Harvard Historical Studies, 110

Published under the auspices
of the Department of History
from the income of the
Paul Revere Frothingham Bequest
Robert Louis Stroock Fund
Henry Warren Torrey Fund

The White House in 1823

The Making
of the
Monroe Doctrine

Ernest R. May

Harvard University Press
Cambridge, Massachusetts
and London, England

First Harvard University Press paperback edition, 1992

Library of Congress Cataloging in Publication Data

May, Ernest R.
     The making of the Monroe doctrine.

     Bibliography: p.
     Includes index.
     1.   United States—Politics and government—
1817–1825.   2. Presidents—United States—Election—
1824.   3. United States—Foreign relations—1817-
1825.   4. Monroe doctrine.   1. Title.
E371.M38   327.73   75-11619
ISBN 0-674-54340-8 (cloth)
ISBN 0-674-54341-6 (paper)

to
William L. Langer

Preface

At latest count, the Library of Congress card catalogue had 359 entries under "Monroe Doctrine." The bibliography includes some of the best works in diplomatic history—among them Samuel Flagg Bemis's *John Quincy Adams and the Foundations of American Foreign Policy*, Bradford Perkins's *Castlereagh and Adams*, Dexter Perkins's *The Monroe Doctrine, 1823-1826*, Harold W. V. Temperley's *The Foreign Policy of Canning*, and Arthur P. Whitaker's *The United States and the Independence of Latin America*. Why, then, another study?

My answer has to start autobiographically. About ten years ago, I went through some of the John Quincy Adams manuscripts in the Massachusetts Historical Society. The supervisor of the Adams Papers project had invited me to edit a definitive edition of John Quincy Adams's diary. In considering the proposal, I examined what the archive contained for the period, 1817-1825, when Adams was secretary of state—his diary, his calendar, his wife's diary, his letterbooks, and his incoming correspondence. Although I decided not to do the editing, I learned a good deal about the man and the period.

Not long afterward, I started to write a short account of the making of the Monroe Doctrine. It was to be for nonscholarly readers, simply recounting the decision. I could not write it. Trying to do so, I found that I could not explain even to myself why the Monroe administration had acted as it did.

Books on the doctrine analyzed the principles which had

been announced: European powers should not help Spain regain her former colonies; European monarchies should not impose their ideology on nations in the New World; and there should be no future European colonization in the Americas. Dexter Perkins made a convincing case that the dangers envisioned had been unreal. To the extent that statesmen on the continent contemplated aiding Spain, overturning American republics, or establishing new colonies in the Western Hemisphere, they were deterred by fear of Britain, not by concern about the United States.

It was clear from the record, however, that the American doctrine had been developed in large part because Monroe and his advisers faced issues which seemed to require decisions. They had an invitation to join Britain in resisting the alleged European threat to Latin America. Everyone recognized that acceptance would mean abandonment of the posture previously held and, as Monroe put it, entanglement "in European politicks, & wars." On the other hand, Monroe, and most of those whom he consulted, saw the offer as so advantageous that it should not be turned down. Except for the maxim that there should be no future colonization, the Monroe Doctrine expressed general agreement with British positions.

Coincidentally, the administration faced the question of whether to recognize or aid Greeks who were fighting for independence from the Ottoman Empire. There was loud public demand to do so. The argument for resisting this demand was again to avoid entanglement in European politics. Daniel Webster summarized a popular view, however, when he asked how the United States could defend liberty in Latin America and ignore the same cause in Europe.

In the upshot, the British alliance did not materialize, and the United States did not lead in recognizing Greece. These decisions, even more than the rhetoric that accompanied them, reaffirmed a policy of nonentanglement. But why?

The literature on the Monroe Doctrine did not answer this question—at least not to my satisfaction. Among those who knew of the British alliance overture, everyone except Secretary of State Adams favored acceptance. Adams was the only member of the administration consistently to oppose recognition of Greece. Explaining why the outcomes were victories for Adams, Bemis says simply that his "views by the force of their reason had prevailed over everybody." (p. 390) The same explanation appears in other accounts. In fact, however, there is no evidence that Adams changed anyone's opinion. His own diary records that his colleagues held much the same views at the end as at the beginning. Yet Adams got what he wanted.

When puzzling about what besides Adams's persuasive powers might have produced this outcome, I remembered what had struck me when poring through his manuscripts—the quantity of diary entries and especially correspondence that had to do with the approaching presidential election. It was a preoccupation in his household. His wife characterized the coming contest as "a mighty struggle which arouses alike all the passions and most ardent feelings of mankind." And, as it happened, most of his rivals were in one way or another participants in the foreign debate. William H. Crawford and John C. Calhoun were fellow members of Monroe's cabinet. Henry Clay was the speaker of the house. Andrew Jackson, who had just begun to be talked of as a candidate, was a newly elected member of the Senate. None of the existing accounts of the Monroe Doctrine makes more than passing reference to the "mighty struggle" which filled the mind of Mrs. Adams. Yet the more I thought about it, the more I became convinced that the struggle for the presidency might provide a key to understanding why the foreign policy debates came out as they did.

In this book I explore three hypotheses. The first is that the positions of the various policymakers were largely determined by their ideas of national interest and their personal interplay—in other words, that Adams's convictions were more definite and firm and he more stubborn and forceful than the others. The second is that the outcomes are best understood as products of international politics. The hypothesis is that, in view of what other governments were doing, the range of options open to Americans was very narrow, and the choices actually made were those which would have been made in the same circumstances by almost any reasonable men. The third hypothesis is that the whole process was governed by domestic politics. The positions of the policymakers were determined less by conviction than by ambition. They had different stakes riding on the outcomes, and Adams had a greater stake than the others.

No one of these hypotheses seems to me inherently the more plausible. In a study of American foreign policy during and after World War II, I concluded that convictions about "lessons" of history were a controlling force. Examining in more detail the China policy of that period, I found the strength of character of Secretary of State Marshall a critical determinant. In analyzing American policy during World War I, I was most impressed by the extent to which international politics constrained decision-makers in Washington. In the case of the Monroe Doctrine, however, my conclusion is that the outcomes are best explained in terms of domestic politics.

This is not to say, of course, that individual convictions and personalities were of no consequence or that the international system did not limit Americans' freedom of action. Nor is it even to assert that the evidence is conclusive. Indeed, the direct evidence of connections between the foreign policy debates and the presidential contest is sparse and ambiguous. It is not at all surprising that scholars have overlooked it. American statesmen have always had an aversion to admitting, even to themselves, that their opinions on foreign policy could be affected by private interest. This aversion has been stronger in Washington than in any other major capital, not excepting the Vatican. Hence the conclusion argued here is based chiefly on inference from circumstantial evidence, and because this is so, I would urge readers to review the evidence in their own minds before uncritically accepting my verdict.

If a reader finds my reconstruction plausible, however, I hope he will be driven to more wide-ranging reflection. If the Monroe Doctrine was actually a by-product of an election campaign, one may wonder if some shortcoming in methodology has prevented historians from perceiving the fact. One may also begin to wonder if the sources of wise policy reside in statesmen or in political systems. But these are subjects best reserved until the story has been told.

E.R.M.

Acknowledgments

Without help from scores of librarians and archivists, no scholarly book could be written. My own largest debts are to the staffs of the Massachusetts Historical Society and the Adams Papers project which it houses, the Archives du ministère des affaires étrangères in Paris, the Public Record Office in London, the Library of Congress, the New York Public Library, and, above all, the Harvard University Library.

I also owe thanks to people in the many historical societies and libraries that house manuscripts of the 1820s. Among individuals who went well beyond the call of courtesy in assisting me were Carolyn W. Baldwin of the New Hampshire Historical Society, Linda V. Bauch of the Tennessee State Library and Archives, Marie T. Capps of the United States Military Academy Library, John C. Dann of the William L. Clements Library of the University of Michigan, W. Edwin Hemphill, the editor of the *Papers of John C. Calhoun*, Milo B. Howard, Jr., of the Department of Archives and History of the State of Alabama, George McM. Jones of the University of Pittsburgh Libraries, Archie Motley of the Chicago Historical Society, Nancy Parker of the Woodson Research Center of Rice University, Arlene J. Peterson of the Ohio Historical Society, and Susan B. Tate of the University of Georgia Libraries.

On the substantive side, I owe a great deal more than text or footnote references can suggest to other scholars who have written fundamental works dealing with aspects of the Monroe

Doctrine or European or American Politics, in particular: Harry Ammon, Samuel Flagg Bemis, G. de Bertier de Sauvigny, James A. Field, Jr., Patricia Kennedy Grimsted, Emmanuel Beau de Loménie, Richard P. McCormick, Austin Mitchell, Roy Franklin Nichols, Bradford Perkins, Dexter Perkins, William Spence Robertson, Harold W. V. Temperley, C. K. Webster, and Arthur Preston Whitaker. I hope no reader of this book supposes for a moment that it is intended to replace or supplant Dexter Perkins's classic *Monroe Doctrine, 1823-1826.* It is at most a supplement.

My thinking about the subject benefited greatly from conversations with Frank Freidel, Thomas M. Garwin (who had independently developed a similar thesis), Dorothy G. Harrison, and various individuals who offered comments when they heard the essence of the book presented in the spring of 1974 in a series of public lectures sponsored by the Charles Warren Center of American History and its Director, Donald H. Fleming.

Walter Dean Burnham of M.I.T. was good enough to take time during a sabbatical to read portions of the manuscript dealing with American politics. Aida Donald of the Harvard University Press read all of it not only as an editor but also as a scholar who has done research in the period. Bradford Perkins of the University of Michigan also read the entire manuscript and offered splendidly judicious and helpful comments. To all of them, I am deeply grateful.

Mary Ellen Gianelloni typed several versions of the work as it was revised and rewritten in light of the conversations and comments just mentioned. My wife, Nancy, joined in the substantive criticism and also helped tirelessly in preparing an index. I appreciate this aid more than I can say.

Lastly, I need to express gratitude to students, co-workers, and various loved ones who either suffered hearing about the Monroe Doctrine or suffered lack of attention to their concerns because my mind was wandering away to the 1820s.

E.R.M.

Contents

Tables

Illustrations

*The Making
of the
Monroe Doctrine*

1

The Pressing Problems

On August 16, 1823, Richard Rush, the United States minister in London, came to the British Foreign Office in answer to a summons from the foreign secretary, George Canning. As his carriage turned off Whitehall into Downing Street, he could see to his right, at Numbers 10 and 11, plain Georgian houses which held the offices of the prime minister and the chancellor of the exchequer. Opposite them, on his left, were a run-down Whitbread's pub and a row of ill-kept lodging houses. At the dead end of the narrow street stood the cluster of crumbling brick buildings which housed Canning's department.[1]

A lean man with a long, grave face and a bald head framed with grey sideburns, Rush looked older than his forty-three years. Moreover, he had behind him a long history of public service, including three years as attorney general of the United States, and he had represented his government in London ever since 1817. Often before, a messenger had escorted him up the flight of stairs that led to Canning's corridor-like office with its three walls of tapestries and rank of windows looking out on St. James Park.

---

1. Sir Edward Hertslet, *Recollections of the Old Foreign Office* (London: John Murray, 1901), pp. 1-59; [James Grant], *Travels in Town*, 2 vols. (London: Saunders and Ottley, 1839), II, 162-225; Montagu H. Cox and Philip Norman, eds., *London County Council Survey of London*, vol. XIV: *The Parish of St. Margaret, Westminster*, Part III, vol. II: *Neighborhood of Whitehall* (London: B. T. Batsford, 1931), passim.

On this day, Rush probably had a presentiment that something important was to be said. Parliament had just recessed. Being also leader of the House of Commons, Canning had had an exhausting schedule and should by now have been off to the country. Only a few days earlier he had written a friend that he longed for some weeks of rest: "I want them exceedingly, for I am worn down with work and anxiety."[2] Yet he remained in London for this meeting.

Rush could speculate that Canning wanted to talk about Russia. In 1821, the tsar had decreed that only Russians could use the North Pacific. Since both English and American ships sailed there and both governments had claims to land, a dispute ensued. The English and American envoys in St. Petersburg were trying to get the decree rescinded. After exchanging greetings with Canning, Rush commented that he expected fresh instructions from Washington relating to the North Pacific and northwest coast but had not yet received them.

Rush could guess that Canning might instead have on his mind Spain and the Spanish empire, for revolutionaries in Spain had recently made a captive of King Ferdinand VII and proclaimed a constitutional monarchy. This event had alarmed Russia, Austria, and Prussia, the so-called Holy Alliance, which avowed the principle that legitimate kings should not be constrained by constitutions. The Holy Allies had put down other constitutionalist movements, and they had encouraged France to send troops to Spain to rescue Ferdinand. If the French overran Spain, which seemed likely, there might follow some move to help the Spanish monarch regain his rebellious colonies in the Western Hemisphere. If so, Rush's government would face a choice between leaving the new Latin American republics to their own devices or supporting them and risking war. Knowing that Canning had tried to prevent the French from marching into Spain and that British merchants were making money in Latin

---

2. Canning to Charles Bagot, Aug. 10, 1823, Josceline Bagot, *George Canning and his Friends*, 2 vols. (London: John Murray, 1909), II, 199.

America, Rush could see that the British government might face a comparable dilemma.

After failing to get a rise from his mention of the Russian issue, Rush offered Canning an opening for discussing Latin America. He asked if there seemed any prospect of the revolutionaries holding out in Spain. Canning answered vaguely. Repeating what he knew his own secretary of state had said recently to the British minister in Washington, Rush observed "that should France ultimately effect her purposes in Spain, there was at least the consolation left, that Great Britain would not allow her to go farther and lay her hands upon the Spanish colonies."[3]

At this, Canning quickened. As Rush later reported to Washington, Canning asked, "what I thought my government would say to going hand in hand with his."

Canning's words undoubtedly startled Rush. Only forty years had passed since the American Revolution. Less than a decade had gone by since Britain and the United States had been at war. Yet a British foreign secretary seemed now to be practically proposing an alliance.

The proposition was flattering. Although the United States had less than half the merchant tonnage of Britain and a navy with only one-sixteenth as many guns, Canning spoke of "the large share of the maritime power of the world" which the two nations possessed.[4] He said that "the simple fact of our being known to hold the same sentiment would, he had no doubt, by its moral effect, put down the intention on the part of France, admitting that she should ever entertain it."

3. This account of Canning's first overture to Rush in based on Rush to John Quincy Adams, Aug. 19, 1823, Despatches: Great Britain, Archives of the Department of State. It has been reproduced many times, as, for example, in Stanislaus Murray Hamilton, ed., *The Writings of James Monroe*, 7 vols. (New York: G. P. Putnam's Sons, 1898-1903) (hereafter, Monroe, *Writings*), VII, 361-365.

4. 17th Congress, 2d session, Report by the Secretary of the Navy, "Condition of the Navy and Its Operations." *American State Papers*, vol. I (Washington, D.C.: Gales and Seaton, 1834), pp. 803-805; C. J. Bartlett, *Great Britain and Sea Power, 1815-1853* (Oxford: Clarendon Press, 1963), pp. 21-43.

Rush already had instructions from Washington emphasizing the common interest in blocking European action in the Americas. He had perhaps also seen a dispatch from Canning's cousin, Stratford Canning, lately British minister to the United States, which described Secretary of State John Quincy Adams as interested in cooperative action.[5] With nothing more than the word of a British diplomat as to Adams's inclinations, however, he could not be certain that his government would approve his grasping the hand that Canning extended. Aware that dispatches took a month to cross the Atlantic, that he held the most important post in the American diplomatic service, and that he had bright prospects for rising to be secretary of state or perhaps even President, Rush hesitated to assume responsibility. Hence, instead of snatching at Canning's offer, he sniffed and probed. What, he asked, was Britain's position with regard to the former Spanish colonies? Did she intend to recognize their independence?

Canning dodged the question. Alluding to an earlier offer to mediate between Spain and the rebel governments, he said that Britain would not again "lend her instrumentality or aid, whether by mediation or otherwise, towards making up the dispute between Spain and her colonies; but that if this result could still be brought about, she would not interfere to *prevent* it." Edging closer to an answer, Canning conceded that he "believed the day had arrived when all America might be considered as lost to Europe, so far as the tie of political dependence was concerned." Then he returned to his own question. Would not the United States agree to adopt the same position as Britain?

Rush closed the conversation by evading Canning's question as Canning had evaded his. He promised to report the foreign secretary's proposal to Washington "in the same informal manner in which he threw it out."

After the interview, Rush returned to his legation. All

---

5. Stratford Canning to Canning, June 6, 1823, C. K. Webster, ed., *Britain and the Independence of Latin America: Select Documents from the Foreign Office Archives*, 2 vols. (London: Oxford University Press, 1938), II, 495-496.

along the route stood reminders of how great was the nation which had just invited the United States into a partnership. Turning left out of Downing Street, Rush's carriage rolled the length of Whitehall, past the Horse Guards and the Admiralty. On top of the latter towered the giant windmill-like semaphore, by means of which the Sea Lords sent commands to warships at the mouth of the Thames. Beyond the Admiralty, near Charing Cross, workmen were demolishing the royal stableyards in Great Mews and Dung Hill Mews in order to clear a square commemorating Admiral Lord Nelson's victory at Trafalgar. On Regent Street, John Nash's newly designed thoroughfare, and then on Oxford Street, so recently the Oxford post road and London town's northern boundary, ran a file of shops, where, as Rush had exclaimed on first arriving in London, "every conceivable article lay before you; and all made in England."[6]

Once back at his legation-residence on Baker Street, one of the many four-story row houses recently built in the Marylebone district, Rush began to prepare a report on his conversation with Canning. Despite the importance of this report, or perhaps because of it, he did not complete and sign a final version until after the weekend. Dated August 19, enclosed in a sealed pouch, it then went off to Liverpool to be placed on an American ship bound for home.

The fastest ships on the Atlantic, the packets of the Black Ball lines, took almost three weeks for the Liverpool–New York run. In fact, it was to be more than six weeks before the message reached Washington. Meanwhile, Rush found that he had more to communicate.

On August 22 he received a letter from Canning, now in the country. It contained a five-point summary of Britain's policy.

> 1. We conceive the recovery of the Colonies by Spain, to be hopeless.
> 2. We conceive the question of the Recognition of them as Independent States, to be one of time and circumstances.

6. Richard Rush, *Memoranda of a Residence at the Court of London*, 2d ed. (Philadelphia: Key and Biddle, 1833), p. 54.

3. We are, however, by no means disposed to throw any impediment in the way of an arrangement between them and mother country by amicable negotiation.

4. We aim not at the possession of any portion of them ourselves.

5. We could not see any portion of them transferred to any other Power, with indifference.

Canning asked Rush if American policy could not be stated in almost exactly the same language. If so, could he and Rush issue concurrent declarations or, better still, sign and publish a joint statement embodying these points? They could thus warn France and the continental powers while at the same time reassuring Spain that they had no designs on her empire.[7]

Rush thanked Canning but remained noncommittal. He had an uneasy feeling that Canning would not be pressing him without evidence that some move against the former Spanish colonies was in the offing. If it came, he might be charged with having encouraged it by being too timid to seize Canning's offer. Fretfully, he made copies of Canning's letter and his own noncommittal acknowledgment and directed that they go off to America by the fastest packet. With these copies he sent a covering note saying that he had "deliberated anxiously" but that he remained hesitant, primarily because of "the danger of pledging my government to any measure or course of policy which might in any degree, now or hereafter, implicate it in the federative system of Europe."[8] If events went badly and Rush were later criticized, he would at least have this explanation to quote in his defense.

Rush found, however, that his plea of lack of instructions did not suffice to stop Canning. Time and again, the foreign secretary wrote him, summoned him to the Foreign Office, or invited

---

7. Canning to Rush, Aug. 20, 1823, Monroe Writings, VII, 365-366. The date of receipt is indicated in Rush to Canning, Aug. 23, 1823, ibid., p. 366.

8. Rush to Adams, Aug. 23, 1823, ibid., pp. 368-369; Rush to Monroe, Jan. 28, 1824, Papers of James Monroe, Library of Congress, confessed: "When Mr. Canning made his approaches to me last summer on this subject of Spanish America, I felt that it placed me in a new and difficult conjuncture, and having to decide upon it in default of instructions, and without any communion with other minds, I became proportionably [sic] anxious about the issue."

him to Gloucester Lodge, his villa in Brompton on the outskirts of London. Canning told Rush in confidence of plans afoot for a conference of great powers. To be held as soon as France completed the conquest of Spain, it would deal with the future of the Spanish colonies. This news alarmed Rush. And the uneasiness he had felt from the beginning increased when Canning said that, if Rush had to wait for instructions from home, "events may get before us."[9]

On September 18, in an interview at the Foreign Office, Canning made his most determined push. A spell in the country had restored his physical vigor. When Rush said that nonentanglement in European politics had hitherto been American policy, Canning countered with an oration: "however just such a policy might have been formerly, or might continue to be as a general policy, he apprehended that powerful and controuling circumstances made it inapplicable on the present occasion . . . They (the United States) were the first power established on that continent, and now confessedly the leading power . . . Were the great political and commercial interests which hung upon the destinies of the new continent, to be canvassed and adjusted in this hemisphere without the cooperation or even knowledge of the United States? Were they to be canvassed and adjusted, he would add, without some proper understanding between the United States and Great Britain, as the two chief commercial and maritime states of both worlds [?] He hoped not, he would wish to persuade himself not."[10]

In the face of such eloquence, Rush found it hard not to bend. During the preceding month he had, however, figured out how to meet Canning part way while at the same time protecting himself against a charge of being either too bold or too cautious. He answered that he appreciated all the points Canning made. The interests of his government and the British government coincided, he said, to the extent that both wanted to prevent France and other continental powers from moving into the

9. Canning to Rush, Aug, 23, 1823, Monroe, *Writings*, VII, 369; Rush to Adams, Aug. 28, 1823, ibid., pp. 370-372; Canning to Rush, Aug. 31, 1823, ibid., pp. 372-374. The quotation is from the latter, p. 373.
10. Rush to Adams, Sept. 19, 1823, ibid., pp. 377-386.

Western Hemisphere. Their positions differed in that the United States had recognized the new American states. Since Britain had not taken this step, the two nations might find themselves at odds if, for example, Spain should strike singlehandedly at one or more of her former colonies. If the British government would extend recognition to the new republics, Rush declared, he would be willing to go beyond his instructions and sign a joint declaration such as Canning had proposed.

As Rush reported to Washington, he did not expect Canning to agree to this condition on the spot. The foreign secretary said "such a measure was open to objection." When pressed by Rush to be more specific, he commented lamely on "the uncertain condition, internally, of these new states, or, at any rate, of some of them."

Meanwhile, Rush's original dispatches made their way across the Atlantic. His reports on the first two interviews and Canning's letters, proposing a five-point joint declaration and warning of a possible great power conference about Latin America, all reached New York early in October and then went on to Washington, either over the post road or by coastal ship via Baltimore.

The question posed by Canning then would confront President James Monroe and his cabinet. Their answer did not have to be given immediately. Before the age of cable, radio, and telephone, statesmen could take their time about making decisions. But an answer would have to be framed. The American government had to decide not just what to say but what to do, and the clear choice would be between two fundamentally different foreign policies.

Yet another pressing problem, posing an equally basic issue, was meanwhile emerging because of the situation in Greece.[11] In the spring of 1821, the first fighting had begun

11. The best recent summary is Douglas Dakin, *The Greek Struggle for Independence, 1821-1833* (Berkeley and Los Angeles: University of California Press, 1973). For the United States, the most extensive study is Myrtle A. Cline, *American Attitudes toward the Greek War of Independence* (Atlanta, Ga.: Higgins-McArthur Co., 1930); the best is James A. Field, Jr., *America and the Mediterranean World, 1776-1882* (Princeton: Princeton University Press, 1969), chap. 4.

between Greeks and Turks. Since Russia was thought to want Turkish territory and some leaders of the Greek revolt were former Russian officials, it was at first assumed that the tsar would intervene. When this did not happen, the Greeks appeared to be left on their own. Turkish forces did not, however, succeed in suppressing their movement. By the end of 1821, there were separate resistance groups in the east, the west, and the south. Early in the following year, they coalesced, issued a declaration of independence modeled on that of the United States, proclaimed a republican form of government, and petitioned European capitals and Washington for formal recognition.

The Turkish sultan had meanwhile gathered forces for an offensive. Confused and fragmentary news reports told of bloody fighting. In Chios and other islands in the Aegean, the Turks reportedly slaughtered the Greek inhabitants. They reconquered the western part of Greece proper but were halted at the walls of Missolonghi. In eastern Greece, they carried on running battles with elusive guerrilla bands. As in the islands, they resorted to terror. It was said that one Turkish commander seized women, stripped them naked, and caged them with snakes and starved rats. As of the early summer of 1822, the Turks seemed on the verge of triumph. But Missolonghi held out. So did the guerrillas. Turkish supplies did not. By the end of summer, observers' dispatches told of Turkish troops retreating under fire. In 1823, in the face of a renewed Turkish offensive, the Greeks enjoyed further successes. They continued, moreover, to consolidate their government, convening a constituent assembly, passing laws, and sending envoys abroad to press the case for recognition.

Admiring ancient Greek culture, interpreting the conflict as one between Christians and infidels, shuddering at reports of Turkish atrocities, and thrilling to republican rhetoric that resembled their own, Americans developed strong sympathy for the Greek rebels. In October 1822, the Washington *National Intelligencer* alleged that nothing occupied the public mind so much as Greece, and newspapers reported large pro-Greek rallies in various parts of the country.[12] For the most part, speakers and newspaper editors called merely for moral support or private contributions. A minority, however, asked that the government officially extend financial or even military aid to the Greeks.

Monroe's annual message to Congress in December 1822 had taken note of public feeling. Although it went so far as to express hope that the Greeks would achieve independence, it also made explicit, as Adams noted in his diary, "that neither justice nor policy would justify on our part any active interference in their cause."[13] Public enthusiasm for the Greeks nevertheless became increasingly more passionate. Appeals for recognition and assistance formally presented by agents of the Greek rebels were published in newspapers throughout the nation. Even in the remote Ohio valley, editorials endorsed aid to Greece. In October, the prestigious *North American Review*, a quarterly which Americans pridefully compared with the mother country's *Edinburgh Review*, called upon the government to recognize Greece as it had recognized new nations in Latin America. By December public enthusiasm for such a step would seem to be spreading like fire in a dry woodland.[14]

The Greek question and the British alliance question were not directly linked. Despite pro-Greek feeling in England and some possibility of England's intervening in Greece, Canning had not mentioned cooperation there, and only a few Americans suggested it. The two decisions seemed to have no necessary bearing on one another.

Abstractly, however, the issues did have some similarity. Since becoming independent, the United States had had an am-

12. Washington *National Intelligencer*, Oct. 26, 1822.
13. Monroe, *Writings*, VII, 299-300; Adams diary, Nov. 16, 1822, Adams Family Papers, Massachusetts Historical Society. Most passages from Adams's diary relevant to the history of the Monroe Doctrine are reproduced accurately in Charles Francis Adams, ed., *Memoirs of John Quincy Adams*, 12 vols. (Philadelphia: J. B. Lippincott and Co., 1874-1877). I have chosen, however, to cite only the manuscript diary since it is now widely available in a microfilm edition and since the date of entry will enable any curious reader to find the appropriate passage in the *Memoirs*.
14. *North American Review*, 7 (Oct. 1823), 289-424; Louisville *Public Advertiser*, June 6, 1823; Washington *National Intelligencer*, Sept. 26, 1823; New York *American*, Nov. 21, 1823; Baltimore *American*, Nov. 24, 1823; Baltimore *Weekly Register*, Dec. 13, 1823; Philadelphia *Franklin Gazette*, Dec. 16, 1823.

biguous relationship with Europe. Some Americans and most Europeans had thought of the United States as a minor European power, different from Switzerland or the Italian or Scandinavian states chiefly in being farther away, having once been a colony, and being a constitutional republic. Taking account of the potential for territorial growth, some Americans conceived of the United States as an empire rather than merely a nation. This had been the designation preferred, for example, by Benjamin Franklin.[15] But it had remained indeterminate whether the United States was to be an empire within the European political system or instead the sun within a wholly separate system. Canning's offer compelled a choice between these alternatives. The Greek question not only posed the same choice but asked Americans whether theirs was to be a geographical or an ideological empire—a Rome merely of Caesar or a Rome also of St. Paul. The problems were specific and urgent. The policy issues were broad and affected the basic posture of the United States in international relations.

---

15. See Richard Koebner, *Empire* (Cambridge: Cambridge University Press, 1961), chap. 4.

2

The Policymakers

Most debate about the pressing foreign policy issues would involve principally President Monroe and two members of his cabinet, Secretary of State John Quincy Adams and Secretary of War John C. Calhoun. Though bedridden throughout the autumn and winter of 1823-1824, Secretary of the Treasury William H. Crawford would also be a participant, owing simply to the fact that he had a large following in Congress, the press, and the country and Monroe, Adams, and Calhoun therefore had to take into account what he might have said or might say later. In the same vicarious way, Henry Clay and Andrew Jackson would also take part, for they too could influence congressional and public reactions.

Although these men had much in common, certainly as compared with contemporaries in England or Europe or with American politicians of any later era, each individual had an outlook shaped by his upbringing, education, and career, by the history which he had watched, and by the fears or hopes with which he had lived.

MONROE [1]

Ultimate responsibility for American policy lay, of course, with Monroe. Sixty-five in 1823, he was near the last year of his

---

1. Except where otherwise noted, this sketch of Monroe draws on Harry Ammon, *James Monroe and the Quest for National Identity* (New York: McGraw Hill, 1971) and,

second term. Tradition dictated that he not seek a third. He could look forward only to retirement.

As a token of his age and a reminder to others of his service in the Revolution, he continued to wear eighteenth century clothing—a cutaway coat, frilled neckcloth, waistcoat, knee breeches, long hose, and buckled shoes. One biography of him is entitled *The Last of the Cocked Hats*. Monroe was not, however, an elegant man. Just under six feet, with sloping shoulders, long arms, a lanky frame, and a weathered face, he looked like what he was—a hard-working Virginia farmer.

Despite the eminence he had attained, Monroe had behind him a career marked more by frustration than success. He came from a family which just barely qualified as gentry. His father and grandfather had had to work in the fields with their hands and had had little time for schooling. Entering William and Mary in 1774, he became the first of his line to go beyond country tutoring. His education was interrupted by the Revolutionary War, and, though he later studied law, acquired some French, and sampled writings of the *philosophes*, he never matched in learning such friends or patrons as Jefferson, Madison, John Randolph, and John Taylor of Caroline. He was also poorer than they. His plantations barely paid for themselves, and his speculations in Virginia and Kentucky lands turned out unprofitably. Although he married the daughter of a rich New York merchant, his father-in-law lost all his money in the Revolution. Throughout his life, Monroe had to fret and scrimp and borrow. Even in the final year of his presidency, he was worrying about how to meet his bills.[2]

During the War for Independence, Monroe experienced his first great disappointment. Joining up as a soldier at the age of eighteen, he had the exhilaration of serving as a lieutenant with Washington, fighting in New York, and taking part in the crossing of the Delaware. After being wounded at the battle of Trenton, however, he could not get another command. Though

to a lesser extent, on William P. Cresson, *James Monroe* (Chapel Hill: University of North Carolina Press, 1946) and Arthur Styron, *The Last of the Cocked Hats: James Monroe and the Virginia Dynasty* (Norman: University of Oklahoma Press, 1945).

2. Monroe to Joseph G. Swift, Jan. 4, 1823, Private Papers of Joseph G. Swift, United States Military Academy.

Virginia eventually made him a lieutenant colonel, thus enabling him to be "Colonel Monroe" for the rest of his life, his efforts to recruit volunteers failed; and he put away his uniform before the war was over. The chance to be a military hero passed him by.

Monroe's early political career was similarly flawed. After leaving the army, he became a protégé of Jefferson, the wartime governor of Virginia. He went to the state legislature and then to the Continental Congress. He failed, however, to be chosen a delegate to the contitutional convention in Philadelphia. He concluded sourly that his presumed friend, Madison, had deliberately thwarted him.

After the new Constitution went into effect, Monroe ran against Madison for a seat in Congress, but lost. Although the state legislature sent him to the United States Senate, the Senate was then less in the public eye than the House. Madison was more conspicuous doing Jefferson's work in the House than was Monroe doing the same in the upper chamber. And when Jefferson and Madison made their celebrated tour of the North in 1791, laying groundwork for a nationwide Republican party, Monroe could not join them because he had to stay home working his farms.

Monroe's next opportunity to achieve independent distinction came in 1794. In company with Jefferson and Madison, Monroe had been criticizing the Washington administration's coolness toward Revolutionary France and apparent drift toward reconciliation and possibly alliance with her chief enemy, England. They fought the appointment of Chief Justice John Jay as special envoy to London, alleging that Jay was an Anglophile, but they lost. Then Monroe was asked by President Washington to become minister to France. Offered the chance thus to repair relations with the French and offset whatever harm Jay might do, Monroe was exultant.

He set out, however, with handicaps. Washington had appointed him solely to appease Jeffersonians in Congress. The secretary of state gave him scanty instructions and told him almost nothing about the actual mission assigned to Jay. When

Monroe arrived in France, he made public statements in support of the French and in criticism of the British. He denied that Jay would negotiate a treaty of friendship and trade with Britain. It soon became evident that he did not know what he was talking about, for Jay signed just such a treaty. When Washington recalled Monroe, few Frenchmen lamented his departure. Although Jefferson and some of his allies tried to fête Monroe as a martyr when he got home, their efforts did little to salve the hurt. His mission to France had ended humiliatingly.

In the late 1790s, during John Adams's presidency, Monroe missed another opportunity. When Jefferson and Madison engineered the Virginia and Kentucky resolves protesting alleged repressive measures by the administration, Monroe was sick and unable to lend a hand. In the turn of events that resulted in Adams's failing to be reelected and Jefferson's becoming President, Monroe returned to public life as governor of Virginia. It was a largely honorific office, entailing no power except in wartime when it involved command of the militia. After serving three years, Monroe prepared for permanent retirement to life as a farmer and an occasional practitioner before the courts in Richmond.

By asking him to return to Paris on a special mission, Jefferson gave Monroe a fresh shot at a place in history. Napoleon, now the ruler of France, had acquired the vast Louisiana territory from Spain, and Jefferson wanted Monroe to join Minister Robert R. Livingston in negotiating for purchase of the mouth of the Mississippi River. Seeing a chance to redeem himself as a diplomat, Monroe scarcely hesitated, and, of course, he and Livingston succeeded in buying all of Louisiana. At last, Monroe had the applause and fame for which he had yearned.

Unfortunately, Monroe did not then come home to enjoy his triumph. He accepted appointment as minister to Britain. There he had to deal with issues arising out of renewed war between Britain and France, especially the impressment of American seamen and the seizure of American cargoes and ships. Failing to understand that many Americans regarded impressment as a worse grievance than interference with trade, he signed a treaty in 1806 that conceded impressment in return for commercial concessions. Jefferson refused even to submit it to the Senate. Monroe's second period as a diplomat thus ended even more badly than the first. Upon his return he was welcomed only by dissidents who were trying to form an opposition in Virginia.

Always worshipful of Jefferson, Monroe blamed his disgrace on Madison, who was Jefferson's secretary of state. He lent himself to the opposition only as it became apparent that Madison would be Jefferson's successor. In 1808 he permitted a slate of electors pledged to him to run against those pledged to Madison. For a third time he suffered defeat, losing in Virginia by more than four to one. With Madison in the White House, it seemed as if Monroe were surely doomed to finish his career with no memorable public accomplishments besides a wound at Trenton, the Louisiana treaty, and two failed missions as an envoy in Europe.

Once again, however, his fortunes rose. As Madison lost popularity because of his apparent inability to solve problems rising out of the continued and increasingly ferocious Anglo-French war, the Virginians who had earlier supported Monroe became more powerful in the legislature. Symbolically, they returned Monroe to the governorship. Madison had already judged it expedient to seek a reconciliation. Early in 1811 he invited Monroe to become secretary of state.

Of course, Monroe accepted the post. He could interpret Madison's offer as giving retroactive approval to what he had done in London. He could hope others would do likewise. With a fresh chance to prove his merits as a diplomat, he might earn the place in history thus far largely denied him. Also, he might possibly put himself in position to be the fourth Virginia President.

Monroe collaborated with Madison in the complicated maneuvers that thrust upon congressional Warhawks responsibility for hostilities with Britain. Once war was declared, he wanted to leave the State Department, exercise military command, and become the conqueror of Canada, but Madison and the senior members of Congress would not even let him become secretary of war. Monroe stood by as an impotent critic while John Armstrong, who did become secretary of war, allowed the British almost unopposed to enter and burn the capital. Only after that disaster did he get to take over the War Department.

There was little glory in his service in Madison's cabinet. The most that could be said was that the worst mistakes had been the responsibility of others. Nevertheless, he became almost by default the choice of Republicans as Madison's successor, and he was elected President in 1816.

In this up-and-down career, some beliefs had taken root in Monroe's mind. They were not immutable. They were not even wholly consistent. But one or another could serve him as a postulate when he reasoned for understanding of a new situation.

For one thing, Monroe believed that the American Revolution had been more than a mere revolt for independence. During the fighting, according to his latest biographer, he shared with the more impassioned revolutionaries an "identification with a force greater than themselves."[3] He saw the French Revolution as the second wave of a movement which Americans had initiated. Though somewhat shaken by the later French turn to Bonapartism, he continued to hold that the lead given by the United States would eventually be followed by the rest of the world. As President, he wrote to a friend, "Our revolution gave birth to that of France, and it is our successful career, and the glorious example which is exhibited by it, that produced the movment [sic] in So. America, & is now producing another great movment in Europe."[4]

At the same time, Monroe felt that the United States had unique advantages. In one of his annual messages as governor

3. Ammon, Monroe, p. 19.
4. "Aratus" letters of 1791, quoted ibid., pp. 87-88; Monroe to Madison, Sept. 2, 1794, Stanislaus Murray Hamilton, ed., The Writings of James Monroe, 7 vols. (New York: G. P. Putnam's Sons, 1898-1903) (hereafter, Monroe, Writings), II, 38-40; Monroe to Archibald Stuart, May 27, 1821, Papers of Archibald Stuart, Virginia Historical Society.

of Virginia, he identified these as the absence of "hereditary orders," the fact that all citizens were "born with equal rights and expectations," the character and extent of the land, and habits and institutions developed through history. Even so, he said in the same message that "America will remain an instructive, an illustrious example to nations."[5] If called upon to reconcile the two lines of argument, he might have replied that other nations would not match the United States but that they would try, and would benefit by doing so.

Mixed with hope for world revolution and pride in his country was fear lest the American experiment be undone. In the early years Monroe shared with many of his contemporaries concern that a monarchist party might emerge and perhaps provoke a civil war or at least incite foreign intrigue. The result could be to put America back under the British crown. In 1791 he was alarmed by essays in a Boston newspaper signed "Publicola," which answered Thomas Paine's recent *Rights of Man* by contrasting the constitutional order of Britain and America with the mob rule alleged to be developing in France. These essays were attributed to Vice President John Adams and only later discovered to be by his twenty-four-year-old son, John Quincy Adams. In Monroe's reading, "Publicola" seemed to be arguing for monarchy not only in Britain but in America. He drew the same inference from a later series of essays by John Quincy Adams denouncing the behavior of Citizen Genêt, the militant revolutionary who in 1793 temporarily represented France in the national capital. The object of the "monarchy party," wrote Monroe, was "to separate us from France and pave the way for an unnatural connection with Great Britain."[6]

Although this particular concern wore off, Monroe remained apprehensive about possible dissolution of the nation or loss of independence as a result of conflict among sections or classes. Experience in the Continental Congress and the first Senate, together with travel to Kentucky and the Old North-

---

5. Message of Dec. 7, 1801, Monroe, *Writings*, III, 318.
6. Monroe to John Breckenridge, Aug, 23, 1793, Ammon, *Monroe*, pp. 103-104.

west, had early convinced him that northerners, southerners, and westerners had profound differences in outlook.[7] The controversy early in his presidency as to whether slavery should extend into the Missouri territory reinforced his opinion by dividing Congress into northern and southern blocs. Meanwhile, disputes about trading rights in European wars, a national bank, protective tariffs, and internal improvements persuaded him that conflict between commercial and agricultural interests was almost equally likely.[8] He felt distaste for the materialism of the commercial interests. When secretary of state, he had burst out to the French minister: "People in Europe suppose us to be merchants, occupied exclusively with pepper and ginger. They are much deceived. . . . The immense majority of our citizens . . . are . . . controlled by principles of honor and dignity."[9] Nevertheless, he carried in his mind the maxim that national policy needed to reconcile the interests of diverse sections and diverse economic groups.

Monroe believed the United States to be in some danger from other nations even if it retained internal unity. During the 1780s and 1790s he regarded all European monarchies as hostile to the American republic. He said that revolutions in the Old World helped to protect liberty in the New. The English he assumed to be always bent on diminishing if not subjugating the United States. In London he had found contempt or hostility toward his country among not only the aristocracy but also backbenchers in the House of Commons and the merchant class. He commented repeatedly that English ministers, no matter what their personal dispositions, would never be able to pursue a policy friendly to the United States.[10]

After the war, when monarchy had been restored in most of

---

7. Monroe to Jefferson, Jan. 19, 1786, Monroe, *Writings*, I, 117-118.

8. Monroe to Madison, May 14, 1815, quoted in Ammon, *Monroe*, pp. 340-341.

9. Henry Adams, *History of the United States*, 9 vols. (New York: Charles Scribner's Sons, 1891-1896), VI, 58.

10. E.g., Monroe to Madison, March 3, 1804, Monroe, *Writings*, IV, 151; Monroe to Jefferson, March 15, 1804, ibid., p. 155; Monroe to Jefferson, April 14, 1823, ibid., VI, 304-307.

Europe, Monroe's apprehensiveness increased. Continuing to hold that republican movements there helped to protect America from monarchical animosity, he saw the United States as less strong when republicanism in Europe was at low ebb. After becoming President, he once commented to his secretary of state:

> The movement in Europe forms an issue between most of the sovereigns and their subjects, & the United States are regarded as the natural ally of the one & enemy of the other, without other agency than the mere force of example. If the progress should be such as to make our overthrow presumable, or to excite despair with the sovereigns, the attempt may be apprehended.[11]

To defend itself against Europe, Monroe had concluded, the United States needed to play the game of European politics. Originally, he had believed simply that the United States should maintain the Revolutionary War alliance with the French. The reasons for doing so had seemed to him all the more cogent when France appeared to be copying the American example. He deplored Washington's Farewell Address, with its counsel against political involvement with Europe. By the time Napoleon dominated Europe, he had begun to think that America's safety might best be protected by a connection with the English, despite their untrustworthiness and hostility. As he explained to Jefferson, "It is important for us to stand well with some power."[12] Although he made no effort to ensure that the United States had a powerful ally when it went to war in 1812, that fact did not. necessarily indicate a change in view, for he faced a situation in which the United States stood on the edge of war with both Britain and France. If anything, the experience probably strengthened his earlier attitude.

Above all, Monroe believed that Americans should do what-

---

11. Monroe to Adams, July 24, 1821, Adams Family Papers, Massachusetts Historical Society, partially reproduced in Worthington C. Ford, ed., *The Writings of John Quincy Adams*, 7 vols. (New York: The Macmillan Co., 1913-1917) (hereafter, Adams, *Writings*), VII, 138-139.

12. Monroe to Jefferson, Jan. 11, 1807, Monroe, *Writings*, V, 2.

ever they could to make Europeans see the United States as a nation of consequence, deserving to be both feared and courted. He came to this conviction during service in France in the 1790s when he discovered with shock that many Frenchmen did not care whether the United States were an ally or not. So dismayed was he that he urged a war with Britain and the conquest of Canada or the British West Indies; "this would be acting like a nation, and we would then be respected as such here and in England."[13]

This theme recurred continually in Monroe's later speeches and private letters. He became a relentless advocate of greater military preparedness, nearly always arguing, as in 1804, that the United States should "become an object, commanding the respect of every power, and of political calculation of each" and that the "respect, which one power has for another is in the exact proportion of the means which they respectively have of injuring each other with the least detriment to themselves."[14]

As President, Monroe thus brought to the issues of 1823 a set of beliefs developed in the course of his previous life. Some of these beliefs were held by large numbers of Americans. Some were shared by other men involved in policymaking. None was unique to Monroe. The clustering, however, was distinctively his. While he believed that the rest of the world would eventually imitate the republicanism of the United States, he held at the same time that the United States had unique strengths which would give it continued superiority. He was fearful that internal sectional or class conflict might undo the nation's promise, and he thought it still vulnerable to attack from monarchies abroad. For Monroe, the prudential rules for American statecraft were: (1) to conciliate all sectional and economic interests; (2) to play European powers against one another; and (3) to build up national power to the end of making the United States in European eyes an enemy to be feared and an ally to be desired.

---

13. Monroe to Madison, Nov. 30, 1794, Ammon, *Monroe*, pp. 128-129.
14. Monroe's journal of 1804, quoted ibid., p. 23.

James Monroe, age 28, artist unknown

James Monroe as President, 1817, by Gilbert Stuart

While Monroe's career had given him these settled convictions, it had also shaped his personality in such a way to give him less than total confidence in his opinions. His history appeared in his features and bearing. In his twenties, he had had an open face with wide, bright eyes, and it was said of him that he lighted up when he smiled. By the time Monroe became President, lines crossed his forehead, drawing his widow's peak so near his eyebrows that a tourist once exclaimed, "He hasn't got brains enough to hold his hat on!" His eyes were hooded and watchful; his mouth was tight and cautious. He remained, as always, slow in comprehension and judgment, and he displayed such reserve as President that Mrs. John Quincy Adams once described him as having *"congealing* qualities."[15]

As his presidency drew to an end, Monroe's chief motive was to protect his reputation. In 1807 Madison had commented on "how dear to Mr. Jefferson his popularity must be, and especially at the close of his political career."[16] In view of the many past occasions in which Monroe had suffered humiliation, this was all the more true of him. As he came nearer and nearer to retirement, he became more and more sensitive about the possibility of offending factions in his party or of taking some action which, like his treaty with Britain, might be criticized as a blunder. In the debate that led to the Monroe Doctrine, he would therefore insert his opinions but above all seek courses that would keep the peace within his cabinet, his party, and his country.

ADAMS[17]

The career of Secretary of State John Quincy Adams had been different from Monroe's in almost every respect. A New

---

15. Cresson, *Monroe*, pp. 47, 95; S. G. Goodrich, *Recollections of a Lifetime*, 2 vols. (New York: Miller, Orton, and Mulligan, 1856), II, 401; Louisa Catherine Adams to Adams, Aug. 3, 1822, Adams Papers.

16. Henry Adams, *History of the United States*, IV, 189.

17. Except where otherwise noted, this sketch of Adams draws on Samuel Flagg Bemis, *John Quincy Adams and the Foundations of American Foreign Policy* (New York: Alfred A. Knopf, 1950) and *John Quincy Adams and the Union* (New York: Alfred A. Knopf, 1956).

Englander rather than a southerner, he came from a town instead of a farm and from a family in which not only formal education but lifelong immersion in books was taken for granted. He had a father to whom he could look up as a man not only of learning but also, of course, of practical accomplishments—a hero of the Revolution and ultimately vice president and President. The fact that the electorate repudiated the elder Adams in 1800 rankled in the son's mind but in no way diminished his family pride.

Adams's first experience of the world across the Atlantic came before his teens when his father went to France to help negotiate the Revolutionary War alliance. He acquired enough education and maturity to be sent to Russia at fifteen as French translator for the American envoy to Empress Catherine the Great. After that he served in Paris, the Netherlands, and London as his father's private secretary. It was with this cosmopolitan background, abetted by private study of Latin classics and modern French literature, that he returned to attend and graduate from Harvard College, study law, and begin practice as a lawyer in Boston.

Adams remained in the United States for only nine years before President Washington appointed him minister to the Netherlands. He went there in the same year that Monroe first went to France. Subsequently, he served temporarily in London. Through most of his father's presidency, he was minister to Prussia.

Following Jefferson's election, Adams again came home. Mixing legal work with politics, he won a seat in the Massachusetts Senate as a Federalist. He then suffered the pain of losing a race for Congress. Since it was a party contest, Adams had some solace in the fact that Federalists were losing everywhere and that his margin of loss was only 59 votes out of 3,739. Also, his friends did exactly what Monroe's friends had done in Virginia thirteen years earlier. They saw to it that the legislature chose him for the United States Senate. Since the Senate had become a more prestigious body than in Monroe's day, this was more than enough to make Adams feel that his defeat had been fortunate.

Adams served in the Senate from 1803 to 1808. He early parted company with the Federalist bloc by endorsing the Louisiana purchase. Later he broke with the Federalists altogether and supported Jefferson's embargo. Consorting more and more with Republicans, he took part in 1808 in the Republican congressional caucus that nominated Madison as Jefferson's successor. When the Federalist-controlled Massachusetts legislature censured his actions, he resigned and returned to the practice of law.

The interlude proved brief, for Madison named him minister to Russia. Confirmation was delayed because of opposition by old Republicans who objected to any favors for Federalists, apostate or otherwise. Eventually, however, Adams went to St. Petersburg. Toward the end of the War of 1812, he joined the delegation which negotiated peace with the British at Ghent. He then became minister to Great Britain. It was while in that post that he received and accepted Monroe's invitation to join the cabinet.

All in all, therefore, Adams had spent most of his mature life abroad. Since growing up, he had had only two intervals in the United States, one of nine years and the other of eight. He had had to form his opinions of American affairs during these two periods or on the basis of letters and other reports sent to him while abroad. This fact did not make Adams any less sure that he understood what had been in progress and what it signified.

One abiding conviction which Adams had developed was that America's attainment of independence constituted one of the great benign events in human history. Despite the suspicions which his Publicola essays aroused in Monroe, the notion that the United States ought to return to the British Empire never even crossed Adams's thoughts. To be sure, he rejoiced that the United States was a republic, but he knew that there were other republics and that there had been many in past history. To him it seemed much more remarkable that a group of remote colonies had separated from their mother country and formed an independent state.[18]

---

18. "Publicola" letters of 1791, Adams, *Writings*, I, 65-109.

Adams did feel that the American republic might outshine all others. Though at first dubious about the Constitution drawn up in Philadelphia in 1787, he shared with his father an enthusiasm for constitutions as such. What he wanted to say when writing as Publicola was that constitutions protected the people against impetuous majorities; and he quickly became a defender of the Constitution which his countrymen had adopted.

Adams's hope that the American republic might distinguish itself from others rested in part on his perception that most of the people belonged to the middle class. He was not so impressed as Monroe with the nation's freedom from "hereditary orders." To him it seemed a more important difference that the United States had no capital like Paris crowded with idlers whom demagogues could turn into mobs. In addition, he thought the United States blessed because it was largely Protestant and nonconformist and thus in his estimate relatively free of superstitions.[19]

Holding these views and, with them, a well-informed and highly critical opinion of European and English society, Adams never saw much reason to suppose that American republicanism would be successfully imitated in the Old World or elsewhere. When the Spanish colonies revolted, he expressed pleasure that they emulated the United States but doubt that they would ever develop comparable institutions. "They have not the first elements of good or free government," he commented to Clay in 1821. "Arbitrary power, military and ecclesiastical, was stamped upon their education, upon their habits, and upon all their institutions."[20] While Adams thought that the United States should in some respects set an example for the world, he did not share the belief of Monroe and others that the nation had a mission to lead others, nor did he see much prospect of success if the experiment were tried.

The great fear in Adams's mind in his early years was that the United States would lose or abandon its hard-won inde-

---

19. Ibid., p. 82; "Columbus" letters of 1793, ibid., p. 156; draft of speech of July 4, 1821, Adams Papers.
20. Adams diary, March, 9, 1821, Adams Papers (hereafter cited simply as Adams diary).

pendence. He saw Europe as posing a constant threat. In the mid-1790s, at the very time when Monroe and other Jeffersonians suspected him of wanting a return to the British empire, he was cautioning Federalists in the administration to expect no favors from the English and writing to his father, "Between the United States and Great Britain no *cordiality* can exist." After the Napoleonic wars, Adams saw England and all of Europe as hostile to the United States and hoping for its overthrow.[21]

Against loss of independence, the best safeguard was, in Adams's view, the preservation of national unity. In notes for an autobiography drawn up in 1809 he wrote:

> There are two political principles that form the basis of the system of policy best suited to the interests and duties of this country. One in relation to its internal concerns, UNION, the other in respect to its intercourse with foreign nations, INDEPENDENCE. These principles are the keys to my political creed.[22]

Like Monroe, Adams worried about possible sectional conflict. He repeatedly expressed fear lest the Virginians pursue their interests so single-mindedly as to drive the North into secession. At one time, while still a Federalist, he characterized as inevitable a "serious struggle . . . between the Ancient Dominion and the Union."[23] Enough of this apprehension survived to make Adams later, as a Republican and an officeholder, a wholehearted supporter of Monroe's inclination to respect the interests of other sections. "The government of this country," he was to write in 1824, "ought to be administered on the principle of conciliated and not of conflicting interests."[24]

In the event of internal conflict, Adams feared England or Europe might strip the United States of its independence. In his essays attacking Citizen Genêt, he observed that Sweden,

---

21. Adams to Timothy Pickering, Dec. 22, 1795, Adams, *Writings*, I, 464; Adams to John Adams, Feb. 10, 1796, ibid., p. 478; Adams diary, May 13, 1818, Nov. 16, 1819.
22. Adams to Skelton Jones, April 17, 1809, Adams, *Writings*, III, 300.
23. Adams to Pickering, Sept. 3, 1798, ibid., II, 358.
24. Adams to Robert L. Walsh, March 1, 1824, Adams Papers.

Geneva, Holland, and Poland had all fallen because of "association of internal faction, and external power." When defending his support of Jefferson's embargo, he argued that "war with England would probably soon if not immediately be complicated with a civil war, and with a desperate effort to break up the union." Reports reaching him in Europe of the secessionist movement that actually took form in New England during the War of 1812 convinced him even more of the peril. When warned by Calhoun in 1820 that the slavery issue might cause the South to secede and ally with Britain, Adams responded that in such event the South would become a colony again.[25]

To avert the danger, Adams held, the United States should resolutely avoid any embroilment in European politics. In an essay published in April 1793, shortly after the outbreak of war between France and Britain, he wrote: "as the citizens of a nation at a vast distance from the continent of Europe; of a nation whose happiness consists in real independence, it is our duty to remain the peaceable and silent, though sorrowful, spectators of the sanguinary scene." He was delighted by Washington's Farewell Address not only because it expressed the same idea but also because his father intimated to him that it had been directly influenced by Adams's writing. This probably helped to fix Adams's conviction. He said to Clay in 1821, "The principle of neutrality to all foreign wars was, in my opinion, fundamental to the continuance of our liberties and of our Union."[26]

Adams did not disagree with Monroe that the United States should and would become more powerful. He had written in 1796, "we should proceed with gigantic strides to honor and consideration, and national greatness, if the union is preserved." He favored stronger military forces, especially a larger navy, and he more than shared Monroe's interest in territorial expansion.

25. "Columbus" letter of 1793, Adams, *Writings*, I, 160; Adams to Ezekiel Bacon, Nov. 17, 1808, ibid., III, 248; Adams diary, Feb. 24, 1820.
26. "Marcellus" letters of 1793, Adams, *Writings*, I, 140; Bemis, *Adams and the Foundations*, pp. 63-64; Adams diary, March 9, 1821.

He said to the President as early as 1819 that it was the destiny of the United States to control all of North America.[27]

Adams nevertheless came to the cabinet debates of 1823 with attitudes quite different from those of Monroe. He thought it the mission of the United States to protect its independence and unique virtue rather than to lead the rest of the world, and he was convinced that the nation should avoid mixing in European politics. While in no sense a pacifist, he shared none of the liking for war and military conquest which Monroe sometimes exhibited, for Adams, as he was to say to Clay in 1823, regarded *any* war "as necessarily placing high interests of different portions of the Union in conflict with each other, and thereby endangering the Union itself."[28]

In cabinet sessions and private meetings with the President, Adams—if his diary is to be trusted—stated his opinions with vigor and at length. He showed little of the cautious reserve characteristic of Monroe. The few setbacks in his life had left no visible marks upon him. A portrait by Gilbert Stuart of the late 1820s can be compared with one by Copley done in 1795. It shows a short muscular man who had put on flesh and grown bald but who retained a serenely self-confident face with shining eyes and a mouth set in an uncompromising line. Combative, immensely learned, quick in mind, and tireless as a debater, Adams was much more forceful than Monroe.

Differences between the two in 1823 were not all matters of belief or personality. Perhaps more important and more subtle in influence were differences in interest. While Monroe's convictions were to some extent subordinated to desire that his presidency end happily, Adams's enthusiasm for principle was corrected in some degree by yearning to be Monroe's successor. Adams did not want this ambition to influence him. In neither the literal nor the popular sense was he a Puritan. His religious opinions were indefinite, and his recreations included dancing,

27. Adams to Charles Adams, June 9, 1796, Adams, *Writings*, I 494; Adams diary, Nov. 17, 1819.

28. Adams diary, Dec. 2, 1823.

card-playing, and madeira-tippling; but he had a Puritan conscience which insisted upon hard work, attention to duty, and abnegation of self. When a friend warned him in 1818 that he might lose the presidency if he did not work to win it, he responded primly, "my business was to serve the public to the best of my abilities in the station assigned to me, and not to intrigue for further advancement."[29]

Yet Adams's conscience did not tell him that he should disdain the presidency. Quite the contrary. His sons and his wife wanted him to be so honored. He could well see his election as a vindication of his father. Indeed, he was to write that he would welcome being elected "for the gratification which it would afford to the declining days of my surviving Parent." If chosen President, he would have proof that the people approved his own past services. He boasted to his wife in 1822, "Of the public history of Mr. Monroe's administration, all that will be worth telling to posterity hitherto has been transacted through the Department of State," and he was to write in his diary in 1824: "To suffer without feeling is not in human nature; and when I consider that to me alone, of all the candidates before the nation, failure of success would be equivalent to a vote of censure by the nation upon my past service, I cannot dissemble to myself that I have more at stake upon the result than any other individual in the Union."[30]

With increasing insistence, Adams's conscience told him that it would be wrong to stand by and permit any of the other candidates to be elected. As early as 1819, he saw in the cabinet and Congress "continual and furious electioneering for the succession." Because he saw his department as central, he concluded that "*all* these exertions hitherto have been directed to the positive purpose of excluding me from the field of competition."[31]

---

29. Adams diary, March 13, 1818.
30. Adams to Henry Coleman, March 18, 1825, Adams Papers; Adams to Louisa Catherine Adams, Oct. 7, 1822, Adams, *Writings*, VII, 316; Adams diary, May 8, 1824.
31. Adams diary, Nov. 27, 1819; Adams to John D. Heath, Jan. 7, 1822, Adams, *Writings*, VII, 193.

John Quincy Adams, age 28, by John Singleton Copley

John Quincy Adams as secretary of state,
by Gilbert Stuart (head) and Thomas Sully (body)

Adams quickly developed a low opinion of Crawford, who was generally regarded as Monroe's likely successor. "Crawford's point d'honneur is to differ from me, and to find no weight in any reason assigned by me," Adams observed. He came to believe that Crawford opposed a treaty with Spain advantageous to the United States solely because it would be to Adams's credit. As early as the autumn of 1820, he was convinced that Crawford was "an intriguer of the first water."[32]

Adams also thought ill of Clay. They had been together at Ghent negotiating peace with Britain in 1814, and had often disagreed. While Adams had developed a respect for Clay's intelligence and debating skill, he had found him wanting in seriousness. He interpreted Clay's various moves in Congress in opposition to the Monroe administration as wholly opportunistic. Summing up, he wrote in his diary in 1820: "Clay is essentially a gamester, . . . with a vigorous intellect, an ardent spirit, a handsome elocution, . . . a mind very defective in elementary knowledge, and a very undigested system of ethics."[33]

Of Calhoun, Adams originally had a higher opinion. After a few months' acquaintance, he commented, "Calhoun thinks for himself . . . , with sound judgment, quick discrimination, and keen observation." Adams made this observation, however, before Calhoun began to be talked of for the presidency. Once that occurred, Adams changed his mind. He thought such an aspiration absurd in so young a man. By the autumn of 1823, he had concluded that Calhoun was as much an intriguer as Crawford. He said to a New Hampshire congressman that even Clay would be better, for he had "a root of principle, which made him a safer man than Crawford or Calhoun."[34]

Adams also started out with a good opinion of Andrew

32. Adams diary, Jan. 6, 1818, Jan. 7, 1819; William Plumer, Jr., to William Plumer, Sr., Nov. 24, 1820, Everett S. Brown, ed., *The Missouri Compromise and Presidential Politics, 1820-1825, from the Letters of William Plumer, Jr.* (St. Louis: Missouri Historical Society, 1926), p. 56.

33. Adams diary, March 31, April 6, 1820.

34. Ibid., Jan. 6, 1818; William Plumer, Jr., to William Plumer, Sr., Dec. 3, 1823, Brown, *Missouri Compromise*, p. 86.

Jackson, but that was at a time when most politicians thought Jackson had little or no chance of being in the presidential race. When the movement for Jackson gained strength in 1824, Adams began to have misgivings. He told a supporter that he thought Jackson qualified for the *second* office in the nation: "the Vice-Presidency was a station in which the General could hang no one, and in which he would need to quarrel with no one . . . It would afford an easy and dignified retirement to his old age."[35] Surveying the opposing candidates, Adams therefore found abundant reason for judging it his duty to obstruct their ambitions, even if it entailed promoting his own interest.

In addition, there worked upon Adams's conscience the alluring argument that public policy in a democracy should commend itself to the people. Soon after becoming secretary of state, he commented in his diary, "These Cabinet Councils open upon me a new scene and new views of the political world. Here is a play of passions, opinions, and characters different in many respects from those in which I have been accustomed heretofore to move."[36] In the cabinet he found himself increasingly applying a test which had seldom entered his reasoning when a diplomat or even when a senator—that of whether or not a policy would be popular. With regard to Jackson's unauthorized seizure of territory in Spanish Florida in 1818, Adams opposed disavowal of the act, contending that it would, among other things, "give offence to all his friends [and] encounter the shock of his popularity." On the issue of whether to recognize the new republics in Latin America, Adams early conceded that the administration might "go farther if such were the feeling of the nation and of Congress." Although he delayed recognition in order to pry territorial concessions from Spain, he said repeatedly that public opinion would ultimately control policy.[37] To the extent that Adams saw the satisfaction of the public as a matter of principle, he could further his own political interest without any reproach from his conscience.

---

35. Adams diary, May 15, 1824.
36. Ibid., Jan. 9, 1818.
37. Ibid., March 28, July 21, July 28, 1818, Dec. 3, 1819.

The influence of ambition on Adams's performance as a policymaker was by no means all a matter of unconscious rationalization. In March 1820 he wrote in his diary:

> The selfish and the social passions are intermingled in every man acting in a public capacity. It is right that they should be so, and it is no just cause of reproach to any man that in promoting to the utmost of his power the public good, he is desirous at the same time of promoting his own.[38]

In the debates of 1823, when seeking prescriptions consistent with the convictions he had matured over time, Adams had abundant resources for both rationalizing and reasoning out positions that would serve his interest in becoming President.

CRAWFORD[39]

It is not easy to reconstruct the positions that Treasury Secretary Crawford would have taken if he had been well enough to sit with the cabinet. He wrote no philosophical essays, kept no diary, delivered matter-of-fact speeches which seldom wandered into abstract speculation, and wrote letters which were equally to the point.

As of 1823 Crawford was fifty-one—fourteen years younger than Monroe and four years younger than Adams. Born in the Virginia Piedmont, he came from a family much like Monroe's but one which had risen in the world as a result of moving first to South Carolina and then to northeastern Georgia. Since these regions were comparatively primitive, Crawford received a fitful education at various schools and academies, but he inherited a prosperous plantation and status as a member of the Georgia

---

38. Ibid., March 4, 1820.
39. Except where otherwise noted, this sketch of Crawford is based on Chase C. Mooney, *William H. Crawford* (Lexington, Ky.: University Press of Kentucky, 1974) and, to a lesser extent, on Philip J. Green, *The Public Life of William H. Crawford* (Chicago: no publisher, 1938).

aristocracy. He then studied law and, like Monroe, combined the management of a farm with practice at the bar.

Crawford was a big man, well over six feet tall, and burly. He had sandy hair, pink cheeks, large blue eyes, and a firm, heavy jaw. His recreations were riding and shooting. He fought at least two duels and, in one, killed his opponent. In appearance and manner, he could have modeled for one of Fielding's country squires. His speeches and letters, however, display a fastidious intelligence and a sense of irony.

Though Crawford became active in politics in the late 1790s, the issues that engaged him were local, not national. Probably, he paid relatively little attention to affairs outside of Georgia prior to 1807, when he was elected to the United States Senate. If that is the case, he perceived and judged issues rather differently from Monroe and Adams, for his ideas did not take form when the critical alternatives were subordination or independence, Confederation or Constitution, or support for France or reconciliation with England. Instead, Crawford matured intellectually at a time when debate centered on whether the nation should or should not risk war in order to defend its honor, status, and alleged rights.

With regard to this issue, Crawford had been ambivalent. He initially opposed the embargo despite Jefferson's plea that it might prevent war. On the other hand, after most of his colleagues had judged the embargo a failure, Crawford argued for retaining it. While conceding that it hurt the economy of Georgia and the South in general, he said that it served to defend the "sectional honor" against the British. In particular, he contended that it should not be given up because of complaints from northern shippers and merchants or the "argument *in terrorem*" that the North might secede. "I will persist in the course which I believe to be right," he declared, "at the expense even of the Government itself."[40]

Crawford continued to lament abandonment of the embargo. He opposed voting money for an increase in the navy,

---

40. 10th Congress, 2d session, *Annals of Congress* (Nov. 22, 1808), pp. 63-73.

William H. Crawford, by John Wesley Jarvis

John C. Calhoun as secretary of war, by Charles Bird King

asking his fellow senators in 1810 "whether the present situation of the world does not solemnly admonish this nation to stand aloof from the dreadful convulsions with which Europe for years past has been agitated to its centre." He continued also to indicate doubt as to the wisdom of making great exertions to preserve the union. Indeed, he once said in a different context that the time would certainly come when some or all of the mercantile states would be "in a state of hostility to the National Government."[41]

When war came to seem inevitable in 1812, Crawford accepted the fact grudgingly. People of the South and West had no grievances against England, he asserted. On the contrary, they profited from commerce with the English. The war would largely benefit people in the North; and if they complained of its burdens, said Crawford, they should do so knowing that southerners and westerners would never again make sacrifices in their behalf. He spoke in favor of taking Florida and Canada, but chiefly on the ground that other Americans besides merchants and shippers should get something in return for what the nation would have to spend.

Although seeming in his speeches to be solely a spokesman for his section, Crawford quickly became a commanding figure on Capitol Hill. A friendship developed between him and Albert Gallatin, the ugly, clever, Swiss-born Pennsylvanian who was secretary of the treasury under both Jefferson and Madison. Crawford impressed Gallatin as uniting "to a powerful mind a most correct judgment and an inflexible integrity," and Gallatin enlisted him as, in effect, the Treasury spokesman in Congress.[42] In March 1812 Crawford's colleagues selected him as president pro tempore of the Senate and thus as third in line for succession to the presidency.

After the war broke out, Crawford left the Senate to become minister to France. The experience added to his education, even

---

41. 11th Congress, 1st session, ibid. (Jan. 23, 1810), pp. 541-546; 11th Congress, 3rd session, ibid. (Feb. 8, 1811), p. 144.
42. Gallatin to John Badollet, July 29, 1824, quoted in Mooney, *Crawford*, p. 26.

if he did not approve of all he learned. In a briefly kept diary, he noted of the statuary in the Tuileries gardens, "I am not pleased with their nudity. If I was supreme legislator of the United States I would prohibit the importation and even the manufacture of naked people, in marble, plaster, or paper."[43] Crawford was a witness in Paris of Napoleon's fall, the Bourbon restoration, the hundred days, and the conclusion of peace. To his irritation he was not included in the delegation that negotiated the Treaty of Ghent with England. Coming back to the United States, he took over the War Department from Monroe and before long shifted to the Treasury. In the Republican congressional caucus of 1816, he ran a close second to Monroe as the nominee to succeed Madison, and then stayed on at the Treasury during Monroe's presidency.

Crawford's philosophy can only be guessed. With regard to the central difference between Monroe and Adams as to whether the United States was the forerunner and leader of a world revolution or a unique and inimitable phenomenon, Crawford evidenced no opinion. While Monroe and Adams were more or less at one in regarding disruption of the union as a potential catastrophe, Crawford appeared to differ with both. He seemed to feel that the connection with the seafaring North was sufficiently disadvantageous to the agricultural South and West to make a rupture tolerable. Certainly, that had been his attitude before the war, and his behavior during the Missouri controversy suggested that this attitude remained unchanged. Although one of his adherents proposed the compromise formula eventually accepted, the senators and representatives closest to him were said to talk "of a dissolution of the Union with perfect nonchalance and indifference"; and Crawford did nothing to discourage such talk.[44] Whereas Monroe and Adams took it as axiomatic that national policies should conciliate diverse interests, Crawford evidently did not.

---

43. From the journal which Crawford kept while in Paris, quoted ibid., p. 58.
44. Charles M. Wiltse, *John C. Calhoun, Nationalist, 1782-1828* (Indianapolis: Bobbs-Merrill Co., 1944), p. 195.

To the extent that Monroe and Adams differed concerning the best means of preserving America's safety, Crawford seemed to side with Adams. Certainly, he said little to suggest that the United States should mix in European politics. He spoke of the United States and France having a special relationship, but he emphasized commercial rather than political reasons for maintaining it. And he parted company with Adams and the President alike in that he opposed spending large sums on the navy and army. He saw the maxim of nonentanglement as following from the premise that the United States was too weak to get involved in games with the great powers. Both before and after the War of 1812, he argued that discrepancies in financial resources between the United States and the cisatlantic powers were so wide that any notion of engaging in war with them was unrealistic.[45]

On only one point was Crawford known to concur with the President and secretary of state. He shared their view that the United States should expand its territory. At the first moment when he judged that it could be done without risk of war, he advocated seizure of Florida, and he expressed hope that opportunities would materialize for safely taking Cuba. To be sure, except for a mention of Canada in connection with the War of 1812, he spoke exclusively of adding territory which would have slavery and be connected politically with the South; but he was in principle an expansionist.[46]

While Monroe, Adams, and the others may have been uncertain just what convictions Crawford would express if sitting with the cabinet, they could have had no doubt that any opinions he voiced would be influenced by his ambition to be President. For it was well known that Crawford regarded himself as *the* Republican candidate—the only one standing on the old Republican principles, defending states' rights against central

---

45. 11th Congress, 1st session, *Annals of Congress* (Jan. 23, 1810), p. 545; Crawford to Monroe, July 20, 1821, Papers of James Monroe, Library of Congress.

46. Adams diary, May 20, 1820, Nov. 28, 1822; Crawford to Monroe, Nov. 10, 1813, cited in Mooney, *Crawford*, p. 62.

power, and opposing Hamiltonian programs. He regarded all of his opponents as, in effect, tools of the detested Federalists, and it seemed clear that he would say or do almost anything to ensure that they did not defeat him.

CALHOUN[47]

At forty-one, Secretary of War Calhoun was much younger than his colleagues. Although not a giant like Crawford, he was taller than Monroe and hence stood well above the stubby Adams. He had a mass of black curls, a dark complexion, prominent cheekbones, and a wide, thin-lipped mouth. His brown eyes, large, close together, very deepset under wing-like brows, were the features best remembered by people who knew him. They used such adjectives as "burning" and "blazing" in part perhaps because Calhoun was so energetic and excitable that his eyes seemed peepholes on a roaring inner furnace.

Born to an Irish family which had emigrated from Scotland to northern Ireland to Pennsylvania to Virginia and thence finally to the South Carolina frontier, he had grown up on a plantation which had been rich by local standards but remote, isolated, and in country where people still had vivid reminiscences of Indian raids. In an undisciplined childhood, spent occasionally working in the cotton fields with slave children but mostly riding, shooting, fishing, and attending local schools which fitfully formed and dissolved, he acquired the elements of an education. At eighteen, he went north to Yale and afterward studied for the bar at Judge Tapping Reeve's celebrated new law school in Litchfield, Connecticut.

Returning to South Carolina, Calhoun quickly became successful as a lawyer. When approaching twenty-nine, he married into the close-knit aristocracy of coastal Charleston. With his

---

47. Except where otherwise noted, this sketch of Calhoun is based on Wiltse, *Calhoun,* and Margaret L. Coit, *John C. Calhoun, American Portrait* (Boston: Houghton Mifflin, 1950).

own inheritance and the property of his bride, he no longer had to earn a living. He could more freely pursue a career in politics, and the combination of his own connections in the uplands and his wife's in the lowlands gave him advantages.

After three years in the state legislature, Calhoun went to Congress in 1810 as one of the young Warhawks. Quickly becoming an important figure in the House, he helped to write the resolution for war in 1812. After peace came, he put forward an elaborate program for capitalizing on the economic changes produced by events since Jefferson's embargo and ensuring that the nation would never again be so unready for war as in 1812. Specifically, he championed a tariff to protect manufactures, a national bank to promote trade, federal help in building of canals and roads, and a relatively large peacetime navy and army. After becoming Monroe's secretary of war, he sponsored construction of a network of military roads in the interior and the fortification of harbors, and he pleaded annually for higher spending on the armed forces.

Calhoun had, of course, formed his attitudes much after Monroe and Adams had formed theirs, for he had been a child in the backwoods when the Constitution, the Anglo-French war, the Genêt mission, and the Jay treaty had been focuses of national debate. Although he claimed later to remember the debate in South Carolina over the Constitution, he recalled his father as having been an opponent of ratification when, in fact, he had been on the other side.[48] In all probability, he did not begin really to think about national issues before the early 1800s, when he was a student at Yale, or make up his mind about any of them before he ran for the state legislature in 1807. If so, his opinions first took shape, as did Crawford's, in the period between the embargo and the peace of Ghent.

It is not easy to decipher what those opinions were, for, while Calhoun did not have the learning or orderliness of

---

48. Anonymous, *Life of John C. Calhoun . . . from 1811 to 1843* (New York: Harper and Brothers, 1843), p. 5. On the question of whether this was an autobiography or merely an authorized biography, see Wiltse, *Calhoun*, Appendix A.

Adams, he was at least as clever, and he was more lawyer-like. Though Calhoun usually argued as if from a core of principles, he seemed able at a given moment to accept as true almost any proposition that supported his case. His intellect was agile enough to be untroubled by inconsistencies between statements made in different contexts. One Yankee senator of ordinary gifts, taken aback by the words and ideas flashing from Calhoun, condemned him as "too theorizing, speculative, and metaphysical."[49]

In 1816 Calhoun asserted that "but little analogy exists between this and any other government. It is the pride of ours to be founded in reason and equity; all others have originated more or less in fraud, violence or accident." But Calhoun appeared to think, as did Monroe, that the chief distinguishing characteristic of the United States was its lack of "hereditary orders." He wrote that its "position, soil, climate and above all its political character, resulting from freedom and exemption from the taint of fudalism [sic], must place it far before Europe."[50]

To the extent that Calhoun attached greatest weight to the absence of feudalism, he could imagine without inconsistency that European nations would imitate the United States, for he could visualize their ridding themselves of feudal institutions. Even in the period of reaction following the Napoleonic wars, Calhoun perceived exactly that to be happening. "Feudalism is gone," he observed in 1821, "and its effects on the state of society nearly vanished." Hence Calhoun could declare:

> We have a government of a new order, perfectly distinct from all which has ever preceded it. A government founded on the rights of man, resting not on authority, not on prejudice, not on superstition, but reason. If it succeed, as fondly hoped by its founders, it will be the

---

49. Henry Cabot Lodge, ed., "Extracts from the Familiar Correspondence of the Hon. E. H. Mills," *Proceedings* of the Massachusetts Historical Society (1881-1882), 37.

50. Calhoun to H. M. Brackenridge, Oct. 23, 1821, W. Edwin Hemphill, ed., *The Papers of John C. Calhoun*, 8 vols. in progress (Columbia, S.C.: University of South Carolina Press, 1959——) (hereafter, Calhoun, *Papers*), VI, 454; speech of Jan. 9, 1816, ibid., I, 313.

commencement of a new era in human affairs. All civilized governments must in the course of time conform to its principles.[51]

Like Monroe and Adams and unlike Crawford, Calhoun showed great concern lest the union come apart and thus fail to achieve its destiny. During the war, to be sure, he had opposed concessions based on fear that New England would secede. "No menace, no threat of disunion shall shake me, from pursuing that course of measures, which I know to be for the honor and best interest of this nation," he declared. In the Missouri controversy, he took the position that the South would have to make itself a separate nation unless the North tolerated both the continuance and the expansion of slavery. Even so, he spoke as passionately as either Monroe or Adams about the importance of preserving national unity. In 1816, for example, he declared that "the *liberty* and *union* of this country were inseparably united," and in 1817 he characterized disunion as "the greatest of all calamities, next to the loss of liberty, and even to that in its consequence."[52]

In Calhoun's eyes, the danger of disunion stemmed not just from potential conflict between sections or between large economic classes but from the very nature of man. "Interest," he once said, "has a wonderful control over sentiment. Even the most refined and elevated, the moral and religious sentiment may be considered as ultimately resting on it."[53] Like Alexander Hamilton, Calhoun believed that individuals and groups would always pursue their selfish aims, forming alliances with others for that purpose, and that the union could be preserved only if the national government were seen as helping many to achieve their private ends. When explaining why he, as a representative from interior South Carolina, should advocate war with Britain in defense of American shippers and seamen, Calhoun declared:

---

51. Calhoun to John Ewing Calhoun, May 6, 1821, Calhoun, *Papers*, I, 98; speech of Jan. 31, 1816, ibid., p. 329.
52. Calhoun to James McBride, June 23, 1813, ibid., p. 177; speech of April 4, 1816, ibid., p. 355; speech of Feb. 4, 1817, ibid., p. 401.
53. Speech of June 24, 1812, ibid., p. 128.

I only know of one principle to make a nation great, to produce in this country not the form but the real spirit of union, and that is, to protect every citizen in the lawful pursuit of his business. He will then feel that he is backed by the government, that its arms are his arms, and will rejoice in its increased strength and prosperity. Protection and patriotism are reciprocal.[54]

Despite what he said about interest governing emotion, Calhoun also believed that preservation of the union required the nation to become, in effect, an object of religious worship. "Our Union cannot safely stand on the cold calculation of interest alone," he said in 1812. "We cannot without hazard neglect that which makes man love to be a member of an extensive community —the love of greatness—the consciousness of strength."[55]

Holding these attitudes, Calhoun viewed American relations with Europe somewhat as did Monroe. Not having experienced the passions of the 1790s, he was less sensitive than either Monroe or Adams to the possibility that foreign powers might mix into American politics and promote divisions. His concern was instead that Americans might be awed by or fearful of European states and in consequence feel less pride and faith in their own. He held Americans to be a people peculiarly attached to peace. He said in 1816:

In the policy of nations, there are two extremes: one extreme in which justice and moderation may sink in feebleness; another, in which that lofty spirit which ought to animate all nations, particularly free ones, may mount up to military violence. These extremes ought to be equally avoided; but of the two I consider the first far the most dangerous . . . I consider the extreme of weakness not only the most dangerous of itself, but as that extreme to which the people of this country are peculiarly liable.[56]

---

54. Speech of Dec. 12, 1811, ibid., pp. 79-80.
55. Speech of Dec. 8, 1812, ibid., p. 145.
56. Speech of Jan. 31, 1816, ibid., p. 317.

Hence Calhoun held that the United States should not shrink into a self-imposed isolation. Because the Atlantic separated the United States from Europe, he conceded that "we shall never enter into the struggle for continental power in that quarter of the world." But he insisted that Americans should not be "indifferent spectators of the events in Europe, because the changes there may have considerable bearing on the affairs and interests of this country."[57] The European balance of power, he thought, would always shield the United States. After Napoleon's defeat, when Britain seemed free to redeploy most of her forces to North America, Calhoun argued that the period of danger for the United States would be brief, for other nations would inevitably exploit such a situation and strike at British interests elsewhere. He contended that the United States should take advantage of the jealousies among nations in Europe at least for the purpose of winning commercial benefits.[58]

By the early 1820s Calhoun had grown apprehensive lest the European monarchs suspend their rivalries and unite to root republicanism from the world. In such event, he warned, "Neither our distance from Europe, nor our pacific policy, will secure us from great disasters."[59] By 1824 he was to be speaking of conflict as inevitable:

> Our country ought to omit no measures necessary to guard our liberty and independence against the possible attacks of the Armed Alliance. They are on one side, and we the other of political systems wholly irreconcilable. The two cannot exist together. One, or the other must gain the ascendency [sic].[60]

In Calhoun's estimation, England was as much an enemy of the United States as any absolute monarchy of the continent. Nevertheless, Calhoun, like Monroe, was willing to contemplate a

---

57. Speech of April 6, 1814, ibid., p. 243.
58. Ibid., pp. 249-250.
59. "Vauban" letter in *National Intelligencer*, April 10, 1821, ibid., VI, 31.
60. Calhoun to Henry A. S. Dearborn, June 8, 1824, J. Franklin Jameson, ed., "Correspondence of John C. Calhoun," *Annual Report* of the American Historical Association (1899), II, 218-219.

temporary alliance with her or with any other state for the sake of either advantage or safety.[61]

Calhoun's convictions, like those of Adams and Crawford, felt the influence of his ambition to be President. He may have had such an ambition from the day he first ran for office. Certainly, it had become definite and conscious by the time he became secretary of war, for he explained his leaving the House for the cabinet on the ground that no one could be elected President without proving that he had executive and administrative capacities.[62] Equally certainly, he had begun to believe by late 1821 that he had a good chance of being elected as early as 1824.

At that time, Calhoun devised a campaign plan. Recognizing that his youth would count against him, he urged his friends to proceed quietly, building up apparent public demand for him rather than putting him forward as an open candidate. Throughout 1822 and 1823 he gave a great deal of effort to acquiring support among political leaders in various states. To some he put himself forward as a true Republican. Crawford's backers were referred to as "Radicals," and Calhoun wrote to one New York politician, "as we, the Republicans, have defeated the Federalists, so will we trample over the Radicals and intriguers." To others, including Federalists and former Federalists, Calhoun represented himself as the man who could work a reconciliation between the parties. He stimulated press attacks on Crawford, and he set about establishing newspapers which would support his own candidacy.[63]

In making this effort, Calhoun could feel that he was not acting solely in his own behalf. In the cabinet, he had developed a low opinion of Crawford. To Adams, Calhoun once remarked "that there has not been in the history of the Union another man with abilities so ordinary, with services so slender, and so

---

61. Speech of Jan. 31, 1816, Calhoun, *Papers*, I, 320.
62. Anon., *Life of Calhoun* (see n. 48 above), pp. 24-25.
63. Calhoun to Samuel L. Gouverneur, April 9, 1823, Calhoun, *Papers*, VIII, 9-10; Calhoun to Micah Sterling, July 20, 1823, ibid., pp. 172-173; Calhoun to Swift, Sept. 28, 1823, ibid., p. 289; Calhoun to Virgil Maxcy, Dec. 29, 1821, ibid., VI, 582-583; Calhoun to Gouverneur, April 28, 1823, ibid., VIII, 33-34.

thoroughly corrupt, who has contrived to make himself a candidate for the Presidency."[64] Moreover, Crawford had opposed almost every proposal that Calhoun put forward and mustered congressional forces to cut back appropriations for Calhoun's department. Not unnaturally, Calhoun became convinced that Crawford did not have the interest of the nation or the union at heart. He was sure that a Crawford administration would be guilty of the worst of sins—feebleness.[65] It seemed to him of great importance that Crawford be denied the presidency.

Although Calhoun had a much higher estimate of Adams, he believed that Adams could not be elected because of his Federalist past. In any case, he thought that an Adams administration would be feeble because of its narrow, sectional support in Congress. Regarding neither Clay nor Jackson as a serious contender, Calhoun saw himself as the one man who could command support in the South, North, and West and thus pursue policies that would maintain the union and advance its greatness. And he came to believe that his election was essential. He was to write in November 1823 that he regarded the choice to be made in the approaching election as more critical than any since the issue had been whether or not to seek independence from England.[66]

To the debates which produced the Monroe doctrine, Calhoun thus brought a set of attitudes rather similar to those of Monroe. He also brought a passionate dedication to advancing his own prospects for becoming President.

CLAY

Just as Monroe, Adams, and Calhoun had to consider what Crawford might say if he showed up at a cabinet meeting or if he commented later on what they had done, so they also had to

---

64. Adams diary, Aug. 27, 1822.
65. Calhoun to Ninian Edwards, Oct. 5, 1822, Calhoun, *Papers*, VI, 296; Calhoun to Micah Sterling, March 27, 1823, ibid., VII, 547.
66. Calhoun to Gouverneur, Nov. 9, 1823, ibid., VIII, 354-355.

take account of likely reactions among public figures not in the administration. Chief among these was Henry Clay.[67]

Forty-six in 1823, Clay was, like Crawford, a native Virginian who had made his career in another state. He had grown up in a village near Richmond, working in the fields on his parents' small plantation and attending a makeshift school just long enough to learn his letters. At fourteen, he nevertheless qualified to be a pupil of George Wythe, one of the most scholarly members of the Virginia bar. In studying with Wythe, Clay picked up a knowledge of classics, literature, history, and political theory so that he could salt his later briefs and speeches with learned allusions. A lawyer who saw a good deal of Clay in court observed of him accurately, however, that he was "independent alike of history, or the schools . . . His ambition, his spirit, and his eloquence are all great, natural, and entirely his own."[68]

At twenty, Clay left Virginia to join his family in Kentucky, newly a sovereign state. He began to practice in Lexington and was within a few years one of the counselors and trial lawyers most in demand in the state. He married a daughter of Colonel Thomas Hart, one of the richest landowners of the region and proprietor besides of nail and hemp factories. His own fees and his wife's dowry enabled Clay to acquire outside of Lexington a six-hundred-acre plantation surrounding an elegant brick mansion. Clay's success did not free him of financial concern. He loved to gamble and sometimes lost large sums. The postwar depression beginning in 1819 was so to reduce the margin between what his family properties earned and what he had to pay his creditors that he had to resume full-time practice of law to remain solvent. But Clay did not suffer constant money worries like Monroe's, and most of the time he was sufficiently well-fixed to play politics without thinking of private loss or gain.

---

67. Except where otherwise noted, this sketch of Clay is based on Bernard Mayo, *Henry Clay, Spokesman of the New West* (Boston: Houghton Mifflin, 1937), Glyndon G. Van Deusen, *Henry Clay* (Boston: Little, Brown, 1937), and Clement Eaton, *Henry Clay and the Art of American Politics* (Boston: Little, Brown, 1957).

68. Thomas F. Marshall, quoted in Mayo, *Clay*, p. 210.

And Clay entered politics as soon as he could afford to do so. Within a year of migrating to Kentucky, he was speaking and writing on statewide issues. Within six years he had become a member of the state legislature. In 1806 he was chosen by the legislature to fill out four months of an unexpired term as United States senator. He thus served briefly in that body with Adams. He returned to Kentucky to become speaker in the state legislature. In 1810 he went back to Washington once again to fill out a short term in the Senate. Although he was certain of being able to continue for a full six-year term, he chose instead to stand for the House of Representatives, and he was elected without opposition.

With his previous service in the Senate, Clay was one of the most experienced of the many young men newly elected to Congress in 1810. His reputation as an advocate and orator had already carried well outside Kentucky. Tall, slender, and loose-limbed, he had blond hair and blue-grey eyes once described as "catamount eyes." He carried himself erectly with his head at a self-assured tilt. His wide mouth was set in a natural smile, but it was mobile enough so that juries and audiences sometimes saw a "killing countenance." In the Senate his sarcasm had been sharp enough to wound the powerful Crawford, whose role as Treasury spokesman Clay had ridiculed. The other new congressmen judged Clay the one among them best able to cope with John Randolph and other veterans who might try to obstruct their will, and they voted him into the speakership.

As speaker, Clay became the second man in Washington. At least in appearance, it was he who led in forcing a declaration of war in 1812. He raised his voice for more determined prosecution of the war on land and sea. In 1814 he accepted appointment as one of the commissioners to negotiate peace. He was thus a colleague of Adams at Ghent. While in Europe, he visited Sweden and parts of Germany and spent some time in Paris and London, and he stored away many bits of knowledge about places and people abroad to use in oratory much as he used the bits of learning he had collected from Wythe. Reelected to Congress even before his return, he again became speaker. In 1820, he considered but decided against a bid for the vice presidency. His thoughts by then were fixed on being elected President in 1824.

Even more than Calhoun, Clay had the mind of a lawyer. He was far more concerned about the coherence of a particular brief than about consistency between one brief and another. Not having Calhoun's speculative, theorizing turn, he seldom felt a compulsion to frame his arguments around general principles. As a legislator and especially as a presiding officer, he had little need to enter into debates other than of his own choosing. The only pressure on Clay to be systematic was that felt by any politician aware that future opponents might look up what he had said and use it against him.

When a youngster, Clay had simply accepted the views of the Jeffersonian majority around him. He was pro-French and anti-British during the 1790s, and he joined in applauding the Virginia and Kentucky resolves of 1798, the election of Jefferson in 1800, and the acquisition of Louisiana in 1803. It was not until 1806 that his mind focused more on national than local issues. What catalyzed the change was not only his brief experience in the Senate but, earlier in the year, his being engaged to help defend former Vice President Aaron Burr against the charge of conspiracy to mount an expedition against Mexico and to entice the trans-Allegheny states and territories into seceding to join a midcontinental empire. Clay took the brief, believing Burr to be innocent. At the time, most Kentucky Republicans agreed with him. Subsequently, when Jefferson announced that he had evidence proving Burr's guilt, Clay concluded that he had been deceived. He went through an anxious period, striving to persuade Kentuckians that he had not been party to any plots by Burr. In doing so, he had to plead his fidelity to the union. From that time onward, Clay always represented himself as believing that the interests of the nation as a whole should take precedence over those of any one section.

Clay spoke occasionally as if he believed foreign intrigue could menace the union. In a speech in 1811, he declared: "Republics, above all other nations, ought most studiously to guard against foreign influence. All history proves that the internal dissentions [sic] excited by foreign intrigue have produced the downfall of almost every free government that has hitherto existed."[69] But this was not a theme which often appeared in Clay's orations.

In general, Clay voiced a confidence in America's ability to preserve its integrity. While he once referred to the nation's "vast maritime frontier, vulnerable in almost all its parts to predatory incursions," he seemed to believe that such incursions could not reach the nation's vitals. In the same speech, he argued that Americans were more intelligent than Europeans and hence stronger than numbers alone might indicate. Because of the extent of the union, he said, it would be very hard to conquer, and it had the unique advantage of possessing no center comparable to London or Paris, the capture of which could bring about the capitulation of the whole. Boastfully, he asserted that even if all the East were to fall, the West would hold firm. More realistically, he made the point that any European power would find it hard to deploy large naval forces in the western Atlantic for any long period of time. Clay continually accused others of underestimating America's strength and overestimating that of nations in the Old World. "If we are united," he said in 1813, "we are too powerful for the mightiest nation in Europe, or all Europe combined."[70]

In an oration soon after the war, Clay forecast that patriotism "will finally conduct this nation to that height to which God and nature have destined it."[71] Seldom, however, did he describe the vision underlying such rhetoric or even indicate how he defined American interests. Clearly, he felt little concern about the nation's security so long as it remained united. On the other hand, he warned repeatedly of wars to come. In 1812, he said to his colleagues in the House: "if you wish to avoid foreign collision, you had better abandon the ocean—surrender all your

---

69. Speech of Feb. 15, 1811, James F. Hopkins, ed., *The Papers of Henry Clay*, 3 vols. (Lexington, Ky.: University of Kentucky Press, 1959-1963) (hereafter Clay, *Papers*), I, 538.

70. Speech of Dec. 28, 1810, ibid., p. 515; speech of Dec. 31, 1811, ibid., p. 605; speech of Jan. 22, 1812, ibid., p. 621; speech of Jan. 8-9, 1813, ibid., 759; Clay to Jonathan Russell, March 24, 1820, ibid., II, 787-788.

71. Speech of Dec. 31, 1811, ibid., I, 604.

commerce; give up all your prosperity . . . Commerce en-
genders collision, collision war." Four years later, after the peace
of Ghent, he declared: "That man must be blind to the indications of the future, who cannot see that we are destined to have
war after war with Great Britain."[72]

Despite his own involvement in business, Clay shared with
other southerners an ambivalence toward trade. Before 1812 he
sometimes advocated war for its own sake, as a means of building a "martial spirit" to correct the enervating "spirit of
avarice." He clearly thought the nation would be served by
adding to its agricultural lands, for he advocated annexing not
only Canada and the Floridas but also Texas. Often, however, he
gave indications of believing that expansion of commerce was at
least as important. When urging conquest of Canada, he stressed
that one result would be to give Americans the traffic in furs.
When demanding annexation of the Floridas, he spoke of the
need to control waters through which exports from the Mississippi Valley would travel. Leading the postwar campaign for
American aid to rebels in South America, he disclaimed interest
in their territories but argued again and again that their nations
would provide rich markets for American shippers and manufacturers.[73]

Clay also spoke idealistically of the Latin Americans, term-
ing them "our neighbors, our brethren occupying a portion of
the same continent, imitating our example and participating of
the same sympathies with ourselves"; and he used similar language about republicans and liberals in Europe.[74] But Clay said
little to indicate whether he inclined to agree with Monroe and
Calhoun that it was America's destiny to be a guide and model
for other states or with Adams that America was unique. What
Clay did say suggested that he would appraise actions by the

---

72. Speech of Jan. 22, 1812, ibid., p. 619; speech of Jan. 29, 1816, ibid., II, 152.
73. Speech of Feb. 22, 1810, ibid., I, 450; speech of Dec. 28, 1810, ibid., p. 514; speech
of March 24-25, 1818, ibid., II, 508-539; speech of March 28, 1818, ibid., pp. 541-
560; speech of May 10, 1820, ibid., pp. 853-859; speech of March 30-31, 1824, ibid.,
III, 690.
74. Speech of Jan. 24, 1817, ibid., II, 291; speech of May 19, 1821, ibid., III, 80.

administration not by any such abstract criteria but by the practical test of whether they promoted domestic unity and prosperity.

With regard to whether the United States should or should not mix in European politics, Clay seemed equally free of any doctrinaire view. After 1815 he frequently explained that he had been for war in 1812 partly because he thought the United States could take advantage of Napoleon's successes in Europe. He had then settled for a compromise peace at Ghent, he said, because the European balance of power had changed. In fact, he was on record at Ghent as having argued against concessions on the ground that England's continental allies were sure to fall out with her and the United States could obtain some help from them. Subject to a vague caveat against "entering into those connections which are forbidden by the genius of our government," Clay clearly had no objection in principle to understandings with cisatlantic powers.[75]

On the other hand, Clay was very far from being committed to the proposition that the United States ought to pursue its interests by playing upon the European balance of power. He insisted that one point of pride for Americans in the War of 1812 was that they had fought alone and without allies. During the war, he had said, "we have nothing to do with the affairs of Europe, the partition of territory and sovereignty there, except in so far as these things affect the interests of our country . . . Our political relation is much less important than it is supposed to be." During Monroe's first administration, Clay criticized the policy of negotiating with Spain for cession of the Floridas and demarcation of a boundary between the Louisiana territory and Mexico, accusing Monroe and Adams of excessive concern about the balances abroad. He would prefer, he said, "to pursue a course exclusively American, uninfluenced by the policy of My Lord Castlereagh, Count Nesselrode, or any other of the great

---

75. Speech of Jan. 29, 1816, ibid., II, 142-143; Clay to Monroe, April 23, 1814, ibid., I, 885; Clay to James F. Bayard and Albert Gallatin, May 2, 1814, ibid., p. 891; Clay to Crawford, July 2, 1814, ibid., pp. 937-939; speech of Jan. 29, 1816, ibid., II, 142, 155.

men of Europe."[76] Members of the administration must have recognized that, if they agreed to Canning's proposition or if they interfered in some manner in Greece, Clay might approve or be silent, but he might equally well find grounds for charging that what they had done involved "connections . . . forbidden by the genius of our government." The test for him would be whether the administration's actions served the nation's material interests.

Or rather whether they *seemed* to serve those interests, for Clay's reactions were certain to be governed in part by an estimate of whether an attack on the administration would win votes for him in the forthcoming presidential contest. Clay wanted to be President and, like Crawford, felt no need to apologize for or rationalize such an ambition. He had a high opinion of his own abilities and, judging Jackson not a serious candidate, thought himself the only westerner who might be elected. The choice of a western man would itself, he believed, contribute to national unity; and he, as President, could contribute further by pursuing policies advantageous to agriculture, commerce, and manufactures. Hence from Clay's standpoint the greatest immediate national interest was his own election, and his stance would be determined by his estimate of how that interest would be affected.

JACKSON[77]

There were other men outside the administration to whose probable reactions Monroe, Adams, and Calhoun had to be attentive. Certainly, Andrew Jackson was among them, for, even if not a candidate for the presidency, he had a public following.

---

76. Speech of Oct. 7, 1815, ibid., p. 69; speech of Jan. 8-9, 1813, ibid., I, 758; speech of June 7, 1820, ibid., III, 870.

77. Except where otherwise noted, this sketch of Jackson is based on Marquis James, *Andrew Jackson*, 2 vols. (Indianapolis: Bobbs-Merrill Co., 1933-1937) and Robert V. Remini, *Andrew Jackson* (New York: Twayne Publishers, 1966).

Henry Clay

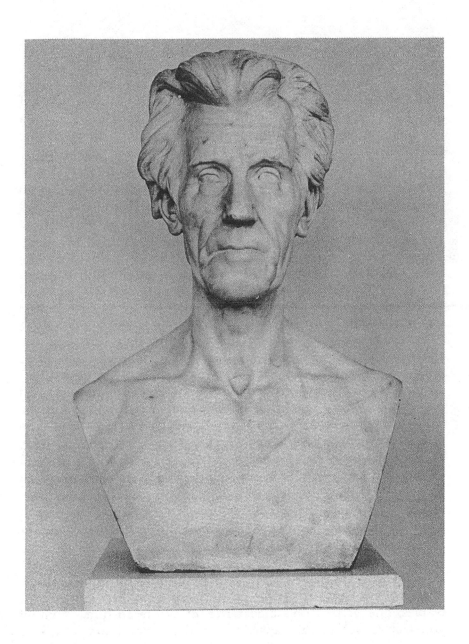

Andrew Jackson, photograph of a bust by an unknown sculptor

Jackson had become a national hero during the War of 1812. Earlier, he had been a lawyer, storekeeper, and planter in central Tennessee. In the late 1790s he had been that state's first delegate to Congress, but he had distinguished himself only by being one of the minority of twelve refusing to vote a farewell compliment to President Washington. Otherwise, he had attracted little notice outside his home state. There, however, he had been elected to the essentially political office of major general of militia. When war was declared, he became an actual field commander. His victories against Indians in the Florida borderland and, above all, his success in marshaling, disciplining, and inspiring troops brought him some fame. His defeat of a British force at New Orleans after the peace had been signed at Ghent gave the American public one triumph to console them for a generally luckless war. Americans in all sections of the union thereafter bracketed his name with Washington's, referring to the two as America's great captains.

Jackson's postwar career kept his fame alive but produced controversy. He conducted another Indian war and served as military governor of Florida. In doing so, he acted both high-handedly and ruthlessly. Among his better publicized acts was the summary execution of two British subjects whom he suspected of aiding Indians in Spanish Florida. Had the British government not shown forbearance, a crisis could have resulted. Without denying Jackson tribute as the victor at New Orleans, some Americans concluded that his gifts were ill-suited for peace. Others, however, acclaimed him all the more fervently. Monroe and his advisers had to recognize that open approval or disapproval by Jackson could influence some of the public reaction to their decisions.

Jackson's probable attitudes, however, were indecipherable. He was assumed by some to be an apostle of liberalism. When word came in 1821 of a contitutionalist uprising in Naples, one of Jackson's oldest friends wrote to him, "I know you will rejoice in the news."[78] On the other hand, much of

---

78. Edward Livingston to Jackson, May 14, 1821, J. S. Bassett and J. Franklin Jameson, eds., *The Correspondence of Andrew Jackson*, 7 vols. (Washington, D.C.: The Carnegie Institution, 1926-1935), III, 56.

what Jackson said about the War of 1812 suggested that he regarded America as uniquely pure and both England and Europe as effete, decadent, and corrupt beyond salvation. There was no way of telling whether Jackson would react unfavorably or favorably to the idea of America's giving some kind of leadership to liberals in Europe.

Nor was it any more clear how Jackson might assess or rank American interests. He certainly believed in preserving the union. While he told Monroe that he would have hanged participants in the Hartford Convention, he also counseled him to appoint some Federalists to office and thus bring them back into the system. With regard to other national interests, Jackson was at best ambiguous. While ardent for taking Florida and, if possible, Cuba, he showed no appetite for Texas. Taking the latter territory would be ill-advised, he wrote Monroe, "until our country . . . is filled with a dense population."[79] Although he reasoned, as did Clay, that Florida and Cuba were important because of exports from the Mississippi Valley, Jackson seemed concerned mostly about markets for agricultural products and very little about manufacturing or shipping. He said nothing to indicate that he shared Clay's hopes in regard to Latin American consumption of what the United States produced. On the contrary, he spoke contemptuously of Clay's riding "his Spanish Jack."[80] It could be inferred that Jackson might view it as America's primary interest to maintain sales of foodstuffs and fibers to England and Europe, in which case he might judge any action which put those sales in jeopardy as imprudent or quixotic.

That Jackson inclined to be violently anti-English was well known. His mother and all of his brothers had died during the Revolutionary War. His own gaunt, furrowed face carried a scar which he attributed to a saber cut received in childhood when he refused to polish the boots of an English officer. During his brief service in Congress, he had been a diehard opponent of the rapprochement with Britain effected by Wash-

79. Jackson to Monroe, June 20, 1820, ibid., p. 28.
80. Jackson to Monroe, Jan. 15, 1820, ibid., p. 8.

ington and the Federalists. In wartime rhetoric he had bracketed the British with the worst savages of the frontier, and, after Ghent, he continued to impute to them malevolent designs against the United States. It was possible that a decision by the administration to go hand in hand with Britain, as Canning proposed, would enrage Jackson. It was also possible that he would react in a wholly opposite way. As of 1823, no one could tell.

Conceivably, Jackson's response would be determined neither by general principles nor by reasoning about current national interests but by prejudices for and against the various individuals in the administration. Only a very skeptical man would have supposed that the determinant might be Jackson's own ambitions, for at the time he disclaimed any. Although only fifty-six and thus an exact contemporary of Adams, Jackson looked much older. His shock-like hair was white. He had twice nearly lost his life in duels, and he lived with a pistol ball in one shoulder. He had also had tuberculosis, and his hollow eyes seemed those of a consumptive staying alive by sheer will power. Jackson said, probably without even self-deception, that he wanted only to retire.

Even so, Jackson's pride and vanity were very much alive. He believed that Crawford had wanted to condemn his conduct in Florida and that Crawford and Clay together were responsible for congressional hearings and debate on the subject which might have eventuated in a resolution of censure. He hated both men. Believing that Adams and Calhoun had defended him in the cabinet, he looked kindly on both of them. In 1821 he let it be known that he thought highly of Adams and would support him for the presidency unless Calhoun should run.[81] Toward Monroe he was ambivalent. It was possible that Jackson's reactions to administration policies would be primarily functions of his attitudes toward the individuals whom he believed to have been their sponsors and opponents.

---

81. Jackson to James Gadsden, Dec. 6, 1821, ibid., pp. 139-141.

With regard to Canning's overture and the Greek agitation, the decisive attitudes would be those of Monroe, Adams,
Crawford, Calhoun, Clay, and Jackson. These were the men
who would claim to speak for large constituencies and who,
because of their positions, could insist that their views be
heard. For practical purposes, they *were* the United States.

The positions of these men would obviously reflect the
beliefs which they had developed out of past experience, observation, and reflection. These beliefs, however, did not
dictate categorical answers to the questions confronting them,
even though the policy issues were fundamental in character.

Monroe, for example, could see an alliance with England
as an appropriate means of protecting American security and
enhancing America's standing. He could also see recognition
of Greece as consistent with the nation's mission in the world.
Equally, however, he could judge that an English alliance
would jeopardize America's safety and make it seem a satellite
rather than an independent power, and he could shrink from
action concerning Greece on the ground that it would needlessly arouse the enmity of European monarchies.

While Adams's convictions were certain to make him skeptical about both concert with England and recognition of
Greece, they did not preclude his deciding that either or both
were in the nation's interest. Attaching highest importance to
the maintenance of peace and domestic unity, he could easily
calculate that action by the Holy Alliance in Latin America
could force war and that an Anglo-American combination was
therefore desirable. After probing Adams's views, the British
minister in Washington concluded erroneously that this would
in fact be his posture.[82] Similarly, it was more than imaginable
that Adams's doubts about recognizing Greece could give way,

---

82. Stratford Canning to George Canning, May 6, 1823, quoted in Bradford Perkins,
Castlereagh and Adams: England and the United States, 1812-1823 (Berkeley and Los Angeles:
University of California Press, 1964), p. 313; Stratford Canning to George Canning,
June 6, 1823, C. K. Webster, ed., *Britain and the Independence of Latin America, 1812-1830:
Select Documents from the Foreign Office Archives*, 2 vols. (London: Oxford University
Press, 1938), II, 495-496; Adams diary, June 20, 1823.

as had his doubts about recognizing Latin America republics, in face of evidence that public opinion strongly favored such action.

Someone living in 1823, foreseeing the issues the American government would confront, and possessing some information about the values and beliefs of key American politicians, would have been able to make guesses about their positions, but he would have been hesitant to back his guesses with substantial bets. Certainly, he could not have placed a bet on how their debates would come out. Trying to find a basis for more confident prediction, he would have had to turn to examination of the international and domestic environments in which the decisions would be made.

3

Foreign Politics

While the questions before the American government involved basic policy choices, decisions had to be influenced by estimates of practical consequences. If the danger were real that European powers would move into Latin America and that England would not resist unless joined by the United States, the case for accepting Canning's alliance offer could have been compelling, even for men opposed in principle to foreign entanglements. On the other hand, if European action were unlikely or if England were sure to act in any case, Americans would have more freedom of choice. Similarly, if the Holy Allies viewed the Greek independence movement as part of an international revolutionary conspiracy, like the constitutionalist uprisings in Italy and Spain, American recognition of the Greeks could not only vex them but possibly affect their attitudes toward intervention in Latin America. If the Holy Allies saw the Greeks instead as oppressed Christians, they would not necessarily take offense. In any event, their reactions would probably be influenced by the attitudes of England. In order to assess the American government's decisions, it is necessary to ask how the actual or apparent policies of powers on the other side of the Atlantic limited the options of American policymakers.

RUSSIA

The dominant member of the Holy Alliance was Russia. As of 1823, its population was half-again that of France, more than twice that of the United Kingdom, and four to five times that of the United States, and it disposed of an army seven to eight times larger than any other in the world.

Russia was an absolute monarchy. Indeed, it was *the* absolute monarchy. With only slight exaggeration, Nikolai Turgenev wrote: "In every absolute monarchy there has been and there is still some class, some body, some traditional institutions, which on certain occasions oblige the sovereign to act in a prescribed manner or set boundaries to his caprice; nothing of the sort exists in Russia."[1]

The dictator of Russian policy as Tsar Alexander I. Everyone who dealt with his government recognized that he alone had the deciding voice. A French diplomat in St. Petersburg once observed that no business could be transacted when the tsar was absent from the capital, and another commented, "the really essential things remain secret, because it is the Emperor alone who decides them."[2] Moreover, the lights which guided these decisions were Alexander's inner lights. In a study of Russian foreign policy during Alexander's reign, Patricia Kennedy Grimsted concludes, "the very concept of Russian national interest or *raison d'état* was hardly meaningful to him, unable as he usually was to separate state interests from his personal interests as monarch."[3]

Since his coronation in 1801, Alexander's notions of Russian interest had fluctuated. Influenced by teachings of the French *philosophes*, he had toyed in his early years with drafts of constitutions and plans for reforming and rationalizing

---

1. Nikolai Turgenev, *La Russie et les russes*, 2 vols. (Paris: Imprimeurs-Unis, 1847), II, 263-264.

2. Patricia Kennedy Grimsted, *The Foreign Ministers of Alexander I: Political Attitudes and the Conduct of Russian Diplomacy, 1801-1825* (Berkeley and Los Angeles: University of California Press, 1969), pp. 19, 23, 30.

3. Ibid., p. 42.

Russian government to make it less arbitrary. In this frame of mind, he felt friendly toward republics such as Switzerland and the United States, and he evidenced this feeling by cordiality toward their representatives. When John Quincy Adams arrived in St. Petersburg in 1809, Alexander declared to him that "the system of the United States was wise and just"; and during Adams's four-and-a-half-year stay, the tsar repeatedly paid him special attentions and stopped to talk with him on the streets or quays of the capital whenever their paths crossed.[4]

Warring with France during most of his first decade and a half of rule, Alexander gradually became less enthusiastic about the principles of the *philosophes*. Experience meanwhile taught him how hard it was to ordain changes and how nearly impossible to effect them while still keeping his own powers intact. By 1814-1815, when peace returned to Europe, he had a much more cautious approach to reform—so cautious, in fact, that some contemporaries and many historians have described his later reign as "reactionary."

Insofar as the label fitted, it was because Alexander had grown increasingly religious and increasingly preoccupied with fear of revolution. One or both of these properties may have been a product of mental disorder, for Alexander possibly inherited some instability from his lunatic father. In any case, he had suffered experiences which might have driven any mind over the edge. In particular, he lived with knowledge that he had known his father was to be murdered and had done nothing to prevent it. Whether or not out of festering guilt, Alexander did come to pray so much that, according to his doctor, he grew great calluses on both knees.[5] He also renounced intimacy with the opposite sex. The Countess of Choiseul-Gouffier recalls discussing with Alexander the affair between King Louis XVIII and Madame du Cayla, saying that

4. Samuel Flagg Bemis, *John Quincy Adams and the Foundations of American Foreign Policy* (New York: Alfred A. Knopf, 1950), pp. 162-163.

5. Grand Duke Nikolai Mikhailovich, *L'empereur Alexadre Ier: Essai d'étude historique*, 2 vols. (St. Petersburg: Papiers de l'Etat, 1912), I, 299.

the relationship was probably platonic. Alexander remarked, "I do not allow even that. I am forty-five, while the king is sixty-seven, and I have long given up that sort of thing."[6] Consorting with mystics such as Sophie, Baroness de Krudener, the tsar came more and more to associate opposition to revolution with reverence for God. The charter of the Holy Alliance, pledging defense of Christianity and legitimacy, was itself an evidence.

In the years following the Napoleonic wars, Alexander displayed commitment to this double cause. He convinced himself that there persisted a powerful conspiracy with headquarters still in Paris, that its goal was to destroy the Christian religion, and that its strategy was to undermine and overthrow princes who were protectors of the faith. He exulted when his partners in the Holy Alliance used their power to put down revolutionary movements. The success of these efforts he interpreted as proof of God's favor. Thus, when Austrian forces rescued and reinstated the barbarous monarch of the Two Sicilies, Alexander described the event as a holy miracle.[7]

Nevertheless, Alexander remained fearful that the struggle would end in victory for the supposed revolutionary conspiracy. His anxiety was stimulated by Prince Metternich, the Austrian prime minister, who shared with him reports from a corps of secret agents, all of whom had strong incentives to magnify or fabricate evidence of revolutionary ferment. Although Alexander's own *haute police* were more careful and objective, courtiers brought him tales of conspiracies in Russia itself. As the Decembrist revolt of 1825 was to show, some of these tales had substance. In any event, there was ample cause for alarm in the fact that the army had to deal each year with dozens of peasant demonstrations. Worse still were occasional signs of unrest in the army itself, where many officers and men had been exposed to the infection of French ideas in the

6. Countess of Choiseul-Gouffier, *Historical Memoirs of the Emperor Alexander I and the Court of Russia*, translated from the French (Chicago: A. C. McClurg, 1900), p. 254.

7. Alexander I to Prince Golitzyn, Dec. 14, 1820, Mikhailovich, *Alexandre Ier*, I, 519.

course of campaigning against Napoleon. In 1820 there was a mutiny in the elite Semenovskii regiment quartered in the capital. Since the regiment was the one which Alexander had commanded when a Grand Duke, this mutiny shocked the tsar to his core.

Together with assassinations in the Germanies and France and constitutionalist uprisings in Italy and Spain, the mutiny in the Semenovskii regiment brought Alexander to the verge of panic. He resorted to new police measures at home, including the dissolution of all secret societies. Showing mistrust for many of his veteran councilors, he took into his household the monk Fotii, a fanatic who anathematized any retreat from the old ways. Meanwhile, he described himself and his partners in the Holy Alliance as engaged in war against an *"empire of evil."*[8]

Only in rhetoric, however, did Alexander travel all the way to hysteria. When actually making decisions, he seemed able to tell a hawk from a handsaw, no matter which way the wind blew. He kept a close eye on the dispositions and morale of his army. Well aware that its elements varied in quality, readiness, and equipment and that many units performed essential police functions, he was chary about committing Russian troops to enterprises of the Holy Alliance. In view of the success of the constitutionalists in Spain and their virtual imprisonment of King Ferdinand, he assembled a large army in Poland and talked of marching it through the Germanies and France and across the Pyrenees, but he meanwhile exhorted the French to send in their army instead, and he told the King of Prussia that his whole motive in threatening Russian intervention had been to force action by the government in Paris.[9]

Similarly, in dealing with the Greek question, Alexander

8. Alexander I to Princess Meshcherska, Oct. 22, 1820, quoted in Grimsted, *Foreign Ministers of Alexander I*, p. 62.

9. Alexander I to Frederick William III, Paul Bailleu, ed., *Correspondance inédite du Roi Frédéric-Guillaume III et de la Reine Louise avec l'Empereur Alexandre ler* (Leipzig: S. Hirzel, 1900), pp. 327-328.

moved coolheadedly. The first uprising in Greece was led by Alexander Ypsilanti, who had once been a member of the tsar's entourage. The news of it thrilled clerics and devout aristocrats in St. Petersburg, many of whom held that Russia had a holy duty to help the Greek Christians liberate themselves from the Turkish infidels. According to the French ambassador, Alexander's generals were ardent for war. The tsar thus found himself under heavy pressure to intervene. One of his two foreign ministers, the fervently pro-Greek Ivan Antonovich, Count Capodistria, asked the French ambassador, "Do you think then that the Emperor can account as nothing the opinion of his people and the general outcry of the Russian nation?"[10]

Alexander, however, did not share the enthusiasm of his courtiers and soldiers. In cool appraisal, he described Ypsilanti as "a fool, who will probably himself be lost and will cause the loss of many victims, for they have neither cannon nor resources, and it is probable that the Turks will destroy them."[11] Not only reluctant to engage his army in a war but also fearful lest a Russian campaign against Turkey trouble relations with Britain and produce friction with Austria, the tsar remained skeptical about military intervention.

To rationalize his skepticism, Alexander did not rely on calculations of Russian interest. Instead he resorted to the proposition that the Greek revolt was the handiwork of the conspirators in Paris. Its objective, he argued, was to divide the Holy Alliance and to preoccupy in the Balkans the Russian and Austrian forces that would otherwise be available to suppress revolutions elsewhere. The other argument which he put forward was that Russian intervention could precipitate a general massacre of Christians in the Ottoman Empire.[12]

---

10. Count de la Ferronays to Minister of Foreign Affairs, April 14, 1821, Archives du ministère des affaires étrangères, Correspondance Politique (hereafter CP): Russie, CLXII; La Ferronays to Minister of Foreign Affairs, July 18, 1821, Mikhailovich, *Alexandre Ier*, II, 369.
11. Alexander I to Prince Golitzyn, March 10, 1821, Mikhailovich, *Alexandre Ier*, I, 536.

Facing the pressures to which Capodistria referred, the tsar did not find it easy to maintain this position. According to Capodistria, he had difficulty justifying even to his own cabinet a policy of "allowing the Turks the possibility and even major facilities for preventing a war demanded and awaited with impatience by all those who profess the Greek religion."[13] The Turks, by dealing with the Russian ambassador as if he represented a hostile power, made Alexander's task doubly difficult. In the summer of 1821 the tsar felt compelled to send a threatening note to the Porte and, when the reply proved unsatisfactory, to sever diplomatic relations. By autumn he was having to plead as an excuse for inaction the approach of winter and the consequent need to postpone military action until spring.[14]

When spring came in 1822, Alexander nevertheless held his ground. Doing so cost him the services of Capodistria, who resigned and went off to Switzerland. It also led to a rupture with other intimates and to gossip that the tsar had become a pawn of Prince Metternich. On occasion, Alexander appeased his critics by speaking as if his posture might change. In fact, he remained as circumspect as ever.

With regard to the Spanish colonies, Alexander's stance was somewhat the same. He seemed to see revolutions in the New World as linked with those in Europe. At any rate, he wrote in 1820 of a threat from "the liberal revolutionaries, radical levellers and Carbonari of all corners of the world."[15] Although the American minister saw little sign of it, the British ambassador reported the whole Russian government to be perturbed by United States recognition of Latin American republics. At the tsar's direction, the foreign ministry sent out a

12. Lebzeltern to Metternich, July 15, 1821, Grand Duke Nikolai Mikhailovich, ed., *Les rapports diplomatiques de Lebzeltern, Ministre d'Autriche a la Cour de Russie (1816-1826)* (St. Petersburg: Gosudarstvennie Bymag', 1913), p. 79; La Ferronays to Minister of Foreign Affairs, Aug. 14, 1822, Mikhailovich, *Alexandre Ier*, II, 415.

13. La Ferronays to Minister of Foreign Affairs, July 18, 1821, ibid., p. 369.

14. La Ferronays to Minister of Foreign Affairs, Sept. 19, 1821, CP: Russie, CLXII.

15. Alexander I to Prince Golitzyn, Feb. 15, 1821, Mikhailovich, *Alexandre Ier*, I, 524.

circular arguing vehemently that no European government should copy the action of the United States.[16]

At the Congress of Verona in the autumn of 1822, Alexander sought to commit the great powers to nonrecognition. Largely because of resistance by the British delegates, this initiative failed. Alexander nevertheless impressed upon all those present his own opposition to any action or gesture that would embarrass the beleaguered monarch of Spain.

Until after the French invasion of Spain in 1823, the tsar seemed to think of the colonial question solely in these terms. Even with Ferdinand restored, Alexander continued to feel concern chiefly about the dignity of the Spanish monarch. He held that recognition of any of the new states would be an affront to Ferdinand unless and until Ferdinand himself accorded them independence. Also, however, he entertained doubts as to whether, in any circumstances, the acknowledgment of the New World republics would be right or wise.

In November 1823 the tsar spoke at length with the French ambassador, the Count de la Ferronays. Characterizing the colonial issue as "the great affair today," the tsar said, "this question of the colonies is immense and full of complications. The first thing to do, in my view, is not to depart from principle and not any more to sanction a revolution in America than in Europe." The new republics, he continued, were not comparable to the United States. The latter had been "one people, with leaders, and with estimable leaders," while the Latin Americans had neither unity nor leadership. "Where," he asked, "are the Franklins, the Washingtons, the Jeffersons of southern America?" The tsar concluded, "Everything is still in disarray in America; let us wait a while for the chaos to subside."[17]

---

16. Henry Middleton to John Quincy Adams, July 20, 1822, William R. Manning, ed., *Diplomatic Correspondence of the United States concerning the Independence of the Latin American Nations*, 3 vols. (New York: Oxford University Press, 1925), III, 1866-1867; Charles Bagot to Lord Londonderry, May 6, 1822, C. K. Webster, ed., *Britain and the Independence of Latin America: Select Documents from the Foreign Office Archives*, 2 vols. (London: Oxford University Press, 1938), II, 298.

As of the autumn of 1823, the tsar remained determined to avoid embroilment in Greece, felt strongly that all the powers should refrain from embarrassing Ferdinand by recognizing the independence of Latin American states, but was prepared in practice to see Latin American affairs settle themselves. It angered him that the British seemed inclined to proceed toward recognition whether or not Ferdinand consented, but all he said to La Ferronays was that, in the event Britain acted so, the other powers "should all protest in the strongest possible manner."[18]

As indicated by what he said to the French ambassador, Alexander still had a softness for the United States. In the previous year, when faced with American protests against the ukaz that proclaimed the north Pacific a closed sea, he had retreated, and orders had been given that the United States be pacified.[19] Through reports from officials concerned with naval and colonial affairs, the tsar doubtless appreciated the vulnerability of Russian America in the event of a conflict, but his attitude seemed a product of something more than prudence, something more even than calculation that the United States might be an ally in a war with England. Alexander seemed to feel a genuine affection for the American republic.

One can surmise that the tsar would have been shocked by an Anglo-American alliance to protect Latin America and doubly shocked if there followed U.S. recognition of the independence of Greece. The first would have seemed to him an injury to Spain, a further wedge between the continental powers and Britain, a contribution to the promotion of chaos,

17. La Ferronays to Minister of Foreign Affairs, Nov. 28, 1823, Mikhailovich, *Alexandre Ier*, II, 501-502.

18. Ibid., p. 502.

19. Nesselrode to Poletica, Oct. 15, 1821, "Correspondence of Russian Ministers in Washington, 1818-1825," *American Historical Review*, 18 (Jan. 1913), 329-331; Capodistria to Tuyll, July 25, 1822, ibid., pp. 344-345; Nesselrode to Tuyll, Dec. 14, 1822, ibid., pp. 538-541; Nesselrode to Gur'ev, July 15, 1822, Nikolai N. Bolkhovitinov, "Russia and the Declaration of the Non-Colonization Principle: New Archival Evidence," *Oregon Historical Quarterly*, 72 (June 1971), 111.

and a betrayal of his own friendship. The second would have seemed to him to make more difficult a settlement between Greeks and Turks and, worse still, to be likely to stimulate pro-Greek agitation in Russia. The tsar would almost certainly have felt less friendly toward the United States. It seems unlikely, however, that his decisions would otherwise have been significantly affected.

The tsar's preferences, however, were not the only determinants of Russian policy. Ruling such a vast land, Alexander had to delegate tasks to others. To the extent that he did so, he put himself in the hands of his agents, for he gave them the ability to shape issues in such ways as to make the outcomes very different from what he had intended.

This was all the more true in the 1820s, for Alexander had tired of ruling. The slender, erect, vivacious man who had taken power in 1801 was by now in his fifties, running to fat, stooped, increasingly deaf and shortsighted, easily fatigued, and prone to illness and fits of melancholy. While his impassive, moonshaped face still looked youthful, his balding head showed furrows, and the easy charm that once captivated visitors was no longer so often in evidence. He spoke of "this burden of a crown which weighs on me terribly."[20] Always restless, he spent less and less time in St. Petersburg. Even when there, he preferred to stay outside the city, at Tsarskoe Selo, where, in a palace with walls of lapis lazuli, porphyry, and amber, floors encrusted with mother of pearl, and grounds that included a zoo and a miniature replica of Windsor Castle, he could nevertheless fancy himself living "a simple country life."[21] Much of the time, however, he moved about the country, visiting military garrisons. In 1822, he left the capital in mid-May and did not return for eight months. In August 1823 he departed and was absent until November. After being confined to a sickbed in the winter of 1823-1824, he left again in

---

20. N. K. Shilder, *Imperator' Aleksandr' Pervyï: Ego Zhizn' i Tsarstvovanie*, 4 vols. (St. Petersburg: A. S. Suborin, 1905), IV, 311.
21. Choiseul-Gouffier, *Historical Memoirs*, pp. 274-276.

August 1824 and was gone until October.[22] His physical decline, his moodiness, and his frequent absences from the seat of government gave his adjutants even more discretion and power than they might otherwise have had.

At the time, the tsar transacted business through government departments superficially similar to those in Western capitals. Earlier in his reign, he had relied on a Senate divided up into specialized committees. Although many of these committees still functioned, they now served exclusively as advisory bodies, receiving reports from ministers and offering comments to which the ministers or the tsar sometimes paid attention and sometimes did not. Meanwhile, the functions of ministers had become more and more clearly delineated. There had developed a quasi-cabinet in a Council of Ministers which met with some regularity to consider matters in dispute, and there was even a sort of prime minister in Alexei Andreevich, Count Arakcheev, who headed the tsar's chancery, served as rapporteur for the Council, prepared summaries of documents, and handled the issuance of decrees, commissions, military orders, and the like.[23]

Universally regarded as the second most powerful man in Russia, Arakcheev was a coarse, no-nonsense soldier. When a young officer, just out of artillery school, he had been assigned to the entourage of the Grand Duke Paul. A shared liking for Prussian military customs and discipline drew the two together, and when Paul became tsar the twenty-eight-year-old Arakcheev was made a major general. Although he eventually lost Paul's favor, he served for a time as military tutor to the Grand Duke Alexander. Once again, a friendship developed. When Paul's murder made Alexander tsar, Arakcheev was recalled to duty. He rose steadily thereafter.

---

22. Mikhailovich, *Alexandre Ier*, I, 267-273, 285- 288, 293-299; Lebzeltern to Metternich, Feb. 9, 1824, Mikhailovich, *Rapports diplomatiques de Lebzeltern*, pp. 127-128.

23. The structure of the tsarist government is amply described in Turgenev, *La Russie et les russes*. A reasonably well-documented account of Arakcheev's career is Michael Jenkins, *Arakcheev, Grand Vizier of the Russian Empire* (New York: Dial Press, 1969).

Except for diligence, capacity for work, and loyalty to his master, Arakcheev had no attractive traits. He maintained his residence and office in Liteiniya Street and his country home at Gruzino on the Volkhov as if they were Prussian garrisons, insisting on minimum comfort and maximum discipline. Even the most high-born had to queue up in his anterooms and pass hours waiting for an audience. When he conveyed a decision or order, he did so in few words, offering no explanation.

It has been surmised that Arakcheev's influence with Alexander owed something to his being a living, daily reminder of the guilt which Alexander felt for not having prevented the murder of his father. Another explanation is that Alexander saw Arakcheev as single-mindedly loyal to him and a man who courted no other friends. That he was attached to and dependent on Arakcheev is abundantly evident in letters which he wrote after the prime minister suffered a heart attack in early 1822, for the tsar seemed desolated.[24] He was wholly unwilling to turn to anyone else for counsel, and after Arakcheev began to recover, Alexander eased his burden by replacing, one after another, other high officials who had in the past been adversaries of Arakcheev in policy debates. Men assumed to be subservient to Arakcheev were installed as chief of staff of the army and as ministers of War, the Interior, Finance, and Education, and some of these men were appointed even though Alexander himself had a low opinion of their abilities.[25] Alexander thus made his government at least as much Arakcheev's as his own.

There is no evidence that Arakcheev had any predilections on foreign policy issues. Completely a Russian, he had been out of the country only when visiting battle lines. Unlike most courtiers in St. Petersburg, he neither spoke nor wrote French, and it appears that he treated foreign affairs as a special

---

24. Reproduced in Shilder, *Imperator' Alexandr' Pervyi*, IV, 236-237.
25. Mikhailovich, *Alexandre Ier*, I, 274-279.

category of business best left to the tsar and his foreign ministers and merely kept track of by the chancery.

Nevertheless, Arakcheev had some interests likely to be affected by the emperor's decisions on foreign policy. He was above all the guardian of the army, intent upon keeping its numbers up, and he had a special interest in the so-called military colonies, where conscripts trained part of the time and worked the rest of the time as farmers. Arakcheev's fiercest battles had been with senators and treasury ministers who called for reduction in army expenditures or questioned the utility of the military colonies.

In spite of the ministerial changes authorized by Alexander, Arakcheev in 1823 had to anticipate continued debate on the subjects. As of January 1 anticipated expenditures for the coming year approached 480 million rubles while anticipated revenues were below 464 million. There were already outstanding debts, mostly to foreign bankers, totaling almost 600 million, and neither Arakcheev nor anyone else had a clear scheme for paying off these obligations.[26] It seemed evident that government outlays would somehow have to be cut back. Almost certainly, part of the cutting would have to come from the 40 percent of expenditures budgeted for the army. In these circumstances, Arakcheev may have had reason for wanting the tsar to intervene in Greece, for a state of war would surely quiet criticism of deficit spending for military purposes. On the other hand, Arakcheev could equally well have calculated that, if there were a war and extraordinary military expenses, pressure would increase rather than diminish for trimming the military colonies and other elements of the permanent establishment. Budgetary concerns did not dictate which way Arakcheev would arrange data relevant to the tsar's foreign policy decisions, but they did give him a reason for considering the possible implications of

26. Modest Ivanovich Bogdanovich, *Istoriya Tsarstvovaniya Imperatora Aleksandra I i Rossii v' ego Vremya*, 6 vols. (St. Petersburg: Tipografiya Sushchinskago, 1871), VI, 198-199.

information and advice that filtered through his hands.

Arakcheev also had an interest in replacing Karl Robert, Count Nesselrode, the foreign minister identified with the tsar's relatively prudent policies. To be sure, Nesselrode himself represented no threat to the prime minister. One of the many foreigners in Russian service, he came from a German family, belonged to the Anglican church, and had never learned how to write correct Russian.[27] A career diplomat and bureaucrat, he had been co-foreign minister with Capodistria and reluctantly taken the full portfolio after Capodistria's resignation. He was generally regarded as unimaginative, not particularly energetic, and intent simply on carrying out the tsar's instructions. But he had enemies, especially among partisans of war for Greece who blamed him for the tsar's policy and condemned him as a virtual agent of Prince Metternich. Arakcheev had some reason for wanting to placate these groups, particularly since one consisted of army generals. Moreover, Arakcheev had a personal grievance against Nesselrode owing to the fact that Nesselrode's wife was the daughter of Dmitri, Count Gur'ev, a former treasury minister who had been one of Arakcheev's most prominent antagonists. The rumor circulated in the autumn of 1823 that Arakcheev was seeking to remove Nesselrode and to replace him with Dmitri, Count Tatishchev, then the Russian ambassador in Vienna.[28]

If this rumor was accurate, the implication was that Arakcheev wanted a more activist foreign policy or at least was willing to see such a policy adopted as one consequence of replacing Nesselrode, for Tatishchev was notoriously an advocate of fighting the Turks. Moreover, he had earlier been ambassador to Spain, had then urged direct Russian aid to Ferdinand, and was believed to hold that the Holy Alliance should provide further direct aid in order to help Spain regain

---

27. See Grimsted, *Foreign Ministers of Alexander I*, pp. 196-219, 270-278.
28. La Ferronays to Minister of Foreign Affairs, Oct. 1, 1823, Mikhailovich, *Alexandre Ier*, II, 478-479.

her empire.[29] Possibly, Arakcheev was prepared to further such outcomes in order to remove Nesselrode.

Less powerful figures in the tsar's entourage would probably have welcomed diplomatic if not military conflict with the United States. The directors of the Russian-American Company had long wanted more support in resisting the encroachments of English and American traders and settlers. They had somehow succeeded in getting the tsar's signature on the 1821 ukaz. Mikhail Speranskii, then the governor of Siberia, told an American diplomat that they had done so "surreptitiously"; and the explanation may have lain in relationships between Ivan Vasilevich Prokofev, the manager of the company's Moscow office, and Arakcheev—relationships alleged by the historian of the company to have involved payments of bribes.[30] Some company officials had felt aggrieved when the tsar responded to English and American protests by ordering that the ukaz not be enforced.

If the Russian settlements in the North Pacific should in any way appear to be endangered because of tension with the United States, the company's directors and managers could hope that money would be spent for their defense. Should that occur, the company might be rescued from the impending bankruptcy which had compelled it to suspend dividends in 1822-1823 and which had turned stockholders' meetings into scenes of near riot.[31] It can be surmised therefore that some officers of the company would use such leverage as they possessed to urge that the tsar not recoil from conflict with the Americans.

A number of men in the company hierarchy were naval officers, and they had an additional reason for not shrinking

---

29. William Spence Robertson, *France and the Independence of Latin America* (Baltimore: Johns Hopkins University Press, 1939), pp. 134-135.

30. Middleton to Adams, Aug. 8, 1822, 59th Congress, Senate Document No. 162, Proceedings of the Alaska Boundary Tribunal," II 42-46; S. B. Okun, *The Russian-American Company*, translated from the Russian (Cambridge, Mass.: Harvard University Press, 1951), pp. 105-106.

31. Ibid., pp. 68-69.

from trouble with the United States. For the tsar and Arak-cheev had been niggardly with funds for the navy. The budget for 1823 had reduced these funds while allowing the army a substantial increase.[32] In spite of increasing diplomatic friction, little preparation had been made for conflict with England, and naval officers could reasonably assume that the tsar and his minister would spend money for naval readiness if one prospective enemy were the upstart American republic. Thus there were people in the Russian government likely to try to stir indignation or anger in the tsar if the United States should unite with England to interfere between Spain and her colonies or should by itself meddle in Greece.

On the other hand, there were also people in St. Petersburg who had reason for wanting the tsar not to take offense against the United States. Some of them occupied key positions in the bureaucracy, and it is important to recall that Russia was already the most bureaucratized of all the powers. The Russian foreign ministry had a staff of three hundred, for example, while the French and British had respectively fifty-five and twenty-eight.[33]

In that ministry, correspondence and memoranda concerning relations between the Russian-American Company and the United States passed through the hands of Peter Ivanovich Poletica. A Ukrainian who had been Russian minister in Washington from 1818 to 1822, he was an Anglophile and something, too, of an Americanophile. He had committed himself in print to the proposition that Americans would remain friendly to Russia, and he was in a position to counteract any efforts by the company to aggravate Russian-American relations.[34]

Just as the potential influence of Russian-American Com-

---

32. Bogdanovich, *Istoriya Tsarstvovaniya*, VI, 197-199 and Appendix, pp. 20ff.
33. Grimsted, *Foreign Ministers of Alexander I*, pp. 26-27.
34. Petr Ivanovich Poletika, *A Sketch of the Internal Condition of the United States of America*, translated from the French (Baltimore: E. J. Coale, 1826), p. 72. On Poletica, see Mykhaylo Huculak, *When Russia Was America: The Alaska Boundary Treaty Negotiations, 1824-1825 and the Role of Pierre de Poletica* (Vancouver: Mitchell Press, 1971), pp. 89-103.

pany officials and naval officers depended on Arakcheev, so that of Poletica depended necessarily on the receptiveness of his superiors, especially Nesselrode. Since it was the apparent interest of Nesselrode to maintain the alliance with Vienna and since Metternich and his ambassador in St. Petersburg, Ludwig, Count Lebzeltern, opposed action by the Holy Alliance in both Greece and the Americas, the information and advice passing to the tsar from the foreign ministry seemed likely to encourage caution and restraint.

Officials in St. Petersburg, however, were not the emperor's only agents. In determining his choices and how those choices would be perceived, they were perhaps not even the most important. For Russian ambassadors possessed considerable discretion. In view of their distance from St. Petersburg, the slowness of the mails, and the fact that dispatches often had to catch up with Alexander somewhere on his travel route, these ambassadors would often take positions, report them to their master, and ask that he either approve or disapprove what they had done. The ambassador at Constantinople had contributed to the breach in relations with Turkey, and Tatishchev in Vienna had more than once exceeded his instructions in issuing warnings that, in certain circumstances, his government might intervene in behalf of the Greeks.

With regard to Russian policy toward Spain and Spanish America, the key figure other than the tsar was neither Arakcheev nor Nesselrode but the Russian ambassador in Paris, General Karl' Andrei Osipovich' Pozzo di Borgo.[35] Another cosmopolite, Pozzo di Borgo was a sixty-year-old Corsican, of a family that had feuded with the Bonapartes. He had been one of the island's representatives in the French Legislative Assembly of 1790-1791 but had opposed revolutionary edicts. Subsequently, he held office in Corsica when the island was under British rule. When the French reconquered it, he fled.

---

35. See Adrien Maggiolo, *Corse, France et Russie: Pozzo di Borgo, 1764-1842* (Paris: Calmann Lévy, 1890) and Pierre Ordioni, *Pozzo di Borgo: Diplomate de l'Europe français* (Paris: Plon, 1935).

Tsar Alexander I, engraving from a portrait by G. Doch

Count Nesselrode, drawing by Rooera

Before long he entered Russian service, acquiring his general's commission during the Napoleonic wars but actually serving primarily as a diplomat. Following the defeat of Napoleon, he rejected an offer to join the government of Louis XVIII, remaining in Paris instead as the representative of the tsar.

In view of the dominant position of Russia on the continent, Pozzo was a powerful figure in France. During the first half-dozen years after the war, a number of ministers and many leaders in the French Chambers made their way to his embassy, at the junction of the Place Concorde and the Champs Elysées, to seek advice about policy, both foreign and domestic, from this short, plump,swarthy Corsican with fiery eye and flying hands, who was said to combine with the allure of a cavalry officer "the penetrating look and feline expression of a Roman monsignor."[36] The Duc de Richelieu, French prime minister for most of the period 1815-1821, was thought by many to take most of his cues from Pozzo, and the same was said of foreign ministers in the governments that followed.

With regard to Russian policy, Pozzo was much more of an activist than his emperor. He favored intervention in Greece and tried to further the cause by getting the French to promise naval aid in the Mediterranean in case the British took the side of the Turks. Similarly, he showed concern lest Russia fail to influence events in the Spanish empire. As early as 1819, he had written Nesselrode, "The American broils will do harm to old Europe, who is sufficiently sick herself so as not to be distracted without injury by that which touches her so near."[37] He believed that, once Ferdinand had been restored, the Russians and French should unite in an effort to see that certain of the Spanish colonies became semiautonomous states ruled by Bourbon princes. If France adopted such a policy, he would be

---

36. Count de Carné, *Souvenirs de ma jeunesse au temps de la Restauration*, 2d ed. (Paris; Didier et Cie., 1873), p. 66.

37. Pozzo to Nesselrode, June 29, 1819, Count A. de Nesselrode, ed., *Lettres et papiers du Chancelier Comte de Nesselrode, 1760-1850*, 12 vols. (Paris: A. Lahure, 1908), VI, 94.

able to argue to the tsar that both Russian interests and the cause of legitimacy called for backing her up.

Unless Arakcheev intervened actively in support of a more militant foreign policy, the Russian-American Company officials and naval officers would remain impotent, and Nesselrode, influenced by Poletica as well as by Metternich, would continue to help the Tsar maintain courses that accorded with his instincts. If, however, Pozzo proved able to transform the question into one of whether or not to assist the French, the whole situation would be different. Nesselrode would be handicapped because of his own high respect for Pozzo and because of his knowledge that the tsar not only admired and trusted his ambassador in Paris but attached great importance to keeping France in the legitimist camp. Arakcheev might then be tempted to take a hand, opening the way for Russian-American Company officials and naval officers to do likewise. However reluctantly, the tsar might end up intervening in some fashion in the Americas, even if his policy entailed a possible collision with Britain or the United States or both. The key lay in Paris —in the question of whether or not the French would take an initiative.

FRANCE

Though not quite a constitutional monarchy on the English model, France was very far from being an absolutist state. After the defeat of Napoleon in 1814, King Louis XVIII had been invited to the throne by Napoleon's Senate. He had then issued a constitutional charter, nominally as an act of grace but actually as a precondition for retaining his crown, and this charter guaranteed certain rights to the citizenry and assigned certain responsibilities to a hereditary house of peers and an elected chamber of deputies. Even by the 1820s, when the Restoration regime had gained an appearance of solidity, the monarch ruled by sufferance. When Louis XVIII's successor grumbled that the constraints left the crown hardly any options, Prince Talleyrand observed, "Your Majesty forgets the post-chaise."[38] Louis XVIII could never be unmindful of this truth. Had he wanted to, he could not have imposed his will as could Alexander in Russia.

In any case, the king did not wish to dictate. A younger brother of Louis XVI, he was in his late sixties by the 1820s. Most of his middle years had passed in exile. It was his ambition to arouse so little opposition that the people would consent to keep a Bourbon monarchy after he died. Otherwise he sought to conserve his own privacy and peace of mind. Not even liking to leave the heart of Paris, he deserted the Tuileries for St. Cloud only when the accumulated garbage and offal of his eight hundred retainers made the drainless old palace uninhabitable. He dealt with as little public business as possible, keeping ministers in office so as to avoid having to accustom himself to new faces, attending cabinet meetings infrequently and, when there, either sleeping or interrupting debate to tell stories and display his talent for mimicry, and usually designating someone as prime minister so that each day's court circular could say, whether truly or not, that he had met with his chief minister for so-and-so many hours. Though feeble and often in pain, he performed all his public duties. "A king may die," he said, "but he can never be sick."[39] Clearly, however, he did not exercise personal control over French policy.

Since the monarchy was larger than the monarch, one would nevertheless make a mistake to discount altogether its influence on decisions. For the whole French government was decidedly royalist. Being dedicated to conserving a monarchical system, ministers and agents of the crown and leaders in the legislature responded readily to hints from the Tuileries, and when they received none from the king himself, they heeded

---

38. G. Lacour-Gayet, *Talleyrand, 1754-1838*, 3 vols. (Paris: Payot, 1947), III, 216.
39. Countess de Boigne, *Memoirs*, translated from the French, 3 vols. (New York: Charles Scribner's Sons, 1908), III, 122; Count de Villèle, *Mémoires et correspondance*, 6 vols. (Paris: Perrin et Cie., 1889), III, 8, 39; Baron de Damas, *Mémoires*, 2 vols. (Paris: Plon, 1923), II, 52.

those from courtiers near to him. Some paid special attention to Monsieur, the Comte d'Artois, who was the heir presumptive and who would in fact succeed in 1825 as Charles X. Others listened to Madame du Cayla, the fading beauty who three times a week came in from Saint Ouen, the chateau rebuilt and presented to her by the king, to spend two hours alone with Louis behind locked doors, or to her intimate friend, the pretentious little Sosthènes, Vicomte de la Rochefoucauld. While the advice of Monsieur and the court favorites usually had to do with patronage rather than policy, their suggestions as to who should be in which posts sometimes had far-reaching implications.

The man who bore chief responsibility for assessing the interests of the monarch and the monarchy was the king's prime minister, Joseph de Villèle.[40] Though often described as a Gascon, he was, properly speaking, a Toulousien. Short and slender with a small nose, thin mouth, and pockmarked face, he had trained to be a naval officer, deserted the sea eventually to become a planter on the island of Mauritius in the Indian Ocean, and returned to his native region only late in the Napoleonic period. His provincial accent remained with him. Though describing him as "dull and of a dullness without a distinguishing quality" and characterizing his language as "graceless" and "habitually incorrect," a politician who knew him well said nevertheless that "without ever achieving eloquence, he expressed his thought clearly."[41] Representing Toulouse in the chamber of deputies, Villèle became increasingly influential as he learned how to effect coalitions among the doctrinally antagonistic elements of the right and center. He became a minister for the first time in 1820, grew to be a favorite not only of the king but also of Madame du Cayla and la Rochefoucauld, and in late 1822 was made head of the government.

---

40. In addition to Villèle's own *Mémoires*, see Jean Fourcassié, *Villèle* (Paris: Librairie Arthème Fayard, 1954).

41. Chancellier Pasquier, *Mémoires*, 6 vols. (Paris: Plon, 1894), V, 277-278.

King Louis XVIII, engraving by E. Degebert

Madame du Cayla, the king's mistress,
engraving from a portrait by Gerard (detail)

Villèle's preoccupations were the management of the legislature and of France's finances. Neither task was simple. The
house of peers and the chamber of deputies teemed with factions. The former included noblemen whose primary interest
was compensation for losses during the Revolution and others
who attached chief importance to regaining power in their
localities. Their desires ran at cross purposes with those of a
prime minister who wanted to restrain spending and to conserve the authority of the central government. Villèle had to
retain their support without giving them much compensation,
and he found this all the harder to do because so many resented
being led by a commoner who had been ennobled only after
becoming head of the cabinet.

In the lower house, Villèle could ensure a royalist majority
by using patronage, money, and other means of suasion to
affect the outcome of elections. He could not, however, ignore
the fact that large constituencies were represented by the
minority on the left which was more constitutionalist than
royalist. In view of his responsibility for the treasury, he had to
be particularly conscious that some of them spoke for manufacturing, commercial, and financial interests whose confidence the government had to retain. It followed that Villèle not
only had to muster large majorities for government measures
but to ensure that those majorities included as many deputies
as possible from the center and left-center of the chamber. This
imperative meant in turn that Villèle would be constantly
criticized by his own former associates who were royalists of
the right.

While handling the legislature would have been difficult
in any circumstances, it was made all the more so by the fact
that Villèle became prime minister in a period of relative
depression. Throughout the Atlantic world, the years 1819-
1823 saw declines in prices for both agricultural products and
manufactures, slowdowns in trade and shipping, and increases
in unemployment. Villèle had to expect diminished tax
revenues, tailor his budgets accordingly, and disappoint not
only particular interest groups in the two chambers but also
ministerial colleagues who had followings of their own among
legislators, newspaper editors, and the public at large.

In order to govern, Villèle needed cabinets which commanded support in the house of peers and among right-wing deputies in the chambers. Many of those whom he selected for cabinet posts were not men whom he would voluntarily have chosen. Many had ideas which were at variance with his. While persuading them to accept measures which would win centrist votes, he had to prevent their insisting upon or pursuing policies which he regarded as wrongheaded. When this failed, as it sometimes did, he had to effect the replacement of a minister without thereby driving any significant group into opposition.

Though not titled prime minister until later, Villèle began practicing the arts of cabinet management as soon as he took the treasury portfolio, for his status as leader of the chamber made him necessarily the pivotal member of the government. He advised the king with regard to other appointments in the cabinet. In particular, he recommended Mathieu, Duc de Montmorency, for the foreign ministry. The king expressed reservations. "You don't know him," he said to Villèle. "He is a man of coteries; he is likely to give you a lot of trouble."[42] But Villèle insisted, for Montmorency had friends on the far right of both houses. Moreover, since he was the father-in-law of la Rochefoucauld, his appointment seemed likely to cement Villèle's ties with Madame du Cayla.

At the time, Villèle apparently felt that foreign policy and defense policy were subjects about which he and his right-wing colleagues would have few differences, for he selected two other ultras, the Duc de Bellune and the Marquis de Clermont-Tonnerre, as ministers respectively of war and the navy. The previous government had been dismissed in large part because the king and significant elements of the public had come to regard it as excessively subject to Russian influence. Although Montmorency and the others were friendly with Pozzo di Borgo, Villèle had reason to suppose that they would favor a more independent course. At the same time, he could be almost certain that they would oppose changing front entirely

42. Villèle, *Mémoires*, III, 4.

and siding with the English against Russia, for that was the policy espoused by a member of the house of peers whom they all held in odium—the extravagantly talented opportunist who had served as foreign minister for the Directory, Napoleon's regime, and the Restoration monarchy, Prince Talleyrand. Villèle must have felt that he, Montmorency, Bellune, and Clermont-Tonnerre could find common ground or, at any rate, that he would find it less painful to make concessions to them than if their portfolios embraced domestic rather than foreign affairs.

If this was his expectation, it proved false, for what turned out to be the great issue during the new government's first year and a half was whether or not to use troops to suppress revolution in Spain and restore Ferdinand to his throne. It was Villèle's decided opinion that such action would be wrong. He was apprehensive that French armies would become ensnarled in a long contest with guerrillas, as had been the case when Napoleon invaded Spain in 1808. He feared that the British might back the Spanish revolutionaries, with the result being a new Anglo-French war which would ruin French maritime trade and further cut into his government's revenues. Believing that a good deal of revolutionary sentiment lingered among the French populace, he was loath to see the army sent into battle abroad and thus made incapable of maintaining domestic security. He even felt some concern lest French soldiers be converted into revolutionists by contact with those in Spain. Above all, he worried about possible implications for his legislative and financial programs, for he recognized that the left and some of the left-center in the chamber sympathized with Spaniards who were trying to make their country a constitutional monarchy, and he could foresee that a war in Spain might add hundreds of millions of francs to the government's deficit.[43]

In common with ultras in the legislative bodies, Mont-

---

43. Villèle to Count de Serre, Sept. 27, 1822, Alfred Nettement, *Histoire de la Restauration*, 8 vols. (Paris: Lecoffre fils, 1860-1872), VI, 280; memo by Villèle, n. d., ibid., p. 320.

morency and the others favored intervention in Spain. Any revolution anywhere horrified them. That in Spain seemed all the worse because its target was a Bourbon monarch. Its success, they felt sure, would encourage those of their compatriots who wanted a stronger constitution and a weaker king. Assessing the risks entailed in not intervening as serious, they tended to minimize the probable costs, arguing that there would be no guerrillas because those who had resisted Napoleon had fought for their king and that country people would not take arms for a constitution; that the English monarchy would never go so far as to align itself with revolutionaries; that a war would be short and inexpensive; and that a victory in Spain would restore honor and glory to the flag of France and reinforce royalism among France's soldiers.[44]

Aided by the fact that the king shared most of his fears, Villèle succeeded through most of 1822 in imposing restraint on his colleagues. In the autumn, however, there was a congress of the great powers at Verona. Tsar Alexander and Pozzo had been talking for some time of the necessity of lending aid to Ferdinand, suggesting that the French might find it preferable to send in their own armies rather than having armies from the east march across their territory. If Villèle were to continue to have his way, the French representatives at Verona would have to resist such pressures. But Louis XVIII could not attend, for he was too frail, and though the king urged that Villèle himself go, Villèle did not dare to entrust the management of internal affairs to any of his colleagues. Hence France had to be represented by Montmorency who was personally inclined to promise the Holy Allies that France would intervene in Spain.

Villèle did all that he could to buckle reins on his foreign minister. He composed detailed and precise instructions, telling Montmorency to say only that France would decide her own policy in her own good time. On the eve of departure,

---

44. Emmanuel Beau de Loménie, *La carrière politique de Chateaubriand de 1814 à 1830*, 2 vols. (Paris: Plon, 1929), II, 37-42.

Montmorency was informed by the king that Villèle had become prime minister and that nothing was to be said or done at Verona without his explicit approval. Moreover, against his will, Montmorency was given a delegation which included ambassadors whom Villèle judged likely to be more responsive to him than to the foreign minister. One was François-René, Vicomte de Chateaubriand, the writer and philosopher, then French ambassador to Britain, who, though an ultrarightist and earlier an advocate of intervention in Spain, had wooed Villèle so flatteringly as to create the impression that he would do whatever the prime minister suggested.[45]

All Villèle's devices proved ineffectual. Montmorency would not accept being a mere agent of the cabinet, and he became even less tractable when told that Villèle was prime minister, for he felt outrage that a commoner should have been set ahead of him. From Verona he wrote Villèle that he would have to adapt to conditions as he found them and not necessarily be bound by the letter of instructions from Paris. To the other foreign ministers he began to hint broadly that France would welcome the opportunity to act in Spain if only assured that the Holy Allies would come to her aid in the event of war with England.[46]

The one factor working in Villèle's favor was Montmorency's impatience to leave the conference. His reasons were entirely personal. He was married to a daughter of the immensely rich de Luynes clan. During the Revolution, he and his wife had had a difference of opinion, the consequence of which was that she took a vow of future chastity and humility, exacted the same of him, and then kept him not only celibate but in a state of poverty that made him an object of pity and ridicule in Parisian society. This continued for many years, until a succession of deaths made it apparent that there would be no male heir unless Montmorency and his wife had issue. A family conclave persuaded the lady to renounce her vows

---

45. Ibid., pp. 24-25; Fourcassié, Villèle, pp. 227-228.
46. Beau de Loménie, Carrière politique de Chateaubriand, II, 39-43.

and liberate her husband from his. In the aftermath she became transformed. Her doting passion for Montmorency became the talk of the capital. Having reluctantly allowed him to go alone to Verona, she discovered that she could not bear his absence and wrote that she would join him. Appalled by the thought of her making him an object of mockery by Prince Metternich and others at the conference, Montmorency seized every pretext for discouraging or delaying her departure. When these proved unavailing, he concluded that his own best course was to desert the proceedings, intercept his wife en route, and escort her home.[47] Since he came to this decision before the conference closed, he might have departed with France as yet uncommitted to intervention in Spain.

Had Montmorency's colleagues actually been loyal to Villèle, they might have produced a final outcome corresponding with the prime minister's wishes. Unfortunately for Villèle, Chateaubriand chose to continue Montmorency's work rather than to carry out the wishes of the prime minister. Soon after arriving in Verona, he had contrived an introduction to the tsar. It was one of Alexander's better days, when his charm was on full display. Chateaubriand was captivated. He convinced himself that he in turn had won the heart of Alexander.[48] Aware that Russian favor had theretofore been an asset in Paris, Chateaubriand probably judged that his career would benefit if Alexander found him useful. Though writing dissembling letters to Villèle, he bent his efforts to securing the outcome desired by the tsar. The Congress of Verona thus ended with the French delegation virtually promising that France would send an army across the Pyrenees.

Villèle was not prepared to accept this result. Following the Verona congress there were cabinet meetings almost daily, at the residence first of one minister, then of another. Though acknowledging that the result would be war, Montmorency insisted that France had an obligation to unite with the Holy

47. Ibid., pp. 30-31, 40-42.
48. Viscount de Chateaubriand, *Congrès de Vérone. Guerre d 'Espagne. Negociations: colonies espagnoles*, 2 vols. (Paris: Béthune et Plon, 1838), I, 78-80.

Allies in sending a virtual ultimatum to the revolutionary regime in Madrid. A French army was already stationed along the French frontier, the pretext being need to prevent refugees from bringing in fevers. Bellune was already reinforcing and redeploying it for offensive operations, and Clermont-Tonnerre was positioning elements of the fleet to lend support at sea. But Villèle fought against the ultimatum proposed by Montmorency, advocated that nothing be done militarily other than to continue clandestine aid to royalist guerrillas in Spain, reiterated all his past arguments against intervention, and pointed to tumbling prices on the Paris *bourse* as evidence that war could cause financial catastrophe.[49]

The prime minister, however, found himself alone. Even the king deserted him, taking the position that France was bound by the pledges made at Verona. On Christmas day, 1822, with the king in attendance, the cabinet held its final debate on the subject. Villèle and Montmorency each had in his hand a letter of resignation to pass to the king if the other won. At the end of the debate, Louis summarized the arguments on both sides and announced that he was prepared for the time being to follow the advice of Villèle. Madame du Cayla was later to tell Villèle that the king's original intention had been to rule for Montmorency but that she had threatened to abandon him if he did.[50] Perhaps this was true. Perhaps not, for Louis would have been loath in any circumstances to part with Villèle.

Though the prime minister won a personal victory, he suffered a policy defeat. Montmorency did resign. There followed loud outcries from right-wing deputies and newspapers and anxious dispatches from French ambassadors in Berlin, Vienna, and St. Petersburg, warning that France risked the ire of the Holy Alliance. In choosing a successor to Montmorency, Villèle had to find someone whose appointment would pacify

---

49. Fourcassié, *Villèle*, pp. 234-237; Henry Contamine, *Diplomatie et diplomates sous la Restauration, 1814-1830* (Paris: Hachette, 1970), pp. 59-60.

50. Fourcassié, *Villèle*, p. 237.

the former foreign minister's political allies and signal to the eastern courts that no abrupt change in French policy was in prospect. Hence he offered the post to Chateaubriand. After a period of hesitancy, perhaps feigned, Chateaubriand accepted.[51]

Though Villèle may have been deceived as to the full role of Chateaubriand at Verona, he could have had no doubt that the new foreign minister would be intent on fulfilling the promises made there. Knowing the disposition of his other colleagues and the king, Villèle can have had no illusions as to what was in prospect. After a decent interval, he abandoned opposition to the proposed ultimatum, let preparation for war go forward, and in the spring of 1823 agreed to the actual commencement of military operations.

To the extent possible, Villèle took over administrative supervision of the war. The Duc d'Angoulême, the elder son of Monsieur, was appointed to command the expeditionary force, and Villèle corresponded with him over the head of the minister of war, paying close attention to movements of troops and supplies. Bypassing Chateaubriand, he advised Angoulême on how to deal with Spanish factions, stressing that French commitments should be as limited as possible in scope, duration, and cost. He also corresponded privately with the French ambassador in London, doing his utmost to discourage English aid to the Spanish revolutionists.

Though Villèle remained fearful throughout, the war went much better than he had foreseen. Prorevolutionary guerrilla forces proved negligible. On the whole, the Spanish clergy and gentry welcomed the invaders, and the peasants followed their lead. The revolutionary armies were easily routed. Within a few months, they retreated to the confines of Cadiz. There was momentary alarm in Paris lest they hold out there indefinitely, keeping Ferdinand a prisoner or perhaps transporting him to the Americas. Chateaubriand declared, "If Cadiz does not fall, the French monarchy is in danger. If

---

51. Beau de Loménie, *Carrière politique de Chateaubriand*, II, 54-55.

Joseph, Count de Villèle, engraving from a portrait by Rouillard

François René, Viscount de Chateaubriand, unsigned engraving

revolution triumphs in Spain, all Europe is lost."[52] But Cadiz yielded after a brief siege. Ferdinand was escorted back to his capital. Spain seemed to have been pacified and its legitimate monarchy restored with relatively little cost to France in either life or money.

There remained the question of the Spanish colonies. During the previous half-dozen years, this question had from time to time surfaced in French cabinets. For the most part, however, it had been a concern of lesser officials. In the navy ministry, men in the directorate of colonies had had to take account of how the revolutions in Spanish America might affect French holdings in the Caribbean and on the Guiana coast. They also had to consider the future of that portion of the island of Hispaniola which was nominally a French colony but which in fact had been independent ever since Napoleon failed to reconquer it early in the century. The available evidence suggests that they inclined to view independence movements in the Spanish colonies as threats to the French empire and to argue that France should help the Spaniards and leave the fate of French Hispaniola to be determined later.[53]

Elsewhere within the navy ministry, other attitudes prevailed. Some officials felt concern lest France miss opportunities to develop trade with Latin American republics. From some captains in the fleet came warnings that if the French flag were not seen in the ports of these republics the result would be to give an undesirable advantage to the English and Americans. For purposes of communication to other ministries and the cabinet, these divergent views found reconciliation in a recommendation that France show no favor to the independence movements but reinforce garrisons and fleets in the

---

52. Chateaubriand to Polignac, Sept. 9, 1823, Louis Thomas, ed., *Correspondance générale de Chateaubriand*, 5 vols. (Paris: Édouard Champion, 1912-1924) (hereafter, Chateaubriand, *Correspondance*), IV, 383.

53. Robertson, *France and Latin American Independence*, pp. 125-126, 185-187; Camille Rousset, *Ministre de la Restauration: Le Marquis de Clermont-Tonnerre* (Paris: Plon, 1885), pp. 187-194.

Americas so as to display the flag and be prepared for any contingencies that might arise.[54]

In the foreign ministry, business was divided between a Northern Division and a Central Division. The former dealt with all countries between Russia and Britain, the latter with Turkey, the Italian states, Spain, and the United States. Even before Greek, Spanish, and Spanish American matters reached the forefront of European politics, this compartmentalization was awkward. This was especially so because, as a later foreign minister was to comment, officials of the ministry believed that they should be "discreet, modest, the color of the wall; two people who are concerned with the same business may not speak to one another unless they were formally authorized."[55]

It appears that the Central Division attached greatest importance to actual and potential French trade in the Americas. From it issued memoranda warning that if France lagged in recognizing the independence of Spanish American states she might find them already drawn into the orbits of Britain and the United States. The Northern Division, on the other hand, assigned priority to preserving good relations with the Holy Allies. Hence its officials drew up memoranda pointing out the evils that might follow if France should act independently of Russia, Austria, and Prussia, especially if she seemed to be imitating or following the lead of the British.

At the level of François Rayneval, the political director of the ministry, the views of the two divisions were more or less harmonized. The advice given successive foreign ministers, when they asked about Spanish American affairs, ran roughly as follows: Most of Spain's American colonies were lost to her. She did not have the power or credit to recover them, and they would eventually be independent states. Sooner or later, France would have to extend recognition in order to safeguard her own economic interests. From the standpoint not only of

---

54. Robertson, *France and Latin American Independence*, pp. 181-182.
55. Damas, *Mémoires*, II, 51; Contamine, *Diplomatie et diplomates*, pp. 133-140.

France but of all the powers, including England, however, it was not desirable that the new nations should be republics. That would link them with the United States and make them antagonistic to Europe. Hence France should work with the other powers in an effort to induce Ferdinand to grant independence or at least autonomy to the mainland colonies, installing on the throne of each some prince of the Bourbon line. Something of the sort had already happened in the Portuguese empire, where Brazil had been given the status of a coordinate monarchy and had without difficulty developed independent diplomatic and trade relations with European states. Rayneval and his associates reasoned that something similar would be the most satisfactory solution for Mexico, Gran Colombia, Peru, and the Plata region. Though Rayneval himself was transferred to Berlin when the Villèle cabinet first took office, his successor, Henri de Chastellux, duc de Rauzan, adhered to the same line.[56]

So far as one can ascertain, Villèle and his associates first discussed the matter in the spring of 1822 when news arrived that the United States had recognized republican governments in several of the former Spanish colonies and when left-wing deputies made speeches calling for France to do likewise. Counseled by his permanent officials, Montmorency pressed the view that France should actively encourage the creation of independent or autonomous monarchies. Meanwhile, he signed dispatches drafted by the careerists which at one and the same time warned the Spanish government that France might follow the United States and pleaded with the British government not to do so.[57] The object of the former was to frighten Spain into considering some concessions to the colonies; that of the latter was to prevent Britain from taking action which would interfere with the establishment of Bourbon monarchies in the Americas.

---

56. Robertson, *France and Latin American Independence*, pp. 182, 204.
57. Montmorency to Lagarde, May 7, 1822, CP: Espagne, DCCXIV; Montmorency to Chateaubriand, May 13, 1822, Robertson, *France and Latin American Independence*, pp. 208-209.

Montmorency nevertheless responded negatively to a British suggestion that France and Britain concert their dealings regarding the Spanish colonies. In explanation, he observed that the king of France had a special relationship with his Bourbon cousin in Spain and that, from the French standpoint, a bilateral understanding was less desirable than common understanding among all the powers.[58] In part, this reply reflected the concern of Northern Division officials about a possible breach with the Holy Alliance. Also, no doubt, it reflected Montmorency's own suspicion that any such arrangement with the English might prove an obstacle to France's unilaterally intervening in Spain.

Although Villèle registered no objection, this last point apparently did not escape him. While Montmorency was at Verona, Villèle revived the idea of some coordinated Franco-British action concerning the colonies. He wrote Montmorency that the establishment of independent or autonomous monarchies in the Americas should be a precondition for any offer of support to Ferdinand by the powers. Only such a precondition, he argued, would ensure English cooperation with the Holy Alliance and France. He put great stress on the point and repeated it over and over in instructions to his foreign minister.[59]

Possibly Villèle genuinely felt that some settlement of Spanish colonial issues was of high importance to France and to Europe. Certainly he shared the opinion of his more right-wing colleagues that the spread of republicanism in the Americas could set a harmful example for the Old World, and, as a former *colon*, he appreciated the value of overseas trade. From his vantage point in the treasury, he was interested in commerce with independent American monarchies that would contribute to France's prosperity and increase revenues from customs and taxes. Given his concern with centrist opinion

---

58. Montmorency to Chateaubriand, May 13, 1822, Robertson, *France and Latin American Independence*, pp. 208-209.
59. Villèle to Montmorency, Sept. 23, Oct. 4, Oct. 12, Oct. 15, Oct. 18, Nov. 6, 1822, Villèle, *Mémoires*, III, 69-73, 98-99, 117-118, 123-124, 135, 183-190.

in the chamber of deputies, he could not be indifferent to the voices of merchants who asked that the government promote such commerce.

It seems more likely, however, that Villèle pursued this line primarily because of his desire to avoid intervention in Spain. He could be almost certain that Ferdinand would not oblige the powers by conferring independence or autonomy on parts of his empire or, at any rate, that he would be very slow to do so. If the Holy Allies accepted the French proposal, the French government could postpone military action in Ferdinand's behalf on a pretext which would be understandable both in the eastern courts and among the French public. If the Holy Allies would not make a colonial settlement a precondition, the pretext would still serve. But, of course, Villèle could not persuade Montmorency and his associates at Verona to employ a tactic likely to forestall intervention in Spain. Hence Villèle's efforts had no outcome except to leave him on record as deeply concerned about the future of the Spanish colonies.

During the period when intervention was decided upon and French forces began moving across the Spanish border, little more was said about the subject. It did not recapture the attention of cabinet ministers until the summer of 1823, when the restoration of Ferdidand seemed near at hand.

In the meantime, the new foreign minister, Chateaubriand, had become entranced by the scheme for establishing monarchies in the New World. At fifty-five Chateaubriand remained the romantic who had made out of a tormented childhood, partly passed amid the isolation of a Norman castle in imagined if not real incest with an older sister, the brilliant prose poem *René* and out of brief travel in the wildernessess of the United States and Canada the fable *Atala*, which epitomized what Gilbert Chinard terms France's *rêve exotique d'Amérique*. As moody as ever, he alternated hours of somber silence with periods of such gaiety that Madame de Duras said he had "the soul and heart of

60. Pierre Moreau, *Chateaubriand* (Paris: Hatier Boivin, 1956), p. 89.

a child."[60] Having intrigued with zest to gain his offices, he entertained dreams of going down in history as not only one of France's greatest writers but also one of her greatest statesmen. In fact, his *chef d'oeuvre*, surpassing *René* and *Atala*, was to be his multivolume autobiography. He prided himself on the war with Spain. To the Comtesse de Castellane, with whom he conducted a passionate love affair throughout his term as foreign minister, he sent letters which combined endearments with boasts. Apologizing that he had to cancel a rendezvous on account of the culmination of the Spanish war, he wrote to her, for example: "Forgive me this deliverance of the unfortunate king of Spain. I do not know if you can read my writing; I write to you after having written to all the kings and ministers in Europe. My hand is tired, but my heart is not. It loves you with all the ardor, all the passion of youth. Take a million kisses on your hands, your lips, and your hair."[61] The notion of being the man to give the American Eden its princes appealed enormously to Chateaubriand's vanity.

Even while the upshot of the Spanish campaign remained uncertain, Chateaubriand turned his energies to this project. To the Austrian ambassador he spoke elliptically of possibly putting the French navy at the service of Ferdinand once he had been replaced on his throne. To the Marquis de Talaru, dispatched to Spain as France's ambassador, he sent instructions to advise Ferdinand that the Caribbean islands, Mexico, and Peru could remain nominally Spanish if the king would agree "to establish in America large monarchies governed by princes of the house of Bourbon."[62] While these instructions were probably drafted by the foreign ministry staff, they unquestionably had Chateaubriand's approval.

As the summer wore on, the foreign minister made it clear that he did not desire to share with Britain the credit for achiev-

---

61. Chateaubriand to Madame de Castellane, Oct. 5, 1823, Chateaubriand, *Correspondance*, V, 25.

62. H. W. V. Temperley, "French Designs on Spanish America, 1820-1825," *English Historical Review*, 40 (Jan. 1925), 40; Chateaubriand to Talaru, June 9, 1823, CP: Espagne, DCCXXII.

ing this great result. He directed the French ambassador in London to repel any such overtures.[63] Instead, he seems to have hoped that there would be a new congress of the continental powers and that, by charming Alexander, he could get the Holy Allies to second his advice to Ferdinand. Meanwhile, presumably at his instance, the cabinet resolved not only to continue urging the formula on the Spanish king but to offer as an incentive hints that French warships might transport the Bourbon princes and, together with some contingents of French troops, help them assume their thrones.[64]

Villèle appears not to have opposed Chateaubriand—at least not at first. He did differ with him about the desirability of Franco-British cooperation. When talking with the British ambassador, he stressed the common interest of the two governments not only in upholding monarchism but in curbing the pretensions of the United States.[65] Villèle accepted without demur, however, the recommendation that France risk committing naval and military forces to the project. In fact, he reported the decision to Angoulême, the French commander in Spain, in a letter of his own which implied that it represented *his* policy as much as that of the cabinet.[66] To be sure, Villèle may have remained skeptical whether Ferdinand would yield, even if the Holy Allies and France together exerted pressure, and he certainly recognized that France was as yet very far from actually ordering ships and battalions across the Atlantic. In approving the withdrawal to European waters of fleet elements stationed in the Caribbean and in writing pessimistically to Angoulême about the condition of the armed forces, he indicated at the very least that he had not yet put his mind to the practical aspects of implementing Chateaubriand's policy. "The truth is," he had written to Angoulême, "that we do not have any administration worthy of the name, either at War or at the Navy. It is

63. Chateaubriand to Polignac, July 17, 1823, CP: Angleterre, DCXVII.
64. Sir Charles Stuart to George Canning, Aug. 18, 1823, Foreign Office Records, Public Record Office, Great Britain (hereafter, FO): France, CCXCI; Villèle to Angoulême, July 3, 4, 5, 1823, Villèle, *Mémoirs*, IV, 188, 191, 200-201.
65. Stuart to Canning, June 23, 1823, FO: France CCXCI.
66. Villèle to Angoulême, July 5, 1823, Villèle, *Mémoires*, IV, 200-201.

such that we would now have a hard time sustaining a war even against Bavaria."[67]

Where the compass of French policy would settle remained uncertain. When summer turned to autumn in 1823, France had a vigorous and volatile foreign minister whose imagination was captivated by the idea of establishing monarchies in the Americas and who had important independent constituencies on the right wing of the chamber and in the salons of Paris. The prime minister had shown great cautiousness in the past, had many reasons for continuing to do so, but was committed in writing to support the foreign minister's visionary project. The king and majorities in the two chambers could be counted upon to back whatever decision Chateaubriand and Villèle agreed upon.

If the French ministers resolved to act in the Western Hemisphere in such a way as to advance the monarchical cause and not to provoke protest from the Spanish king, they could be almost certain of winning at least moral support from the tsar.

The key question was whether or not Villèle would continue to favor the policy once he scrutinized its implications. He himself had already stated most of the arguments in favor of it or at least signed documents setting them forth. France could hope for direct benefits from trade with the autonomous monarchies and indirect benefits from the symbolic check to republicanism and from the improvements in metropolitan Spain that seemed sure to result if colonial wars ceased to bleed her. But Villèle had not yet eyed the financial costs of outfitting expeditions to Cuba, Puerto Rico, Mexico, and Peru, nor had he looked at the possible larger costs, both abroad and at home, if the policy should encounter opposition from Britain or the United States or both.

For the moment, Villèle seemed to suppose not only that the British government would not object but that it might even be helpful. Although he perceived that setting up monarchies in the New World would threaten the ambitions of the United States and although he had probably been told by Chateaubriand that

67. Chateaubriand to Polignac, Oct. 5, 1823, CP: Angleterre, CXLV; Villèle to Angoulême, Sept. 14, 1823, Villèle, *Mémoires*, IV, 393.

Gallatin, the American minister, had predicted overt protests by his government, he seemed also to suppose that the Monroe administration would in fact acquiesce. Because of the American Revolution and the War of 1812 and reports of persisting anti-British animus among Americans, it was widely thought among official circles in Paris that the United States was one of France's "natural allies." While Villèle voiced doubt as to whether there were any "natural" alliances, he himself counted the North American republic as in actual circumstances a nearly certain ally in case of war with Britain.[68]

A firm show of resistance by either London or Washington would unquestionably shock Villèle into thinking twice about the balance between benefits and costs. Among other things, he would hear cries of alarm from French shippers, merchants, and bankers. Anyone recalling the strength of his opposition to intervention in Spain would have predicted his turning against Chateaubriand and advocating that the scheme be dropped. It would then remain to be determined whether he could prevail over his foreign minister or whether, even if he kept his place, he would lose the battle, as he had lost that over Spain. As matters stood in the early autumn of 1823, the crucial question was whether Britain or the United States or both would give Villèle reason for second thoughts about the policy pursued by Chateaubriand.

Great Britain

While Britain was far from being what it would become later, it was more nearly a parliamentary monarchy than France. The king had less latitude than Louis XVIII in his choice of ministers and less actual or latent power to determine what they did.

Like his father, George III, the sixty-year-old George IV felt some impulse to "be a king." He struggled against taking

---

68. Chateaubriand to Polignac, March 15, 1824, Chateaubriand, *Correspondance*, V, 180-181; Villèle to Montmorency, Nov. 24, 1822, Villèle, *Mémoires*, III, 240-243.

dictation from the cabinet, protesting any infringement on his prerogatives, and he talked to courtiers as if he could manipulate the government and the parliament by playing one man or faction against another.[69]

Seldom, however, did George IV actually put his capacities to a test. In part, no doubt, this was because he remembered the fates of Charles I and James II and the fact that his own father had been declared *non compos mentis* by the parliament. In part, also, it was because George was easily distracted. For most of his life, he had little to do except follow public business as an impotent heir apparent. He had found diversion in pleasures of the table and the flesh. As regent and then as king, he did not change his ways. Dorothea, Princess Lieven, the wife of the Russian ambassador, wrote of him: "The King makes love, goes out, and every day loses a little of the lively interest he took in affairs."[70] Much of his attention went to comparatively trivial matters. During the first years of his reign, he was preoccupied with winning a divorce from his queen, Caroline, whom he believed to have been his match in infidelity. Then and later, much of his time also went to wrangling with his ministers over offices and titles for relatives of his mistresses. He was further engaged in furbishing the Royal Pavilion at Brighton and developing a project for reconstructing Windsor Castle, and he devoted much of his energy to complaining about the parsimony of the Treasury or architectural interference by the surveyor general.[71] Meanwhile, bouts of gout and erysipelas periodically laid him low.

While George IV interested himself only fitfully in matters of state, he had strong and decided opinions on some of them. He was, for example, a pronounced partisan of legitimacy and mon-

---

69. A. Aspinall, ed., *The Letters of King George IV*, 3 vols. (Cambridge: Cambridge University Press, 1938) (hereafter, George IV, *Letters*), II, 880, n. 1; A. Aspinall, ed., *The Correspondence of Charles Arbuthnot*, Camden Third Series, vol. LXV (London: Royal Historical Society, 1941) (hereafter, Arbuthnot, *Correspondence*), pp. 54-56; Peter Quennell, ed., *The Private Letters of Princess Lieven to Prince Metternich, 1820-1826* (London: John Murray, 1937) (hereafter, Lieven, *Letters*), p. 218.

70. Ibid., p. 286.

71. Arbuthnot, *Correspondence*, pp. 59-60.

archy on the continent. Though he had acquiesced in his government's refusal to subscribe to the Holy Alliance, he took pride in the fact that a more formal alliance, contracted at Vienna in 1815, linked England to Prussia, Austria, and Russia; and he opposed any course of action that might put distance between his country and the eastern monarchies.[72] During the Spanish revolution, when English opinion seemed generally hostile to Ferdinand, George lauded the uncompromising stance of the tsar. And with regard to the Spanish empire he was determined that Britain do nothing to help the colonies become independent or to interfere with the restoration of Spanish rule. It seemed intolerable to him that England should play a part comparable in any way to that of France at the time of the American Revolution. Moreover, he saw the issues in the Americas as identical with those in Ireland.[73] When his cabinet took the modest step of permitting Latin American agents to buy arms in the United Kingdom, George became furious. "I don't think I ever saw him more disturbed," wrote the Duke of Wellington.[74]

Ultimately, however, the power to determine British policy lay not in Windsor Castle but in the houses of parliament. While some members were adherents of the king, either because indebted to him or because ideological monarchists, most looked to their own front benches for leadership, and a government sure of majorities in both the Lords and Commons could virtually defy the monarch.

To be sure of such majorities was by no means a simple task. Both houses had members who rarely put in an appearance. Though the House of Lords clearly did not command the confidence of the people as much as the House of Commons, it was far

---

72. George IV to Sir William Knighton, Nov. ?, 1820, George IV, *Letters*, II, 390-391.
73. George IV to Lord Liverpool, Dec. 17, 1824, Duke of Wellington, ed., *Despatches Correspondence and Memoranda of Field Marshal Arthur Duke of Wellington*, 8 vols. (London: John Murray, 1867-1880), II, 368; Liverpool to Wellington, Dec. 8, 1824, Charles Yonge, *The Life and Administration of Robert Banks Jenkinson, Second Earl of Liverpool*, 3 vols. (London: Macmillan, 1868), III, 305; Arbuthnot to Liverpool, Dec. 29, 1824, Arbuthnot, *Correspondence*, pp. 70-72.
74. Wellington to Canning, ? 1823, Wellington, *Despatches*, II, 22.

from being an insignificant body.[75] Numbers of cabinet members still came from it. Moreover, some of the peers owned or controlled territories represented in the other chamber and could dictate who would hold the seats and how they would vote. One parliamentary manager estimated that, of 658 members of the House of Commons, 276 represented aristocratic patrons.[76] If those patrons were in the cabinet or allied with it, such of these members as could be gotten to Westminster could be counted on to vote with the government. In addition, the government could be sure of votes from occupants of the so-called Treasury boroughs.

There were, however, persistent divisions which complicated the mustering of a majority. Several clusters of members thought of themselves as Whigs. Landowners, townsmen, merchants, and men of very different levels of wealth, these Whigs did not always vote as a unit. Particularly on issues affecting economic interests, they often split. They conceived of themselves, however, as guardians of the principles of the Glorious Revolution and as heirs of the men who had called for compromise with the American colonies and opposed the war with Revolutionary France. When issues touched the relative power of the crown or the state or the role that Britain should play in relation to revolutionary movements in Europe or elsewhere, the Whigs could display solidarity.[77]

The Tories, who controlled the government in the 1820s, had a less well-defined ideology, but more votes. While the Whigs had no more than two hundred seats in the House of Commons, including some seventy-odd under the control of Whig peers, Tory peers owned two hundred seats outright.[78] Even so, a Tory government could not be complacent about its majorities. There

---

75. A. S. Turberville, *The House of Lords in the Age of Reform, 1784-1837* (London: Faber and Faber, 1958), p. 176.

76. Edward Porritt and Annie G. Porritt, *The Unreformed House of Commons: Parliamentary Representation before 1823*, 2 vols. (Cambridge: Cambridge University Press, 1903), I, 310.

77. See Austin Mitchell, *The Whigs in Opposition, 1815-1830* (Oxford: Oxford University Press, 1967).

78. Ibid., p. 61; Porritt and Porritt, *Unreformed House of Commons*, I, 310.

was always uncertainty as to how many Tories would be in the House on a given day. Since there were at least as many factions among them as among Whigs, it was never sure that the Tory peers would vote their members as a unit, and, if an issue pitted the government against the king, there was apt to be defection on a large scale. The government therefore had to concern itself with winning or holding votes among the hundred-odd squires and townsmen known as "country gentlemen" and "indepen-dents," some of whom were grouped in factions led respectively by George Canning, the Grenville family, and the Wellesley fam-ily.[79] Though none of the factions numbered much more than a dozen, their votes could be crucial in a division in the House.

The Tory with chief responsibility for mustering majorities was the prime minister, Robert Banks Jenkinson, the Earl of Liverpool.[80] Though only in his early fifties, he had been in the cabinet almost continuously for more than twenty years, holding successively the posts of foreign secretary, home secretary, sec-retary of state for war, and first lord of the treasury, and he had been head of the cabinet ever since 1812.

A tall man with an astonishingly long neck, Liverpool was noted for physical awkwardness and chronic nervousness. He blinked and fidgeted continuously. One political acquaintance termed him "the grand figitatis at Fife House."[81] By the 1820s, moreover, he was visibly showing the premature physical deteri-oration which long hours, interrupted nights, rich diet, and super-abundant wine brought upon most British politicians of the era. The loss of his wife in 1821 sent him into a fit of depression. Even after he married again in the following year, his letters had a hint of longing whenever they touched on the possibility of resignation or death.

Liverpool probably owed his long tenure in office more to cautiousness than to acumen or skill in managing men. Although

---

79. Mitchell, *Whigs in Opposition*, pp. 61-70.
80. On Liverpool, see Yonge, *Liverpool*; and Charles Alexander Petrie, *Lord Liverpool and His Times* (London: Barrie, 1954).
81. W. R. Brock, *Lord Liverpool and Liberal Toryism* (Cambridge: Cambridge University Press, 1941), pp. 32-33.

his government initiated some reforms, he himself was seldom suspected of being an innovator. Especially after the economic slump commenced in 1819, he put most emphasis on paring government expenditures. Both his personal qualities and his policies thus endeared him to country gentlemen and independents who might otherwise have been drawn to the Whigs by their traditional appeal for less government and less spending.

Meanwhile, Liverpool took care to ensure that the government commanded a maximum number of Tory votes in the two houses. His cabinet was a coalition of diverse elements. The Duke of Wellington was close to the king and more or less shared the king's opinions concerning the danger of revolution in England and Ireland, on the continent, and in the Americas. Lord Eldon, Lord Westmorland, and Lord Bathurst had at least as good claim as Wellington to be considered reactionaries. On the other hand, William Huskisson, Sir Robert Peel, and others in the government were entitled to be considered advocates of change—at least of small-scale change in specified areas. Liverpool was always careful to have represented in the cabinet all segments of opinion that appealed to Tories in parliament.

Even so, Liverpool remained fretful lest the small personal factions join forces with the Whigs. He went to great lengths to bring a member of the Grenville family into the government, and he joined battle not only with some sitting members of the cabinet but with the royal household in order to give offices to Canning and thus assure himself of the Canningites' votes.[82]

Of course, Liverpool had opinions of his own. He believed in free trade. He strongly opposed the notion of doing away with the rotten boroughs and making the House of Commons more representative of the public. Though apprehensive about revolution in the United Kingdom, he felt some mild sympathy for Europeans seeking to impose constitutions on their monarchs and for Spanish Americans struggling for independence.

Most of all, however, Liverpool was dedicated to keeping the Whigs out of office and preserving parliamentary govern-

82. Yonge, *Liverpool*, III, 156-164, 197-199.

ment in England—that is, preventing any increase in royal power. This is not to say he sought to diminish royal power or that he lacked respect either for the monarchy as an institution or for George IV as an individual. On the contrary, he was careful not only to protect royal prerogatives but to consult the king and whenever possible accommodate his opinions. But Liverpool was determined that George IV not make and unmake governments as his father had and that governments responsible to the parliament retain the last say. To these objectives, he subordinated all other prejudices and principles.

For a long period, Liverpool had confided the management of foreign relations and leadership in the House of Commons to Viscount Castlereagh, or Lord Londonderry, as he became in the final years of his life. (As an Irish peer, he sat in the Commons rather than the Lords.) But Castlereagh fell victim to what a later clinician would probably have diagnosed as paranoia and depression. In August 1822 he committed suicide by putting a penknife into his throat. In replacing him, Liverpool faced a difficult choice. Canning, who had previously been attached to the government by lesser offices and had recently accepted an offer to become governor-general of India, was a logical person to assume leadership in the House, but he was unlikely to take that post without the foreign secretaryship or some equivalent post in the cabinet. Eldon, Bathurst, and Westmorland would certainly oppose his becoming a major figure in the government, and the king, who, without real evidence, suspected Canning of being one of his late wife's lovers, would resist with indignation and fury.[83] Alternatively, Liverpool could invite the sometimes refractory Wellington to become foreign secretary and seek someone else to lead the Commons. That would please his colleagues and the king, but it might endanger his primary objective of maintaining a majority at Westminster, especially if Canning should take offense and begin to side with the opposition. On balance, Liverpool decided to brook a row with Eldon and the others and to face down the king. He obtained support from Wellington, who

83. Memorandum by George IV, Nov. 22, 1820, George IV, *Letters*, II, 386.

probably did not relish the notion of managing all the details of diplomacy, and simply informed the king that the continuance of the government required appointing Canning to both offices. With poor grace, George finally assented.

Though Canning had been Liverpool's classmate at Eton and Oxford, he lacked the sense of security derived from breeding that served in Liverpool as a counterweight to natural apprehensiveness.[84] The son of an impoverished Anglo-Irish poetaster who died young and of a mother who turned actress and toured the provinces in company with a lover, he had gone to school as the ward of a banker uncle. Consorting with sons of the aristocracy, he was always striving to prove himself equal to or better than they. Though he succeeded in outdoing most of them in scholarship, oratory, and cleverness as a conversationalist and even as a versifier, and though he later acquired a fortune by marriage, he retained throughout his life some of the sensitivity and pushiness of the self-made man.

A member of parliament for thirty years, he had been originally something of a Whig, then a Tory closely identified with the younger Pitt, then an independent Tory who had to be reckoned with whenever a new government was formed. It was largely his participation in various alliances and coalitions that gave rise to his reputation as an opportunist of whom, as one politician put it, "nobody will believe that he can take the most indifferent step without an ulterior object, nor take his tea without a stratagem."[85]

Like Liverpool, Canning looked older than his years. His hairline had receded, and he had begun to grow stout. Though his eyes could still flash, they often showed strain and weariness, and the small mouth that still so frequently curled around cutting epigrams now seemed to be set in a natural pout. But the quickness of his mind and tongue remained, as did his capacity for cannonading arguments against any adversary who undertook to

---

84. On Canning, see Charles Alexander Petrie, *George Canning* (London: Eyre and Spottiswoode, 1930) and P. J. V. Rolo, *George Canning* (London: Macmillan, 1965).
85. Louis J. Jennings, ed., *The Croker Papers: The Correspondence and Diaries of . . . John Wilson Croker*, 2 vols. (New York: Charles Scribner's Sons, 1884), I, 246.

George Canning, unsigned engraving

debate him face to face either in the chamber of the Foreign Office where the cabinet met or on the floor of the House of Commons. To a much greater degree than Liverpool, Canning wanted to be a leader.

In foreign affairs, Canning saw opportunities to fulfill this ambition. For there seemed no question that parliament and the literate public were more sympathetic to revolutions in Europe and America than were the king and most of the cabinet. The Holy Alliance was condemned by almost all English pamphleteers and leader writers. The Spanish rebels' grievances against Ferdinand were generally thought to be legitimate. While many besides George IV had misgivings about independence for Spanish America, seeing analogies with the American Revolution and the unrest in Ireland, most attentive Englishmen felt that the separation of the Spanish colonies was inevitable. As for Greece, its cause inspired real passion among some elements in England, especially after the reported Turkish misdeeds came to include the killing of Lord Byron and other English volunteers. Nor was sympathy for revolutionaries wholly a matter of sentiment. In London, other seaport cities, and centers where factories were going up, many businessmen believed that more liberal regimes on the continent—and perhaps especially independent nations in Central and South America—would mean more sales of British goods and more traffic for British ships. As spokesman for the feelings of Englishmen who abhorred autocracy and the interests of Englishmen engaged in trade, Canning could hope not only to enlarge his personal following but also to make it necessary for the king to turn to him when a successor to Liverpool had to be chosen.

Canning could not court popularity too boldly. As of 1823 he could be none too sure of keeping the offices that provided his forum. He knew that Eldon, Bathurst, Westmorland, and other reactionaries in the cabinet disliked him and would gladly see him lose his seals. Although Wellington had obliged Liverpool by advising the king to agree to Canning's appointment, he had become outspoken not only in criticism of Canning but in criticism of the prime minister for his closeness to Canning. Princess Lieven heard the duke say of Canning "that he is often carried away by his own cleverness and that he wants tact." She also heard him say in front of twenty people, "My Lord Liverpool is neither more nor less than a common prostitute."[86] Since Canning had few friends in the cabinet other than Liverpool, he had to be wary about forcing a test between himself and his colleagues. He had, after all, been about to accept exile to India at the time of Castlereagh's death, and he recognized that, if he went out of office, he might lose his last chance of exercising influence, let alone becoming prime minister. His situation therefore compelled him to be vigilant, prudent, circumspect, and politic.

The special object of Canning's concern was Wellington, the member of the cabinet who paid closest attention to foreign affairs.[87] Like Canning, the duke came from a relatively humble Anglo-Irish family. He had been at Eton briefly, just when Canning was its star pupil, but his father had not been able to continue paying the fees. Wellington had therefore received his schooling in a French military academy, a fact which accounted for his being able to speak and write French more fluently than either Canning or Liverpool and perhaps for his success in divining the enemy's intentions when leading armies against Napoleon and his marshals. He had emerged from the war with a reputation as the greatest general in English annals and for much of the public as the greatest Englishman. Having served then as ambassador to Paris and a delegate to the Congress of Vienna and later interallied congresses, he appeared also to be an authority on the diplomatic arrangements designed to secure lasting peace. Certainly, he thought of himself in such a light. Holding only the post of master general of ordnance in addition to his seat in the cabinet, he had minimal departmental responsibilities, and he expected to receive copies of all important dispatches from British ambassadors and to be given opportunity to comment on drafts of instructions to them. He had such an expectation even

---

86. Princess Lieven to Prince Metternich, Jan. 17, July 18, 1823, Lieven, *Letters*, pp. 224, 274.

87. Princess Lieven to Prince Metternich, Jan. 26, 1823, ibid., p. 230. On Wellington, see particularly Elizabeth Pakenham Lady Longford, *Wellington*, 2 vols. (London: Weidenfeld and Nicolson, 1969-1972).

when the Foreign Office was managed by Castlereagh, whose diplomatic experience exceeded his own, whose judgment he trusted, and whom he regarded as a close friend. With Canning in Castlereagh's chair, the duke took it as his duty to exercise much closer oversight.

Wellington's inclinations contrasted with Canning's. He had compensated for disadvantages of birth in a different way. In fact, he had been compelled to do so, for the qualities that distinguished him from other men only began to become visible when he took command of troops in the field. Meanwhile, he had already assimilated himself by becoming more identified with the aristocracy than were the aristocrats with whom he consorted. So much was this the case that he accepted pedigree as a prime qualification for high rank in the army, becoming thus in some degree the man responsible for the army's later humiliations in the Crimean War.

Nor was it only with the aristocracy at home that Wellington identified, for he developed after 1814 a mutually sympathetic relationship with the French Bourbons and Prince Metternich of Austria. He also came to view the alliance of Britain with the monarchs of the continent as fundamental to British foreign policy. Arguing that this alliance offered the best security against a new world war and that Britain's paramount interest was to have a generation of peace, he opposed as a matter of principle any statement or action by the government that would win favor among those elements of the British public that disliked the Holy Alliance.

Wellington saw nothing inherently wrong in the Allies' attempting to suppress revolutions. Indeed, he rather welcomed their doing so in hope that it might discourage those in England who protested the existing order. In regard to Spain, Wellington's sympathies were with Ferdinand. In regard to the Spanish colonies, he had reached the regretful conclusion that independence was a near certainty, but he still hoped for monarchies instead of republics, and he felt passionately that England should not encourage their revolutionary leaders. Even more than the king, he saw these leaders as counterparts of the rebels seeking

Robert, Second Earl of Liverpool

The Duke of Wellington,
engraving from a portrait by Sir Thomas Lawrence

in Ireland to overturn a system of governance that he cherished. As for Greece, the only question for Wellington was whether its independence would enhance or weaken the relative position of Britain in the Mediterranean. On all major issues therefore, the long-nosed, tight-mouthed duke, with his haughty carriage and custom of speaking in terse commands, wanted policies quite different from those which seemed most likely to win Canning an increase in personal popularity.

At the time when Canning took over the foreign secretary-ship, Spain and Spanish America were already central issues for the government. Though the positions which Castlereagh was to take at the Congress of Verona had been debated by the cabinet, he had drafted his own instructions. Characteristically, they were so broadly phrased as to leave him freedom to negotiate.[88] Partly because Canning had not heard the debate and therefore lacked ability to interpret these delphic documents, partly to reassure the king and the duke, Liverpool commissioned Wellington to go in Castlereagh's stead. Hence the positions of the government were those of Castlereagh as articulated by Wellington. Regarding Spain, Britain held a stance in opposition to intervention by anyone, declaring that her own policy would be rigid noninter-ference in Spanish internal affairs. For Spanish America, the basis of policy was an unambiguous forecast that direct rule from Madrid could never be restored. From this forecast fol-lowed a recommendation that Spain accept outside mediation to establish new relationships and a warning that, in the absence of a mediated solution, recognition of independent Latin American states would eventually become inevitable. Castlereagh had told more than one foreign ambassador privately that Britain would be happier if monarchies rather than republics emerged in the New World. Without saying so explicitly, Wellington intimated that this remained the case.[89]

---

88. C. K. Webster, *The Foreign Policy of Castlereagh, 1812-1822*, 2 vols. (London: G. Bell and Sons, 1934), II, 432-435.

89. Villèle to Montmorency , Sept. 22, 1822, Villèle, *Mémoires*, III, 59-60; Chateau-briand, *Congrès de Vérone*, I, 58-64. Much the best account of British policy is William W. Kaufmann, *British Policy and the Independence of Latin America* (New Haven: Yale University Press, 1951).

While the Congress of Verona was in progress, French intervention in Spain came to seem more and more probable. Since this contingency had not been much discussed while Castlereagh was still alive, it presented Canning with his first challenge and his first chance to stamp his own mark on policy. It was clearly in his interest to take a hard line, advocating at least a strong protest against France's invading Spain and an intimation that Britain might aid the Spaniards in resisting. Such a stance was sure to win some popular support and to deny the Whigs a rallying cry against the government. The alternative of advocating a cautious policy would gain him little, for such a policy would be applauded mainly by his inveterate opponents.

Whether from such calculation or simply as an expression of his own preferences, Canning did in fact adopt a posture of opposition to the French. He drafted instructions to the British ambassador in Paris and paragraphs for the king's address to parliament which warned that Britain might not be able to stand idly by if faced with a threat that France would gain control of Spain. Since these documents had to circulate in advance, Liverpool, Wellington, and other members of the cabinet had opportunity to tone them down, and Canning could take the line he wanted to take only in informal conversations with foreign diplomats. He did so, thus gaining advantage from the fact that they let slip to acquaintances in London reports that he was more bellicose than his colleagues.[90]

Wellington was adamant in opposition to any British involvement in Spain. Calling attention to the weakness of the army and its preoccupation with police duties in Ireland, he pointed out that Britain could aid the Spaniards only with sea power; that this would be of little help to them in ground fighting against the French; that if an Anglo-French war developed, the French were likely to attack Hanover, the Netherlands, and Portugal, none of which Britain would be capable of defending; and that such a war would be ruinous.[91] On every possible occasion,

---

90. H. W. V. Temperley, *The Foreign Policy of Canning, 1822-1827* (London: G. Bell and Sons, 1925), pp. 75-90.

91. Wellington to Canning, Feb. 10, 1823, Wellington, *Despatches*, II, 31-33.

Wellington counseled Canning to be circumspect.

In the end, Canning yielded gracefully to the duke. Perhaps he intended to do so all along and merely wanted to exploit the situation for such credit as he could earn among the opposition and the public sympathetic with the Spanish revolution. In any case, he did not force an issue which might have jeopardized his continuance in the cabinet. After the French moved into Spain, Canning made a speech in the Commons in defense of the cabinet's decision to reaffirm a policy of nonintervention. When Whig leaders criticized this policy, Canning forced a vote. Doubtless, he sensed that, while many members were sympathetic with Spain, very few were prepared to say that they favored war. Canning won a 372-20 vote, and, because of the way he managed the debate, it appeared to be a vote of confidence in him as an individual. He felt much strengthened as a result.[92]

In the meantime, Canning improved his relations with the king. After getting refusals from several others, he hit upon the idea of offering the undersecretaryship in the Foreign Office to Lord Francis Conyngham, the son of the king's reigning mistress. Afterward, George showed a more kindly attitude toward Canning, going so far once as to invite him to dine at Windsor. There is no evidence that the king gave up his suspicions about Canning's relations with Queen Caroline, and he was to say later that his detestation of Canning never diminished. But the outward signs of change, including remarks to courtiers about the usefulness of having Canning in the cabinet, produced at least the illusion that Canning was no longer his bête noire. Rumors circulated that, in the event of a breach with Liverpool, George might turn to Canning to form a government.[93]

In the summer and autumn of 1823, when the future of the former Spanish colonies commanded urgent attention, Canning occupied a stronger position within the government. While by no means able to force the acceptance of his views, he felt more free-

---

92. Canning to Charles Bagot, July 14, 1823, Josceline Bagot, *George Canning and His Friends*, 2 vols. (London: John Murray, 1909), II, 179-180.

93. Arbuthnot to Liverpool, Oct. 7, 1823, Arbuthnot, *Correspondence*, pp. 46-48; Lord Eldon to Lord Stowell, Sept. ?, 1823, Horace Twiss, *The Public and Private Life of Lord Chancellor Eldon*, 2 vols. (London: John Murray, 1844), II, 484.

dom to attempt maneuvers which might result in policies to his liking.

For the moment, Canning had the advantage of dealing only with Wellington. After parliament recessed, the others, including Liverpool, scattered to the country. From August until November there would be no sitting of the cabinet. Canning thus had a free hand at the Foreign Office, subject only to the constraint of having to get the duke's approval for any formal note to a foreign government or any important instruction to a British ambassador.

With regard to Spanish America, Canning favored a clear declaration that Britain would oppose any military intervention and any acquisition of territory by European powers other than Spain. He also favored extending diplomatic recognition to Latin American states that had organized or succeeded in organizing effective governments, regardless of whether Spain and the Holy Allies approved and regardless of whether their forms of government were republican or monarchical. He could perceive that a declaration of opposition to European intervention would win him credit with the Whigs and with all those who had felt misgivings about the government's policy regarding Spain. He had reason to believe that recognition would gain him applause not only in these circles but also among bankers and merchants.[94]

On the first point, Wellington's differences with Canning had to do with tactics, for the government had long ago agreed that in practice it could not permit any continental power to gain new advantages in the Western Hemisphere. Castlereagh, Wellington, and Liverpool had all said as much, but had kept their statements in low key. It was Wellington's view that nothing more needed to be done. Feeling certain that neither France nor any of the Holy Allies intended to act, he held that a well-publicized warning could be gratuitous and would jeopardize the alliance between Britain and the continental monarchies.[95]

On the second point, Wellington differed in principle. Like the king, he opposed formal diplomatic recognition unless and until Spain had conceded it. Commercial agents had already been

94. Temperley, *Foreign Policy of Canning*, pp. 142-144.
95. Wellington to Canning, July 31, 1823, Wellington, *Despatches*, II, 108-109.

sent to the capitals where governments were functioning, and Wellington felt that this represented the maximum concession which the government should make to groups interested in trade.[96]

Earlier, Canning had tried to move Wellington and his allies by playing on their antipathy toward the United States. He had raised an alarm about possible American designs on Cuba, pressed for sending more warships to the West Indies, argued that an emphatic public expression of concern about Latin America would serve as a deterrent in Washington as well as European capitals, and suggested that diplomatic recognition by Britain might be necessary to counteract American influence in the new capitals. Except for getting an augmentation of the West Indies squadron, Canning had had no success with these maneuvers. The duke even protested the idea of Canning's receiving a special envoy sent by Mexico. If there were reason to fear any action by the United States or by France, the duke argued, Britain should first address her continental allies, describe the grounds for such fear, and explain the responses that seemed called for. Not to do so would jeopardize the alliance. For his part, the duke said, he saw nothing as yet that called for such a step.[97]

After the recess of parliament, Canning tried to make more of the French bogey. From Sir Charles Stuart, the British ambassador in Paris, he received a series of reports crying alarm about French plans to move into Latin America as soon as the Spanish campaign ended. Although Canning thought Stuart incompetent and although Stuart offered little evidence to back up his warnings, Canning took them seriously or at least pretended to do so. Passing them on to Wellington, he argued that the point of danger had arrived and that some further declaration of British policy was imperative. But the duke remained unmoved. He wrote calmly to Canning: "it is impossible that either France or

---

96. Ibid.

97. Canning memorandum for the cabinet, Nov. 15, 1822, Webster, *Britain and the Independence of Latin America*, II 393-398; C. J. Bartlett, *Great Britain and Sea Power, 1815-1853* (Oxford: Clarendon Press, 1963), pp. 68-69; Wellington to Canning, July 31, Sept. 23, 25, 1823, Wellington, *Despatches*, II, 108-109, 134-135, 139.

all the powers of Europe can intend to carry troops, whether French or Spanish, to America to conquer the Spanish colonies without the consent of this country."[98]

In the meantime, Canning had commenced and pursued discussions with Rush about a possible joint statement. In all probability, Canning thought then that the predictions from Stuart would have more effect on Wellington. One can infer that he hoped to work out an accord with the United States and then exhibit it to the duke, arguing to him that it was an appropriate means of checking the French, that it provided insurance against America's exploiting the situation to its own advantage, and that, in any case, it was a *fait accompli*. One can also infer that Canning believed the issuance of a joint Anglo-American declaration would prepare the way for early recognition of Latin American governments, for Britain would be associated with a nation that had already extended recognition, and it would have made a complete break with the continental powers at least in regard to dealings with the Spanish empire. Canning would have attained one of his ends and be on the way to attaining the other. In the process he would have attached to himself some of those Englishmen who idealized the United States and wanted closer relations with the former colony.

If these were Canning's hopes, they were disappointed. He found Rush obstinate in insisting that recognition be a precondition for a joint declaration, and he could not alarm Wellington.

The most that Canning could get from the duke was approval for his holding an interview with the French ambassador, Prince Polignac, in order to restate the position the government had adopted earlier. When once convinced that neither Rush nor Wellington would bend, Canning arranged to see Polignac. He told him in firm language that Britain would not tolerate European intervention in Spanish America. Afterward, he tried to persuade Wellington that this step had been insufficient. Sending

---

98. Temperley, *Foreign Policy of Canning*, pp. 508-509; Stuart to Canning, Sept. 22, Oct. 16, 1823, Wellington, *Despatches*, II, 141, 149-150; Canning to Wellington, Sept. 24, 25, Oct. 21, 1823, ibid., pp. 136-138, 140, 154; Wellington to Canning, Sept. 25, 1823, ibid., p. 139.

the duke a memorandum recording the discussion, Canning alleged that Polignac had been evasive. "I fear very much," he wrote, "that nothing is to be gained by more *verbal* communications with Frenchmen, and I am quite sure we gain nothing by leaving our meaning unexplained." But Wellington proved unresponsive, telling Canning that the memorandum was "most satisfactory" and that nothing more needed to be done.[99]

The issues between Canning and Wellington had much more to do with the relative standing of Canning in the cabinet and the country than with the prospective behavior of Britain toward other nations. None of the jockeying between the two men affected basic British policy. In the mind of neither was there any question that Britain should oppose an overt military move against Latin America by France or any other European power. Although Wellington was more sympathetic to the idea of Spain's regaining her empire, he was no more prepared than Canning to see French ships or troops lent to Spain for the purpose.

Were either British politics or British policy likely to be significantly affected by decisions in Washington? Certainly Canning would have been able to play out his game of presenting Wellington with a *fait accompli* if the American government responded promptly and favorably to his proposals. Whether or not he would have succeeded is an open question. In any case, it is almost unimaginable that any feasible action by the United States could have increased or diminished more than marginally the resoluteness of the British government with regard to Latin America. Similarly, it seems improbable that American recognition of Greece could have done more than add slightly to the pressure from philhellenes which the government could already anticipate.

In short, the prospective policies of Russia, France, and England set no clear boundaries for the choices to be made in Washington. Alexander was most unlikely to act except in support of

---

99. Memorandum by Polignac, Oct. 12, 1823, Webster, *Britain and the Independence of Latin America*, II, 115-120; Canning to Wellington, Oct. 21, 1823, Wellington, *Despatches*, II, 154; Wellington to Canning, Oct. 24, 1823, ibid., pp. 154-155.

France. It was virtually certain that Villèle would not move if he had reason to believe that England would oppose. If his influence proved less strong than that of Chateaubriand, the French government might make more of an effort to arrange the establishment of Bourbon monarchies in the New World. Even so, it would not take a serious step in the face of British opposition. And the British government, whatever its complexion, would not permit the use of force by France either in its own behalf or in the behalf of Spain. At least in retrospect, it seems evident that the American government could decide whether it wished a partnership with Britain and whether it wished to encourage the Greeks without fear that its actions would affect the fate of Latin America or affect more than marginally its own relations with any of the major cisatlantic powers.

And this state of things should have been evident to the men deciding American policy. While many of the details which we have inspected were unknown to them, the essential facts were fully visible. Dispatches from American diplomats sketched accurately the standing and sympathies of the tsar and his lack of the wherewithal to lend practical support to Spain except as an auxiliary of France. They reported Russia to lack the naval forces needed for unilateral intervention. If anything, they minimized the danger that Russian policy might be controlled by the tsar's sympathy for the Spanish monarchy.[100] American diplomats in Paris meanwhile described Villèle's opposition to intervention in Spain, forecast that he would be bearish about any action in the Americas, and expressed complete confidence that France would not make any move in face of opposition from Britain.[101] And Rush, despite his complaints of being cut off from good sources of political intelligence, gave his government a full pic-

---

100. George W. Campbell to Adams, May 3, 1819, Manning, *Diplomatic Correspondence of the United States concerning the Independence of the Latin Amercan Nations,* III, 1862; Middleton to Adams, July 20, 1822, ibid., pp. 1866-1867.

101. Gallatin to Adams, Feb. 5, 1823, Papers of Albert Gallatin, New-York Historical Society; Gallatin to Monroe, March 1, 1823, Papers of James Monroe, Library of Congress; Gallatin to Adams, June 24, 1823, Manning, *Diplomatic Correspondence of the United States concerning the Independence of the Latin American Nations,* II, 1397-1398.

ture of the public and parliamentary pressures affecting the British cabinet. To the extent that his cautious nature permitted, he ventured the prediction that Britain would oppose European intervention in the Western Hemisphere, regardless of what the United States did.[102]

Diplomatic dispatches were supplemented by newspaper reports. The Washington *National Intelligencer*, the Baltimore *Weekly Register*, and the Philadelphia *National Gazette* carried extensive extracts from London and Paris dailies together with letters from traveling Americans, reporting in detail the strains between Villèle and Chateaubriand and between Canning and Wellington. While editors' analyses varied, with some appearing to take more seriously than others the danger of intervention by the Holy Allies in Spanish America or Greece, the differences corresponded more to preferences in the presidential race than to differences in the information presented on their news pages. Pro-Adams organs like the *Weekly Register* and *National Gazette* tended to discount evidence of danger while pro-Crawford and pro-Calhoun journals such as the *National Intelligencer*, the Richmond *Enquirer*, the Philadelphia *Franklin Gazette*, and the New York *Patriot* were prone to crying alarm.

Given the accurate intelligence supplied by diplomats and journalists, probably supplemented by oral reports from foreign visitors and Americans returning from abroad, together with the fact that Monroe and Adams knew most of the members of the British cabinet, that Adams knew also the principal figures in St. Petersburg, and that Crawford was well acquainted with many of those in Paris, it is probably fair to judge that the American decision-makers had adequate evidence for a just assessment of the situation abroad. If they chose to make unrealistic estimates of the possible consequences of the options before them, they were rationalizing arguments for courses of action which they pre-

---

102. Rush to Adams, April 22, July 24, July 26, 1822, Aug. 23, 1823, ibid., III, 1464-1465, 1468-1469, 1472-1473, 1480-1481; Rush to Monroe, Dec. 3, Dec. 17, 1821, Oct. 20, 1822, Jan. 30, June 20, 1823, Monroe Papers; Christopher Hughes to Adams, June 10, 1823, Adams Family Papers, Massachusetts Historical Society.

ferred for other reasons. In any case, it is certainly fair to say that a careful appraisal of the foreign scene as of the autumn of 1823 would not have discovered constraints likely to determine the choices of the American government. It would not have permitted an observer to make a confident bet on the course or outcome of the administration's debates on foreign policy.

4

Domestic Politics

There remains one more element of background to canvass. The men who constructed the Monroe Doctrine were all deeply interested in the approaching presidential election. Indeed, it is not too much to say that this subject preoccupied most of them. Mrs. Adams's diary and letters testify that this was the case for her husband, and his own diary suggests the same. Calhoun's nonofficial correspondence for the period dealt with little else. The same is true of Crawford and Clay. We should therefore examine the stakes for which these men were competing and the strategies which they had adopted, for it seems likely that expectations and fears related to the election could well have influenced their reasoning about the pressing issues of foreign policy.

Men who wanted to become President had to think first of how they might be nominated; second, of how they might win in the electoral college; and third, in case no one had a majority, of how to win in the House of Representatives.

THE CAUCUS

For some years, Republican senators and representatives had met prior to elections to select the party's candidates for President and vice president. Owing to the fragmentation and decline of the Federalist opposition, nomination by this Republican congressional caucus had become equivalent to election.

The practice had drawn increasing criticism. Some of it was

on the ground that the caucus blurred the line between legislative and executive power; some on the ground that senators and representatives had been elected to represent localities, not to judge which President would be best for the nation; some on the broader ground that the caucus needlessly narrowed the choice for the people. As 1824 approached, many newspaper editors outside of Washington were contending that no caucus should convene or that, if it did, the people should ignore it. On the other hand, many Republican congressmen and editors said a caucus was more needed than ever. Otherwise, they argued, four or five candidates would run. None would get a majority. The House of Representatives would choose among the top three. Federalists in the House would then have some say in who would win.

As of late 1823, no one knew whether a congressional caucus would be held in 1824. Even if there were a caucus, it might be so poorly attended as to seem unrepresentative, or it might be so divided as to seem inconclusive. Even if well attended and more or less united, it might still be ignored by the people. Each candidate had to think of these contingencies and decide which he would prefer and what he should do.

Assuming that there were twenty to forty Federalists in the House and Senate and a dozen or so Republicans who would refuse to attend as a matter of principle, the candidates could calculate that a caucus might draw up to 230 representatives and senators.[1] If the nomination were to impress the electorate, it would probably have to be made by a caucus as well attended as that which had chosen Monroe in 1816. In other words, it would have to include at least 160 to 190 senators and representatives. And the nomination itself would have to be voted by something more than a bare majority. The winner would not win much unless he received 100 to 120 votes.

---

1. Only twelve members of the House can be definitely identified as Federalists. See Appendix A. The figure, twenty to forty, was, however, used in most newspaper calculations about the caucus. An estimate that there were forty-five Federalists in the House and Senate appeared in the pro-caucus Washington *National Intelligencer*, Feb. 11, 1824, and this figure was cited without quarrel in the anticaucus Baltimore *Weekly Register*, Feb. 14, 1824. The "official" account of the caucus in the *National Intelligencer*, Feb. 16, 1824, reduced the figure to forty.

TABLE 1. Estimated presidential preferences of members of the Senate and House who might take part in a congressional caucus in 1824

Region	Total	Adams	Calhoun	Clay	Crawford	Jackson
New England	*30-45*	*12-27*	4	*0*	*14-16*	*1*
Me.	5-8	3-6	0	0	2-3	1
N.H.	7-8	2-3	1	0	4	0
Vt.	3-8	1-6	0	0	2	0
Mass.	5-10	4-9	0	0	1-2	0
R.I.	3-4	1-2	0	0	2	0
Conn.	7	1	3	0	3	0
Mid-Atlantic	*48-73*	*19-31*	*9-18*	*0*	*18-27*	*2*
N.Y.	28-36	19-27	0	0	9-17	0
Pa.	12-21	0	7-16	0	4-5	1
N.J.	2-8	0-4	0	0	1	1
Del.	0	0	0	0	0	0
Md.	6-8	0	2	0	4	0
South	*43-54*	*0*	*2-7*	*0*	*41-48*	*0*
Va.	18-21	0	0	0	18-21	0
N.C.	10-14	0	0	0	10-14	0
S.C.	6-11	0	2-7	0	4	0
Ga.	9	0	0	0	9	0
West	*30-57*	*6-7*	*1*	*7-15*	*3-5*	*13-18*
Ohio	5-15	0-1	1	2-3	0	2
Ind.	4-5	3	0	0	1-2	0
Mo.	2-3	1	0	0	0-1	1
Ky.	6-13	1	0	2-9	0	3
Tenn.	4-8	0	0	0	0	4-8
Ala.	3-5	1	0	0	1	1-2
Miss.	1-3	0	0	0	1	0
La.	5	0	0	3	0	2
National	*151-229*	*37-65*	*16-30*	*7-15*	*76-96*	*16-21*

Source: Supporting data appear in Appendix A. Where no contrary evidence exists, I have assumed that members from New England were disposed to favor Adams, members from Pennsylvania and South Carolina to favor Calhoun, members from Kentucky to favor Clay, members from Virginia and North Carolina to favor Crawford, and members from Tennessee to favor Jackson.

From newspaper reports and gossip in private letters, one can guess how the candidates visualized the range of possible outcomes. As table 1 suggests, Crawford was the only candidate within striking distance of the necessary vote total.

Whatever the outcome of the congressional caucus, a determined candidate could still run. All he needed was enough supporters to sign a petition to put him on the ballot or, in states where the legislatures still chose presidential electors, to have one legislator propose his name. In almost every state, each of the major candidates could be sure of getting before the electorate. Nomination was thus the least of their problems, and the congressional caucus concerned them chiefly in terms of how it might affect later voting in the states.

THE STATES

There would be twenty-four states at the time of the 1824 election. Each, of course, would have as many presidential electors as it had senators and representatives in Congress, and most would cast their electoral votes on a winner-take-all principle. In theory, a candidate could become President with New York, Pennsylvania, and Virginia and three of the four next most populous states: Ohio, Massachusetts, North Carolina, and Kentucky. In practice, no one seemed likely to carry six of these seven. The winning candidate would probably have to take large and small states within two or more sections: New England, the South, the West, and the Middle Atlantic region.

At the time, the part of the United States inhabited by Americans other than Indians lay mostly east of the Mississippi. In fact, great tracts between that river and the Appalachians remained frontier land, where game and fish were still staples, the cleared fields showed their newness in the dark or clayey color of the soil and in the shine on ax-marked stumps surrounding them, the land routes from settlement to settlement continued to be trails through forests of oak, pine, and gum trees, and handhewn canoes and rafts plied the rivers. Even east of the Alleghenies, the Cumberlands, and the Blue Ridge there were great stretches of wilderness. In this long-settled region, most families lived on far-apart farms or plantations. The large majority of the population earned its living on the land, and most of those who did not kept stores or stables, tended forges, taught school, or hawked services in villages, for less than a million of the nation's almost eleven million residents dwelt in towns of more than 2,500.

Since the nation was made up of not much more than two million families, spread over an area so large that there were six to seven square miles for each inhabitant, it ought to be possible to generalize about politics in such a way as to spare the need for looking at separate jurisdictions. Unhappily, this is not so, for political affairs were for the most part local and peculiar to particular counties and towns, with the interests of most voters and politicians seldom transcending the boundaries of their states.

As of 1823, no national issues gripped the electorate or created strong bonds within or between regions. The battles having to do with forming a federal government lay far in the past. No general European war gave foreign policy the importance it had had between 1793 and 1815. National questions concerning the extension of slavery into the West and programs for building canals and roads appeared to have been settled by compromises not likely to be altered more than marginally during the next few years. Protective tariffs were not much discussed, and the relationship between the federal government and state banks had yet to attract much notice. To an even greater extent than ordinarily, people interested in politics focused on such matters as who would become governor, which faction or factions would control the state legislature, and which parts or sections of the state would benefit most from the state government's patronage and other favors. Although the presidential race inevitably aroused some interest, if only as a major sporting event, it engaged politically active people primarily to the extent that it became entwined with contests for local and state office, including, of course, contests for the national House and Senate.

Anyone who would see the domestic stakes of participants in the Monroe administration's foreign policy debate must therefore look at the states one by one, taking comfort—if any is to be found —from the fact that there were not as many states then as later and perhaps from the thought that the task would be harder if the chief stake in question were not the presidency of the United States but the crown of the Holy Roman Empire.

New England: In the election of 1824, the six New England states would have fifty-one electoral votes—almost 40 percent of the total needed for election. They were assumed to lean toward Adams.

Yet not even Adams's home state of Massachusetts was certain. The regional managers of his campaign, Henry A. S. Dearborn, a Boston businessman and brigadier general of the state militia, and Peter P. F. Degrand, an emigre Frenchman who owned a fleet of ships, judged most politicians and businessmen to be for him. On the other hand, many Massachusetts Republicans remembered that Adams was the son of the last Federalist President and had himself served in the Senate as a Federalist. The Boston *Statesman* argued that true Republicans should be for Crawford.[2] At the same time, many Federalists remembered that Adams, while in the Senate, had deserted the party and supported Jefferson. They looked on him as an apostate, and they still had strength in Massachusetts—enough to win the governorship in every election up to 1823.[3]

Some Federalist leaders opposed Adams because they hoped to build a new national party. They reasoned that if they threw New England votes to a southerner or westerner, they would have more leverage with him than with any fellow New Englander. A few leaned to Crawford, even though he represented himself as the arch-anti-Federalist. Led by Congressman Daniel Webster,

2. Dearborn to Adams, Jan. 2, Aug. 13, 1822, Adams Family Papers, Massachusetts Historical Society; Degrand to Adams, Oct. 8, 1821, Jan. 23, Sept. 25, Oct. 15, 23, Dec. 24, 1822, March 17, April 22, 1823, ibid.; Washington *National Intelligencer*, Sept. 2, 1823; Charles Shaler to Adams, Jan. 9, 1822, Adams Papers; Dearborn to Adams, Jan. 14, 1822, ibid.; Degrand to Adams, Oct. 23, 1822, Feb. 8, 1823, ibid.

3. George W. Erving to Crawford, July 25, 1823, William H. Crawford Papers, Duke University Library. Se Shaw Livermore, Jr., *The Twilight of Federalism: The Disintegration of the Federalist Party, 1815-1830* (Princeton: Princeton University Press, 1962), pp. 117-119, Richard P. McCormick, *The Second American Party System: Party Formation in the Jackson Era* (Chapel Hill: University of North Carolina Press, 1966), pp. 36-42, and Arthur B. Darling, *Political Changes in Massachusetts, 1824-1848* (New Haven: Yale University Press, 1925), chap. 1.

most turned to Calhoun. In September 1823, a pro-Calhoun newspaper commenced publication in Worcester, and in November 1823, a New Bedford paper shocked Adams's friends by endorsing Calhoun. At that time, Representative George McDuffie of South Carolina, one of Calhoun's managers, predicted that Calhoun would carry Massachusetts.[4]

Crawford and Calhoun were, however, the only threats to Adams in his home state. Even the fretful Degrand saw no reason to fear Clay. When a physician friend said seriously that he leaned toward the Kentuckian, Degrand laughed, saying, "you Doctors are always trying hard to turn your Patients to Clay." And until well into 1824 admirers of Jackson in Massachusetts contented themselves with advocating that the general be made vice president under Adams.[5]

In January 1823, the Republican caucus in the state gave a strong but qualified endorsement to Adams. Addressing the points made by Crawfordites, the resolution cautioned that the election should not go to the House, and, on that account, that Adams should not be supported "at all events and under all possible circumstances. Such inflexibility of opinion might destroy that common principle of action from which is to be expected a harmonious and useful result."[6] In a cool assessment of his own prospects, Adams could have concluded that he would probably win Massachusetts but that victory was not a certainty.

Maine, the second most populous New England state, was akin to Massachusetts in many respects. It had, of course, been

4. Webster to Ezekiel Webster, March 25, 1823, J. W. McIntyre, ed., *The Writings and Speeches of Daniel Webster*, 18 vols. (Boston: Little, Brown, 1903) (hereafter, Webster, *Writings*), XVII, 322-323; Degrand to Adams, June 8, Oct. 16, 1822, Feb. 8, 1823, Adams Papers; Washington *Republican*, Sept. 16, 1823, reporting the opening of the Worcester *Yeoman*; Washington *Republican*, Nov. 20, 1823, and Philadelphia *Franklin Gazette*, Nov. 18, 1823, reporting endorsement of Calhoun by the New Bedford *Gazette*; Degrand to Adams, Dec. 9, 1823, Adams Papers; McDuffie to ?, Nov. 21, Dec. 26, 1823, A. R. Newsome, ed., "Correspondence of John C. Calhoun, George McDuffie and Charles Fisher relating to the Presidential Campaign of 1824," *North Carolina Historical Review*, 7 (Oct. 1930), 489, 493.

5. Degrand to Adams, Feb. 8, 1823, Adams Papers (cf. Webster to Adams, Feb. 17, 1823, ibid.); Degrand to John Bailey, March 19, 1824, ibid. .

6. Baltimore *Weekly Register*, Feb. 1, 1823.

part of Massachusetts until the Missouri Compromise of 1820. Politically, it was different chiefly in having many fewer Federalists. Indeed, Massachusetts Federalists had been enthusiastic about its becoming a sovereign state from hope, as one of them put it, of having "a snug little Federal State for the rest of our lives."[7] In consequence, there was no counterpart in Maine to Webster's campaign for Calhoun.

On the other hand, there was much more lively support for Crawford. Both of Maine's United States senators, John Chandler and John Holmes, were active partisans of the secretary of the treasury. So was General William King, the first governor of the state and reputedly its most powerful politician. In addition, the oldest and best-known newspaper in the state, the Portland *Evening Argus*, was decidedly hostile to Adams, declaring that his Federalist background unfitted him for the presidency.[8]

For a time, Maine seemed likely to go for Crawford. In January 1822, Republicans in the legislature adopted a resolution saying, in effect, that Maine would abide by the outcome of a congressional caucus. Opponents of Chandler, Holmes, and King, however, sensed popular opposition to Crawford which was partly sectional feeling against a southerner, partly sentiment against slavery, partly revulsion against someone who had fought duels and killed a man, and partly a result of effective campaigning

---

7. Edmund Quincy, *Life of Josiah Quincy* (Boston: Ticknor and Fields, 1868), p. 374.

8. See Louis Clinton Hatch and others, *Maine: A History*, 3 vols. (New York: American Historical Society, 1919), I, 175-187; on the leanings of Chandler, Holmes, and King: John Maguire to Adams, April 3, 1822, Adams Papers; Chandler to King, April 10, 1822, Papers of John Chandler, Maine Historical Society; Degrand to Adams, Aug. 26, 1822, Adams Papers; Adams diary, Jan. 2, 1823; Rufus King to Edward King, Feb. 23, 1823, Papers of Rufus King, Cincinnati Historical Society; diary, Feb. 23, 1823, Papers of Rufus King, New-York Historical Society; Washington *National Journal*, Nov. 22, 1823; on pro-Crawford manifestations: John Wingate to Adams, Nov. 27, 1821, Adams Papers; Lewis Williams to Ruffin, Dec. 22, 1821, J. G. de Roulhac Hamilton, ed., *The Papers of Thomas Ruffin*, 4 vols. (Raleigh, N. C.: Edwards and Broughton, 1918-1920) (hereafter, Ruffin, *Papers*), I, 258; William Plumer, Jr., to William Plumer, Sr., Dec. 30, 1821, Everett S. Brown, ed., *The Missouri Compromise and Presidential Politics, 1820-1825, from the Letters of William Plumer, Jr.* (St. Louis: Missouri Historical Society, 1926), pp. 69-70; Edward Williams to Adams, Aug. 5, 1822, Adams Papers; Degrand to Adams, Oct. 23, 1823, Adams Papers; diary, Feb. 2, 1823, Rufus King Papers (New-York Historical Society); Webster to Jeremiah Mason, March 23, 1822, Webster, *Writings*, IV, 67; Portland *Evening Argus*, Jan. 26, Oct. 10, 1822.

by the Maine branch of the Dearborn family. When a new legislature convened, these rebels arranged for a new caucus. One of them presided and ruled out of order a motion for a roll call. This had the effect of permitting Federalists to remain and vote. With Federalists accounting for some of the margin of victory, the caucus passed 77-37 a resolution commending Adams and explicitly denying that Maine was for Crawford. Although the *Argus* exposed the ruse, the resolution and the subsequent defeat of a candidate for Congress committed to Crawford made it seem likely but not certain that Adams would carry Maine.[9]

In New Hampshire as in Maine, Federalists were weak.[10] New Hampshire Republicans were, however, divided into factions led respectively by Isaac Hill, a self-made insurance and river boat magnate who published the Concord *New Hampshire Patriot*, and Levi Woodbury, a well-educated, well-connected Portsmouth lawyer.

In the presidential race, Hill leaned to Crawford. Though Woodbury tried to be neutral, he inevitably became identified with Adams. When he won the governorship in September 1823, observers interpreted the vote as signifying that Adams would win New Hampshire. Hill protested accurately that Woodbury had won because of Federalist support.[11] Since Federalist leaders in New Hampshire were for Calhoun, it was possible that Woodbury votes would not all translate into Adams votes. It was also

---

9. Hatch, *Maine*, I, 183-185; diary, Feb. 9, 1823, William M. Meigs, *The Life of Charles Jared Ingersoll* (Philadelphia: J. B. Lippincott, 1897), pp. 114-115; entry of Sept. 20, 1823, *The Journals of Hezekiah Prince, Jr., 1822-1828* (New York: Crown Publishers, 1965), p. 91. William King believed, however, that the legislative vote had been engineered by the Dearborn family in coalition with Federalists and that the state could still be captured for Crawford, and Crawford himself remained sanguine: diary, Feb. 23, 1823, Rufus King Papers (New-York Historical Society); Crawford to John M. O'Connor, May 16, 1823, Papers of William H. Crawford, Rice University Library.

10. See Donald B. Cole, *Jacksonian Democracy in New Hampshire, 1800-1851* (Cambridge, Mass.: Harvard University Press, 1970), pp. 1-58.

11. Degrand to Adams, Oct. 23, 1822, Adams Papers; William Plumer, Jr., to Adams, June 15, 1823, ibid.; William Plumer, Sr., to William Plumer, Jr., Dec. 23, 1822, Papers of William Plumer, Sr., New Hampshire Historical Society; John Wingate to Woodbury, March 21, 1823, Papers of Levi Woodbury, Library of Congress; Seth Hunt to Adams, July 31, 1823, Adams Papers; Sprague to Adams, Sept. 12, 1823, Adams Papers; Cole, *Jacksonian Democracy in New Hampshire*, pp. 50-51.

possible that there would be a reaction among Republicans. (In fact, in 1824 a candidate backed by Hill would unseat Woodbury.) As of the autumn of 1823, however, New Hampshire seemed likely to go for Adams, even if not securely his.

The same held true for Vermont. There, presidential electors would be chosen by the state legislature. Meeting in caucus in the autumn of 1823, Republicans in the body had debated whether or not to endorse Adams and decided not to do so. They resolved that any action would be "premature." How they ultimately voted seemed to depend mostly on the leadership given by Cornelius P. Van Ness, who was to be the state's governor in 1824.[12]

A New Yorker by birth, Van Ness had been brought up in the same small town with Martin Van Buren, now a United States senator from New York and a principal manager of the Crawford campaign, and he had two brothers active in politics, one in New York and the other in Washington, both of whom supported Crawford. It was rumored, however, that Van Ness felt antislavery feeling to be too strong to permit his identifying himself with a southern slaveholder and that he would therefore part company with his friend and his brothers and come out for Adams. This rumor made Adams's friends optimistic. There remained some chance, however, that it would prove wrong and that Van Ness would endorse Crawford or even Calhoun.[13] If so, it was quite possible that Adams would not carry Vermont.

In Rhode Island, both Republicans and Federalists were divided. Crawford had backing from devout Jeffersonians and also from Federalists whom he had wooed by means of a few patronage appointments in the Providence customhouse. Adams's informants assured him that he had stronger support than Craw-

---

12. Washington *National Intelligencer*, Nov. 19, 1823; Baltimore *Weekly Register*, Nov. 30, 1822; T. D. Seymour Bassett, "The Rise of Cornelius Peter Van Ness," *Proceedings* of the Vermont Historical Society, New Series, 10 (March 1942), 1-20.

13. Crawford to Bolling Hall, Nov. 20, 1821, J. E. D. Shipp, *Giant Days, or the Life and Times of William H. Crawford* (Americus, Ga.: Southern Printers, 1909), p. 230; Seth Hunt to Adams, April 9, July 31, 1823, Adams Papers; Calhoun to Virgil Maxcy, April 15, 1823, W. Edwin Hemphill, ed., *The Papers of John C. Calhoun*, 8 vols. in progress (Columbia, S.C.: University of South Carolina Press, 1959——), (hereafter, Calhoun, *Papers*) VIII, 21; Calhoun to Micah Sterling, April 28, 1823, Calhoun, *Papers*, VIII, 36-38; Calhoun to Henry Wheaton, Sept. 26, 1823, Calhoun, *Papers* VIII, 286-287.

ford among Republicans. On the other hand, they also warned him that Calhoun was more popular than either he or Crawford among the Federalists and that Calhoun partisans included army officers stationed in the state, lawyers who had known him at Yale or the Litchfield Law School, and friends of Carolinians who summered in Rhode Island (including Calhoun's mother-in-law, a summer resident of Newport). Presidential electors would be chosen by popular vote but by a limited electorate, for only property owners had the franchise, and as of late 1823, Adams's managers thought he would carry Rhode Island but that he might possibly lose it to Calhoun.[14]

In Connecticut, Adams's prospects were even more dubious. Political alignments in the state were less a function of cleavages over national issues than of rancorous battles over whether or not Congregationalist churches and clergy were to continue to be privileged and receive state support. "Toleration Republicans" who opposed the Congregationalist establishment identified themselves with the national party of Jefferson and Madison and were more disposed than Republicans in most other parts of New England to look to southerners for leadership. Although Adams's friends felt that he had a good chance of winning Connecticut, they saw the same evidence that led Crawford's lieutenants until the winter of 1822-1823 to be sanguine about taking the state.[15] Then, during 1823, they saw Calhoun surge forward, largely, as in Rhode Island, by virtue of his Yale and Litchfield ties and the aid of army officers and itinerant Carolinians. In September 1823, when the state legislature filled a vacancy in the United

---

14. J. D. Pierce to Degrand, n.d., enclosed in Degrand to Adams, Dec. 10, 1823, Adams Papers; Pierce to Adams, Dec. 10, 1823, ibid.; Degrand to Adams, Dec. 22, 1823, ibid.; Washington *National Intelligencer*, Nov. 27, 1823, Feb. 9, 14, 1824; Washington *Republican*, Jan. 7, 1824; Wheeler Martin to John Bailey, Jan. 21, 1824, Papers of John Bailey, New-York Historical Society. One Calhoun supporter in Massachusetts, however, thought Crawford to be ahead of Adams in Rhode Island: Lewis Williams to Virgil Maxcy, Sept. 15, 1823, Papers of the Galloway, Maxcy, and Markoe Families, Library of Congress.

15. See Jarvis Means Morse, *A Neglected Period in Connecticut's History, 1818-1850* (New Haven: Yale University Press, 1933), pp. 1-73; diary, Feb. 9, 1823, Meigs, *Ingersoll*, pp. 114-115; Henry Channing to Adams, Sept. 18, 1823, Adams Papers.

States Senate, it rejected a candidate identified with Crawford and instead chose a partisan of Calhoun. In the aftermath, Adams's friends grew pessimistic about Connecticut, while Calhoun began to list the state among those where his prospects were most bright.[16]

Thus the New England region seemed very far from being in Adams's pocket. While he had strong support in Massachusetts, it was imaginable that he could lose the state to either Crawford or Calhoun. Maine, New Hampshire, and Vermont could easily slip away to Crawford. Rhode Island or Connecticut or both might go for Calhoun. Adams must have been nagged continually by knowledge that he could not take any of these states for granted and that, if he were visibly to lose the lead in any New England state, his supporters in other sections of the country might conclude that his cause was hopeless and desert him for another candidate.

The available evidence indicated that if voters chose Adams they would do so chiefly because he was a fellow New Englander. Here, even more than in the rest of the union, the election of 1824 promised to be influenced mostly by local politics, personalities, and sectional favorite-son sympathies. The chief danger to Adams in his home region was a possible change in this prospect resulting from a reawakening of old ideological divisions or from debate over some issue of foreign policy.

The South: Crawford's situation in the South was similar to that of Adams in New England. Even though Calhoun came from South Carolina and Clay had roots in Virginia, Crawford was thought to be the southern candidate. Even in his own state of Georgia, however, Crawford had enemies. The Clark family led them, and John Clark's election as governor in 1821 encouraged both Adams and Calhoun. When the Clark faction lost the

---

16. Calhoun to Ninian Edwards, Aug. 20, 1822, Calhoun, *Papers*, VII, 248; Calhoun to Joseph G. Swift, Sept. 8, 1823, Calhoun, *Papers*, VIII, 261-262; Calhoun to Henry Wheaton, Sept. 26, 1823, ibid., pp. 286-287; Baltimore *Weekly Register*, Oct. 25, 1823; Robert Fairchild to Adams, Dec. 10, 1823, Adams Papers; Joseph Barbor to W. Palfrey, Dec. 24, 1823, Adams Papers; E. Channing to Dickerson, Dec. 29, 1823, Papers of Mahlon Dickerson, New Jersey Historical Society.

governorship to a Crawford man in October 1823, the hopes of the other candidates cooled but did not die.[17]

Neighboring South Carolina was, of course, the home state of Calhoun. The legislature would cast its electoral votes. When the Republican members first convened in caucus in 1822, they gave a nearly unanimous endorsement to their senior senator, William L. Lowndes. This seemed to leave open the possibility that their electoral votes would go to someone other than Calhoun. After Lowndes fell ill and died, however, the legislators held another caucus, this in November 1823. With not more than 20 out of 155 opposing, the caucus nominated Calhoun. This seemed to make the state almost certainly Calhoun's.[18]

In North Carolina, no candidate had a clear lead.[19] Adams trailed the others, his strongest early support having come from the Federalist enclave of New Bern and his opponents having used this fact to his disadvantage.[20] Calhoun, on the other hand, developed an impressive following. During 1822, the editor of the

---

17. Shipp, *Giant Days*, pp. 161-163; Crawford to Bolling Hall, Nov. 30, 1821, ibid., p. 230; William Clark to Thomas L. McKenney, Aug. 21, 1822, Papers of Peter Force, Library of Congress; Baltimore *Weekly Register*, Oct. 5, 1822; Jonathan Crowell to Adams, Dec. 7, 1822, April 7, 1823, Adams Papers; Calhoun to Joseph G. Swift, Aug. 5, 1823, Calhoun, *Papers*, VIII, 210-211; Calhoun to Maxcy, Aug. 13, 1823, Calhoun, *Papers*, VIII, 225-226; Philadelphia *Franklin Gazette*, Nov. 18, 1823; Henry Wheaton to Levi Wheaton, Sept. 27, 1823, Elizabeth Feaster Baker, *Henry Wheaton, 1785-1848* (Philadelphia: University of Pennsylvania Press, 1937), p. 48.

18. Crawford to Bolling Hall, Nov. 20, 1821, Shipp, *Giant Days*, p. 230; anonymous to Adams, Dec. 25, 1821, Adams Papers; John D. Heath to Adams, Dec. 28, 1821, Adams Papers; Adams to Heath, Jan. 7, 1822, Adams Papers; Lowndes to Mrs. Lowndes, March 24, 1822, Mrs. St. Julien Ravenel, *The Life and Times of William Lowndes* (Boston: Houghton Mifflin, 1901), p. 219; Heath to Adams, Nov. 27, 1822, Adams Papers; Theodore D. Jervey, *Robert Y. Hayne and His Times* (New York: Macmillan, 1909), pp. 125-127, 143-147; John F. Parrott to Jeremiah Mason, Jan. 7, 1823, Papers of Jeremiah Mason, New Hampshire Historical Society; Baltimore *Weekly Register*, Nov. 29, 1823; Charles M. Wiltse, *John C. Calhoun, Nationalist, 1782-1828* (Indianapolis: Bobbs-Merril Co., 1944), p. 429, n. 18.

19. See Albert Ray Newsome, *The Presidential Election of 1824 in North Carolina* (Chapel Hill: University of North Carolina Press, 1939), and Charles S. Sydnor, *The Development of Southern Sectionalism, 1819-1848* (n.p.: Louisiana State University Press, 1948), pp. 277-278.

20. Newsome, *Presidential Election*, pp. 54-56; Charles Fisher to Ninian Edwards, April 21, 1822, Ninian W. Edwards, *History of Illinois from 1778 to 1823 and Life and Times of Ninian Edwards* (Springfield, Ill.: Illinois State Journal Co., 1870), p. 522.

Salisbury *Western Carolinian* took up his cause. Addressing chiefly voters in the poorly represented central and western counties, he invoked local prejudice against Virginians and argued on a more rational level that Crawford would oppose federally funded roads potentially beneficial to inland growers and merchants. The *Western Carolinian* was soon joined by the Raleigh *Star*, whose editor hoped to pry the state printing away from the Crawfordite Raleigh *Register*. By the summer of 1823, Calhoun counted six of North Carolina's twelve newspapers as behind him.[21]

Crawford nevertheless remained a match for Calhoun, most of the other newspapers backed him, and the state's congressional delegation was practically a unit in his support.

Partisans of both Calhoun and Crawford watched intently the elections for the state legislature in August 1823.[22] Afterward, each claimed victory. The *Western Carolinian* and the Raleigh *Star* exulted that many supporters of Crawford had been defeated. The Raleigh *Register* admitted this to be true but denied that presidential preferences had determined the outcome. When the new legislature convened in January, its first action was to elect a speaker. A man definitely known to be for Crawford was defeated by a man thought to oppose him. Calhoun and his friends were jubilant. Almost the second action of the legislature, however, was to reject a proposal for taking the state printing away from the Crawfordite Raleigh *Register*. Along with pro-Crawford organs elsewhere in the union, the *Register* alleged this vote to show that North Carolina still stood with Crawford. In fact, no one could tell. North Carolina seemed as likely to go for Calhoun

---

21. Macon to Bartlett Yancey, April 17, 1821, Edwin Mood Wilson, *The Congressional Career of Nathaniel Macon* (Chapel Hill: University of North Carolina Press, 1900), pp. 61-62; Newsome, *Presidential Election*, pp. 47-56; Charles G. Haines to Swift, May ?, 1823, Papers of Joseph G. Swift, United States Military Academy; Hamilton Louis to Swift, June 24, 1823, Swift Papers; Washington *Republican*, July 2, 1823; Calhoun to Ogden Edwards, Sept. 21, 1823, Calhoun, *Papers*, VIII, 276-277; T. P. Andre to Swift, Aug. 20, 1823, Swift Papers.

22. Romulus M. Saunders to Ruffin, Dec. 15, 1821, Ruffin, *Papers*, I, 254-255; Calhoun to an unknown addressee, March 18, 1823, Calhoun, *Papers*, VII, 530-531; Calhoun to Joseph G. Swift, Aug. 5, 1823, Calhoun, *Papers*, VIII, 210-211.

as for Crawford, and as early as May 1823 one newspaper forecast that it would actually go for Jackson.[23]

Though Virginia was similar to North Carolina in having a number of internal sectional rivalries, it had a more centralized leadership.[24] By agreeing among themselves, twenty men in Richmond could usually determine not only what the state legislature would do but also how statewide elections would come out. Their family and business connections in other parts of the state gave them sufficient influence in other localities. The fact that a high property qualification limited suffrage made it somewhat easier for the influence to be effective.

The symbolic if not real leader of this so-called Richmond Junto was Spencer Roane, a learned lawyer who, as chief justice of the state supreme court, had fought against federal encroachments on state sovereignty. The spokesman for the Junto was the Richmond *Enquirer*, edited by Thomas Ritchie. It was generally assumed that if the Richmond Junto decided to have a legislative caucus endorse a presidential candidate and form a committee of correspondence to campaign for him, that candidate would receive Virginia's twenty-four electoral votes.

During 1821 and 1822, Adams and Calhoun received some hopeful indications. A northerner returning from a trip to the South reported that *"the only Candidate he heard named in Virginia was Adams,"* and Ritchie published in the Richmond *Enquirer* an editorial itemizing reasons why Monroe should perhaps be succeeded by a man from the North.[25] Winfield Scott, a native of the tidewater, a hero of the War of 1812, a general before the age of

23. Newsome, *Presidential Election*, pp. 54-56, 62; Baltimore *Weekly Register*, Nov. 29, 1823; McDuffie to Maxcy, Dec. 11, 1823, Galloway-Maxcy-Markoe Papers; Louisville *Public Advertiser*, May 14, 1823.

24. See Charles Henry Ambler, *Sectionalism in Virginia from 1776 to 1861* (Chicago: University of Chicago Press, 1910), pp. 102-132, and the same author's *Thomas Ritchie: A Study in Virginia Politics* (Richmond, Va.: Bell Book and Stationery Co., 1913).

25. Degrand to Adams, Dec. 4, 1821, Adams Papers; Richmond *Enquirer*, Jan. 26, 1822; Alexandria *Herald*, quoted in Richmond *Enquirer*, Feb. 8, 1822; Charles Yancey to Adams, Dec. 8, 1822, Adams Papers; Alexander McRae to Adams, Feb. 2, 1823, Adams Papers; Degrand to Adams, June 28, 1823, Adams Papers; Adams diary, July 26, 1823; Washington *National Intelligencer*, July 26, 1823; Smoot and Fraser to Adams, July 19, 1823, Adams Papers.

thirty, and now, though not yet forty, a ranking officer of the army, used a pen name to contribute pro-Calhoun essays to the Richmond *Enquirer* and, with some excess of optimism, persuaded Calhoun that his prospects were good.[26]

Shortly after the Richmond *Enquirer* editorial on the desirability of a northern President, however, Senator Van Buren of New York traveled to Virginia. It was later reported that he had met with Roane, that the result was a revival of the New York—Virginia alliance which had elected every presidential ticket since 1800, and that the Virginia-born Crawford would be the alliance's 1824 candidate. By the autumn of 1822 the *Enquirer* was giving out reasonably clear indications that it would endorse the secretary of the treasury. In October 1823 it came out unequivocally for Crawford. The Alexandria *Herald*, which had theretofore seemed pro-Adams, followed suit. The secretary of state, said the *Herald*, had failed to establish his credentials as a friend of states' rights, while Crawford had done so.[27] As of late 1823, it seemed most likely that Virginia's votes would go to Crawford.

The four southern states exhibited enough contradictory tendencies so that no candidate could simply claim or write off the whole region. While Crawford led in Georgia and Virginia, he could not be absolutely certain of either state. South Carolina was firmly Calhoun's. North Carolina was still a prize which almost any candidate might win.

---

26. Calhoun to Maxcy, Dec. 31, 1821, Calhoun, *Papers*, VI, 595-597; Robert L. Garnett to Swift, Feb. 13, 1823, Swift Papers; Winfield Scott to Gouverneur, April 8, 1823, Papers of Samuel L. Gouverneur, New York Public Library; Calhoun to Gouverneur, April 28, 1823, Calhoun, *Papers*, VIII, 33-34; Calhoun to Ogden Edwards, May 2, 1823, Calhoun, *Papers*, VIII, 44-46; Calhoun to Swift, May 10, 1823, Calhoun, *Papers*, VIII, 58-60.

27. Ambler, *Sectionalism*, pp. 127-129; Ambler, *Ritchie*, pp. 87-92; Robert V. Remini, *Martin Van Buren and the Making of the Democratic Party* (New York: Columbia University Press, 1959), p. 29 (which questions whether Van Buren actually met with Roane); Richmond *Enquirer*, Nov. 11, 1822, Jan. 4, Oct. 29, 1823; Washington *National Intelligencer*, May 12, 1823. Thomas Waggaman to Adams, Jan. 3, 1823, Adams Papers, warned Adams that Virginia was certain to go for Crawford. A similar opinion was expressed by Adams's friend Rufus King, and Crawford said he had no doubt he would carry the state: King to Charles A. King, Jan. 9, 1823, Charles R. King, ed., *The Life and Correspondence of Rufus King*, 6 vols. (New York: G. P. Putnam's Sons, 1900), VI, 494; Crawford to Charles Tait, Papers of Charles Tait, Nov. 23, 1823, Alabama Department of Archives and History.

The Wests: As of 1823 the nine Western states had little in common besides newness and remoteness from the Atlantic coast. Within the section itself, moreover, there were marked differences between the three states above the Ohio River and the six below it, where much of the population came from the South, the laws permitted slaveholding, and some of the country-side had plantations similar to those of Virginia, the Carolinas, and Georgia.

Among the southern-oriented states of the West, Kentucky had the largest population. It was, of course, Clay's home state, and his popularity there seemed such as almost to guarantee him a majority vote in every district.[28]

Similarly, Tennessee appeared to belong to Jackson.[29] Though Adams, Calhoun, and Clay all felt hopeful of inheriting the state if the general dropped out, none of them had any doubt that he would carry it if he stayed in the race.

Missouri and Louisiana were offshoots of Kentucky and Tennessee, largely populated by migrants from those states.

In Missouri, Senator Thomas Hart Benton was the most active figure in the presidential contest. He had earlier lived in Tennessee and served under Jackson in the Tennessee militia during the War of 1812. Afterward, he had quarreled with the general, and his brother Jesse had almost killed Jackson in a duel. One reason for Benton's moving across the river to the Missouri territory was to escape Jackson's revenge. Naturally, he opposed

28. See W. E. Connelly and E. M. Coulter, *History of Kentucky*, 5 vols. (Chicago: American Historical Society, 1922), II, 674-678, and Thomas D. Clark, *A History of Kentucky* (New York: Prentice-Hall, 1937), pp. 198-222. Evidence of support for Adams: Degrand to Adams, Oct. 13, 1822, Adams Papers; Louisa Catherine Adams to Adams, Oct. 8, 1822, Adams Papers; John P. Delaney to Adams, July 5, 1823, Adams Papers; Samuel J. Ingerham to Adams, Aug. 4, 1823, Adams Papers. Of support for Calhoun: diary entry of June 30, 1822, Alfred Tischendorf and E. Taylor Parks, eds., *The Diary and Journal of Richard Clough Anderson, Jr., 1814-1826* (Durham: Duke University Press, 1964), p. 104; George McDuffie to Maxcy, March 29, 1823, Galloway-Maxcy-Markoe Papers. On Clay's commanding strength: Adams to Louisa Catherine Adams, Aug. 1, 1822, Adams Papers; Baltimore *Weekly Register*, Nov. 17, 1822; Louisville *Public Advertiser*, May 7, 1823.

29. The best description of Tennessee politics in this period is in Charles Grier Sellers, Jr., *James K. Polk, Jacksonian, 1795-1843* (Princeton: Princeton University Press, 1957), pp. 68-91.

the Jackson-for-President boom. Having warred with Adams, Crawford, and Calhoun both in the Senate and in columns of the St. Louis *Enquirer*, Benton had little choice except to back Clay. Once committed, he put all his force into a campaign in Clay's behalf.[30]

Although Adams had support from New Englanders who had emigrated to Missouri, they were a beleaguered minority. One wrote complainingly to Adams of Benton and his friends: "They belong to that description of persons who seize every opportunity to bear down and abuse all eastern Men without discrimination; they grant no truce nor peace to what they call a *Yankee*, unless he denationalizes himself and adopts a course of Conduct which he would blush at in his Native State." Benton was able to engineer a vote by the Missouri legislature endorsing Clay for the presidency. Thereafter, Missouri seemed even more certain than Kentucky to be in Clay's column.[31]

In Louisiana the counterpart of Benton was Senator James Brown, who was Clay's brother-in-law. Soon after the Louisiana purchase, he had moved from Kentucky to the new territory and become rich. Fluent in French, he sometimes mediated between the American immigrants and the French-speaking natives, and he had some following among both. Although the Yankee editors of Louisiana newspapers created an initial impression that the state might go for Adams, Brown contrived an endorsement of Clay by the Louisiana legislative caucus. Since the casting of Louisiana's electoral votes would be decided by the legislature rather than by popular ballot, this seemed to ensure that the state would go for Clay.[32]

Politically, Mississippi and Alabama were less in the orbit

30. See William M. Meigs, *The Life of Thomas Hart Benton* (Philadelphia: J. B. Lippincott, 1904), pp. 141-142, and Alan S. Weiner, "John Scott, Thomas Hart Benton, David Barton and the Presidential Election of 1824," *Missouri Historical Review*, 60 (July 1966), 460-494.

31. John B. C. Lucas to Adams, Jan. 24, 1823, Adams Papers; Louisville *Public Advertiser*, May 7, Aug. 18, 1823; Calhoun to Samuel Southard, June 14, 1823, Calhoun, *Papers*, VIII, 117-118.

32. Robert Walsh to Adams, Nov. 23, 1822, Adams Papers; John F. Parrott to Mason, Jan. 7, 1823, Papers of Jeremiah Mason, New Hampshire Historical Society; Isaac

of Kentucky and Tennessee. In Mississippi, the towns and counties along the Mississippi River contained a number of people from Ohio or other points to the north. Both states also had many settlers who had come directly from the Carolinas or Georgia.

In Mississippi, the man who resembled Benton of Missouri and Brown of Louisiana was George Poindexter. In regard to the presidential election, Poindexter's chief interest, apparently solely for personal reasons, was the defeat of Crawford. He hesitated about which of Crawford's opponents to support. In the winter of 1822-1823, after the Tennessee legislature endorsed Jackson, Poindexter considered taking up Jackson's cause. He decided instead to back Adams and from May 1823 onward was actively speaking and writing in Adams's behalf. By the autumn of 1823, with Poindexter campaigning for Adams and five of Mississippi's seven newspapers endorsing him, it seemed probable that the state's three electoral votes would go to Adams or possibly to Jackson.[33]

In Alabama the situation was more complicated. Immigrants from Georgia tended to support Crawford while Carolinians, Virginians, and Tennesseeans in the northern and central parts of the state tended to oppose him but not to be united on an alternative. That Crawford's friends were weak seemed to be demonstrated when his supporters were defeated in 1822 and 1823 in races for the United States Senate and the governorship. But it remained uncertain which other candidate would take the state. Most Alabama newspaper editors were New En-

L. Baker to Jackson, Feb. 14, 26, May 3, 1823, Papers of Andrew Jackson, Library of Congress; Washington *National Intelligencer*, March 17, April 30, 1823; Louisville *Public Advertiser*, May 7, 14, 1823; Calhoun to Southard, June 14, 1823, Calhoun, *Papers*, VIII, 117-118. One of Calhoun's lieutenants forecast, however, that the state would swing to Jackson and that Calhoun would inherit it from the general: Henry Wheaton to Theophilus Parsons, Sept. 6, 1823, Baker, *Wheaton*, p. 47.

33. Edwin Arthur Miles, *Jacksonian Democracy in Mississippi* (Chapel Hill: University of North Carolina Press, 1960), pp. 6-8; John F. Parrott to Mason, Jan. 7, 1823, Mason Papers; Isaac L. Baker to Jackson, Feb. 26, 1823, Jackson Papers; George Poindexter to Jackson, May, 4, 1823, Jackson Papers; Lafayette Saunders to Jackson, July 23, 1823, Jackson Papers; H. Johnson to Edwards, Aug. 10, 1823, Edwards, *Illinois*, p. 504; James Cornell to Adams, Sept. 2, 1823, Adams Papers; Louisville *Public Advertiser*, May 14, 1823.

glanders, and seven out of the nine endorsed Adams.[34] Even so, Clay professed to believe that the voters would ultimately be for him. Some of Calhoun's friends felt that he could capture the state. And there was a burgeoning Jackson campaign.[35] As of late 1823, no one could make a confident forecast.

The northern part of the West consisted of the three states of Illinois, Indiana, and Ohio. By road as well as by river, people in these states traded with Kentucky and states to the south. For the most part, however, they themselves had come from the North, emigrating from Pennsylvania, New York, and New England.

Illinois was very much on the frontier. Only a state since 1818, its population was not yet 100,000. The chief political issue under debate was whether or not to retain the prohibition on slavery included in the first state constitution. With a popular vote scheduled for the summer of 1824, alignments tended to be determined more by this issue than by the presidential race.

Nevertheless, Illinois had partisans of various presidential candidates. Senator Jesse B. Thomas, a Marylander by birth who had earlier practiced law in Kentucky, was a Crawford man, who enlisted for Crawford most of those who wanted to legalize slavery. His reelection to the Senate in January 1823, despite a concerted campaign for his defeat, suggested that he might be able to deliver the state to the secretary of the treasury.[36]

34. Thomas Perkins Abernathy, *The Formative Period in Alabama, 1815-1828*, revised ed. (University, Ala.: Universtiy of Alabama Press, 1965) pp. 120-155.

35. Crawford to Bolling Hall, Nov. 20, 1821, Shipp, *Giant Days*, p. 230; Clay to Porter, Oct. 22, 1822, Feb. 2, 1823, Porter Papers; Gabriel Moore to Bailey, July 3, 1823, Bailey Papers; T. P. Andre to Swift, Aug. 20, 1823, Swift Papers; Calhoun to Ogden Edwards, Sept. 21, 1823, Calhoun, *Papers*, VIII, 276-277; J. G. Lynn to Jackson, Aug. 18, 1823, Jackson Papers; Maxcy to Swift, Oct. 5, 1823, Swift Papers; Baltimore *Weekly Register*, Jan. 11, 1823; Louisville *Public Advertiser*, March 22, May 7, June 25, 1823; Washington *National Intelligencer*, Nov. 5, 12, 1823.

36. R. Carlyle Buley, *The Old Northwest: Pioneer Period, 1815-1840*, 2 vols. (Indianapolis: Indiana Historical Society, 1950), II, 15-22; Theodore Calvin Pease, *The Frontier State, 1818-1848*, vol. II of *The Centennial History of Illinois* (Chicago: A. C. McClurg Co., 1922), pp. 93-98; Daniel Pope Cook to Adams, July 30, 1821, Aug. 29, 1822, Adams Papers; John Elliott to General Blackshear, Sept. 4, 1822, Shipp, *Giant Days*, pp. 171-173; Nathaniel Pope to Adams, Oct. 1, 1822, Adams Papers; Ninian Edwards to Adams, Jan. 5, 1823, Adams Papers.

On the other hand, it was generally believed that the most influential politician in the state was Ninian Edwards, the other United States senator. Although Edwards, like Thomas, was a Marylander who had once lived in Kentucky, he opposed slavery and had strong support among the northern-born majority. Though it appeared at first that Edwards would try to carry Illinois for Adams, he developed an ambition to be the first United States minister to Mexico. During 1823, he became convinced that Adams could not or would not get the post for him. Concluding that Calhoun might do so, he became an energetic supporter of the secretary of war.[37] Depending on whether Thomas or Edwards proved the stronger, Illinois thus seemed likely to go either to Crawford or to Calhoun.

Indiana was also a frontier state. As recently as 1818, a traveler had characterized it as "a vast forest, larger than England."[38] In its earlier territorial days, it had attracted a number of immigrants from Virginia. The subsequent tide of settlers from the North had banded together politically to oppose the Virginians. Although they now made up an overwhelming majority of the state's approximately 200,000 people, they retained some degree of unity. The small group of politicians to whom they looked for leadership therefore ruled almost unchallenged. Jonathan Jennings, a New Jersey man brought up in Pennsylvania, was the dominant figure in this group. He was elected governor in 1819 by a margin of five to one. In 1822 his chosen successor, William Hendricks, won almost without opposition.

While Jennings and his coterie were probably powerful enough to throw Indiana's electoral vote to any candidate, they had no wish to alienate any of their following. It was apparent that they would do so if they backed Crawford, for Crawford was not only a southern man but also an opponent of federally funded internal improvements which were popular among Indianans. In addition, people in Indiana identified strongly with

37. Pease, *Frontier State*, pp. 93-98; Calhoun to Edwards, Aug. 20, Oct. 5, 1822, Calhoun *Papers*, VII, 249, 296; Calhoun to Edwards, May 21, July 20, 1823, VIII, 70-71, 171-172.
38. Buley, *Old Northwest*, II, 25.

the Republican party. Without explaining the cause, one historian comments on their "almost insane hatred of Federalists." Although Jennings was personally friendly to Adams and was courted by the secretary of state, he apparently felt that it would be imprudent to support a man with Adams's Federalist background. Such a judgment was justified by, among other things, an election contest for a seat in the state legislature in which all of the candidates went out of their way to declare that they would not vote for Adams.[39] Although Jennings, Hendricks, and others in the ruling junto remained noncommittal, it seemed most likely that they would end up throwing Indiana's five electoral votes to Clay.

Among the western states, Ohio had the largest population. In the census of 1820, it had ranked fourth in the union, just behind New York, Pennsylvania, and Virginia. With sixteen electoral votes, it promised to be one of the great prizes in the general election. As of late 1823, clues as to how these votes would be cast were hard to decipher.

It did appear that Crawford and Calhoun were relatively weak. Although both men initially felt hopeful, each had concluded by 1823 that Ohio was unlikely to be in his column.[40] While Adams's prospects seemed somewhat better, with the Columbus *Ohio Monitor* and the Dayton *Miami Republican* endorsing him as the only major candidate not an owner of slaves and with a Cincinnati businessman assuring him that the ruling group

39. Ibid., p. 14; Adam A. Leonard, "Personal Politics in Indiana, 1816 to 1840," *Indiana Magazine of History*, 19 (March 1923), 1-56; Louisville *Public Advertiser*, May 7, 14, 1823; Washington *National Intelligencer*, Feb. 1, 1824.

40. Lewis Williams to Ruffin, Dec. 22, 1821, Ruffin, *Papers*, I, 258; Harry R. Stevens, *The Early Jackson Party in Ohio* (Durham: Duke University Press, 1957), pp. 45-47; Louisville *Public Advertiser*, May 7, 1823; Charles G. Haines to Swift, May ?, 1823, Swift Papers; Stevens, *Early Jackson Party in Ohio*, pp. 40-42; Benjamin Ruggles to Charles Hammond, Dec. 18, 1822, Papers of Charles Hammond, Ohio Historical Society; McLean to Everett, Aug. 8, 1828, Worthington C. Ford, ed., "Letters between Edward Everett and John McLean, 1828, relating to the Use of Patronage in Elections," *Proceedings* of the Massachusetts Historical Society, Third Series, 1 (1907-1908), 364; Calhoun to Southard, June 14, 1823, Calhoun, *Papers*, VIII, 117-118. Some of Calhoun's advisers were not equally realistic: McDuffie to Maxcy, March 29, 1823, Galloway-Maxcy-Markoe Papers; Lewis Cass to Maxcy, Oct. 8, 1823, Galloway-Maxcy-Markoe Papers; Maxcy to Swift, Oct. 15, 1823, Swift Papers.

in that city was for him, newspapers not only in the interior but even in Cincinnati itself attacked him as a Federalist, an Anglophile, an aristocrat, and an infidel.[41] As of December 1822, the Adams forces, together with the smaller contingents backing Crawford and Calhoun, proved strong enough to block an endorsement of Clay by Republicans in the Ohio legislature. Meeting in caucus, the legislators voted 43-40 against making any nomination. But Clay's partisans did not give up, and in January 1823, another session of the caucus voted 50-5 for Clay. Although disappointed defenders of other candidates pointed out that at least thirty legislators had abstained, it was thereafter generally assumed that Clay led Adams, Calhoun, and Crawford in Ohio.[42]

In politicians' eyes, the West was therefore a patchwork. Kentucky, Missouri, Louisiana, and Indiana seemed probably Clay's, and Tennessee almost as surely Jackson's. Mississippi and Alabama seemed likely to be in Adams's column, though it was possible that Clay might capture Alabama and that Jackson might win either or both. Illinois would go to Crawford or Calhoun. Ohio might go to anyone but more probably to Clay than to any of the others.

The Middle States: Given the apparent improbability of any one candidate's sweeping New England, the South, and the West, a victory in the electoral college would require winning the Middle Atlantic states.

Maryland, the southernmost of these five states, was really part of the South in that it had slaveowners and plantations, but it also had clusters of people who abominated slavery and looked to the development of manufacturing and trade as the way to prosperity. In addition, Maryland had a Federalist

---

41. Stevens, *Early Jackson Party in Ohio*, pp. 39, 56, 81-82; Bellamy Storer to Adams Jan. 18, 1823, Adams Papers; Nathaniel Pope to Daniel Pope Cook, Dec. 31, 1823, Adams Papers; Washington *National Intelligencer*, Nov. 29, 1823; Eugene H. Rosebloom, "Ohio in the Presidential Election of 1824," *Ohio Archeological and Historical Quarterly*, 26 (April, 1917), 153-225.

42. Stevens, *Early Jackson Party in Ohio*, pp. 50-55; Washington *National Intelligencer*, Jan. 20, 1823, Feb. 1, 1824; John McLean to Swift, Aug. 8, 1823, Swift Papers.

minority large enough to influence the outcome of elections.

Until the War of 1812 Federalists had ruled the state. They had then divided among themselves. Those who persisted in opposing the war were called "blue light" Federalists, from the accusation that they sent signals to British warships off the shore. Those who did not openly continue opposition to the war were called "coodies." Afterward, both factions shrank in size in comparison with the Republican majority; but they remained sufficiently numerous so that Republican leaders often sought deals with "blue light" Federalists such as the Eastern Shore planters Robert Goodloe Harper and Virgil Maxcy, or with Baltimore lawyer Roger B. Taney, who was known as "King Coody."

Because of divisions within the state, Crawford's prospects were not particularly bright. While some old-line Republicans supported him, those who opposed slavery or favored internal improvements and a protective tariff did not, and both factions of Federalists viewed him with hostility precisely because Crawford's Republican backers were their unrelenting enemies.[43]

Adams's chances seemed better. In January 1822 he was told that he might be nominated by a caucus of Republicans in the Maryland legislature. Although no such vote took place, Adams remained a favorite of many legislators because, as a former Federalist, he seemed likely to attract some Federalist ballots. On the other hand, some of these same legislators warned Adams that he would lose Maryland if he appeared to have Federalist support.[44]

43. Livermore, *Twilight of Federalism*, pp. 82, 83, 123, 170; J. Thomas Scharf, *History of Maryland from the Earliest Period to the Present Day*, 3 vols. (Baltimore: State Printing Office, 1876), III, 149-150; Carl Brent Swisher, *Roger B. Taney* (New York: Macmillan, 1935), pp. 58-121; Isaac Munroe to Bailey, Nov. 30, 1821, Bailey Papers.

44. W. H. Allen to Adams, Jan. 7, 1822, Adams Papers; William Prentiss to Adams, Feb. 11, 1822, ibid.; Nathaniel F. Williams to Adams, Feb. 12, 1822, ibid.; R. J. Meigs to Adams, Feb. 19, 1822, ibid.; Audley H. Gassam to Adams, April 14, 1822, ibid.; George Webb to Adams, May 21, 1822, ibid.; Robert A. Garnett to Swift, Feb. 13, 1823, Swift Papers; Isaac Munroe to Bailey, April 15, 1823, Bailey Papers; D. Learned to Bailey, June 24, 1823, Bailey Papers; William Thornton to Isaiah Cooper, Sept. 17, 1823, Adams Papers; James Bowdoin Robins to Adams, Nov. 29, 1823, Adams Papers.

The actual enthusiasm for Adams among Maryland Federalists was meager. Recognizing this fact, Calhoun started a correspondence with Maxcy almost as soon as he became an active candidate. Before long he was able to count "blue light" leaders as among his most fervent supporters. With backing also from a Republican newspaper in Baltimore and from some Republicans in the legislature, Calhoun had a basis for hoping that he could win the state.[45]

Clay had some friends in Baltimore. As a champion of internal improvements and a tariff, he could hope to gain additional strength in Maryland's interior counties. There was also a growing Jackson movement.[46] Hence, Adams, Calhoun, Clay, and Jackson all had some chance of carrying Maryland's electoral votes. Since the state's electors were chosen in separate districts, it was even possible that two or more of the candidates might divide up these votes.

Delaware was the smallest of the Middle Atlantic states. Moreover, it was the only state in the union still controlled by Federalists. Since its electors would be chosen by its thirty-member Federalist legislature, the man for whom they balloted would, in effect, have a Federalist endorsement. All the candidates, of course, wanted Delaware's three votes, but none wanted to be seen as seeking or welcoming them. Hence efforts to win those votes were mostly carried on behind closed doors. P. P. F. Degrand, one of Adams's managers in Massachusetts, dealt privately with the influential Delaware gunpowder manufacturer, Eleuthère Irénée du Pont. In a marvelously ingenuous letter, Degrand wrote Adams that du Pont had awakened him "to the Great National Importance of *Good Gunpowder.*"

---

45. Calhoun to Maxcy, Dec. 23, 31, 1821, Jan. 13, 22, March 18, 1822, Calhoun, *Papers*, VI 582-583, 595-597, 620-621, 631, 751-752; Calhoun to Maxcy, April 12, 1822, ibid., VII, p. 30; Calhoun to Ninian Edwards, Aug. 20, 1822, ibid., p. 249; McDuffie to Maxcy, March 29, 1823, Galloway-Maxcy-Markoe Papers; Washington *National Intelligencer*, July 3, 1823, reporting on the Baltimore *Patriot*; Calhoun to Maxcy, June 11, Aug. 6, Dec. 11, 1823, Calhoun, *Papers*, VIII, 212, 402-403; Philadelphia *Franklin Gazette*, Nov. 18, 1823.

46. Louisville *Public Advertiser*, May 7, 1823; J. P. Kennedy to Maxcy, Oct. 11, 1823, Galloway-Maxcy-Markoe Papers; Baltimore *Weekly Register*, Jan. 9, 1824.

Urging Adams to speak publicly for this cause, he continued, "it would, in a very eminent degree, promote the Public Good. It would also promote my own Good & that of . . . Mr. Du Pont." But Calhoun dealt at first hand with du Pont and, moreover, gave him a War Department contract. As a result, du Pont's support went to him rather than Adams. Meanwhile, Crawford allegedly tried to buy the support of Delaware Federalists with Treasury patronage.[47] Probably on the assumption that Crawford had enough patronage to tempt sixteen of the legislators into his camp, most politicians assumed him to be the likely victor in Delaware.

New Jersey resembled Maryland in having a large, influential Federalist minority. It had, however, only a few slaveholding planters. In fact, antislavery elements in the state were sufficiently strong to produce an outcry against those members of the New Jersey delegation to Congress who voted for the Missouri Compromise rather than for abolition of slavery in all western territories. In addition, New Jersey was a state in which manufacturing and trade were on the increase. Because of this combination of factors, it was assumed that people in New Jersey would be reluctant to vote for any of the southern candidates and would probably choose Adams. A majority of the state's eighteen newspapers supported Adams. Some that supported other candidates conceded Adams to be the frontrunner.

Like Maryland, New Jersey was not safely in Adams's camp. At 4th of July observances in 1823, it was reported, Clay received as many toasts as Adams. A Trenton newspaper declared Calhoun to be a close second to Adams in New Jersey. Calhoun himself wrote in September 1823 that he and Adams were neck and neck in the state, and in November one of his partisans assured him that he had outstripped the New Englander. New

---

47. Degrand to Adams, Feb. 8, 1823, Adams Papers; War Department Contract of July 10, 1823, Calhoun, *Papers*, VIII, 160; duPont to his wife, July 5, 1823, B. G. duPont, *Life of Eleuthère Irénée duPont from Contemporary Correspondence*, 12 vols. (Newark, Del.: University of Delaware Press, 1923-1926), XI, 84; duPont to Thomas L. McKenney, Sept. 10, 1823, ibid., pp. 93-94; Louis McLane to James A. Bayard, Dec. 16, 22, 1823, Papers of Louis McLane, Delaware Historical Society.

Jersey's eleven electoral votes, it seemed, might go to Adams or Clay or Calhoun.[48]

Pennsylvania, the second most populous state in the union, had more electoral votes than Maryland, Delaware, and New Jersey combined. With well over a million people, Pennsylvania was a miniature nation. Its internal regionalism was as marked as that of North Carolina or Virginia, for the Alleghenies divided it into separate eastern and western halves, the former oriented toward the Delaware and Chesapeake bays and the Atlantic, the latter toward the Ohio and Mississippi rivers and the Gulf of Mexico. At the same time, the competing attraction of the Great Lakes tended to separate people in northern counties from those in the south, whether east or west of the mountains.[49]

As in the colonial era, religious differences also divided Pennsylvanians. Quakers had formed the state's original elite. Presbyterians, Lutherans, and Reformed Church members had gradually become more numerous, and Anglicans and Roman Catholics had grown to respectable numbers. And often involved in both sectional and religious conflicts were stresses between English, Scotch-Irish, and German ethnic groups.

Although Pennsylvania had a substantial number of Federalists, it was emphatically a Republican state, with the critical political divisions usually those between relatively conservative Republicans on the one hand and relatively Jacobinical Republi-

---

48. James Otis Morse to Adams, Dec. 5, 1821, Adams Papers; Calhoun to Ninian Edwards, Aug. 20, 1822, Calhoun, *Papers*, VII, 247-249; Washington *National Intelligencer*, April 19, 1823; Hezekiah Niles to Bailey, April 21, 1823, Bailey Papers; D. Thompson, Jr., to Southard, May 14, 1823, Papers of Samuel L. Southard, Princeton University Library; Washington *National Intelligencer*, July 8, Aug. 1, 1823; Eph Bateman to Southard, Aug. 12, 1823, Southard Papers; L. Q. C. Elmer to Southard, Aug. 13, 1823, Southard Papers; Calhoun to Maxcy, Aug. 13, 1823, Calhoun, *Papers*, VIII, 225-226; Calhoun to Ninian Edwards, Sept. 23, 1823, Calhoun, *Papers*, VIII, 281; Baltimore *Weekly Register*, Oct. 11, 1823; J. N. Simpson to Southard, Oct. 15, 1823, Southard Papers; George Holcombe to Southard, Nov. 1, 1823, Southard Papers; J. N. Simpson to Southard, Oct. 15, 1823, Southard Papers; Samuel Southard, Sr., to Southard, Nov. 4, 1823, Southard Papers; Samuel D. Ingham to Southard, Nov. 12, 1823, Southard Papers; Webster to Jeremiah Mason, Nov. 20, 1823, Webster, *Writings*, IV, 77-78; Washington *National Journal*, Dec. 13, 1823; Winfield Scott to Swift, ?, 1823, Swift Papers.

49. See Philip Shriver Klein, *Pennsylvania Politics, 1817-1832: A Game without Rules* (Philadelphia: Historical Society of Pennsylvania, 1940), pp. 3-175.

cans on the other. As of the early 1820s leadership among the former lay with Richard Rush and Albert Gallatin, both of whom were ministers abroad, and, nearer at hand, with a so-called "Family Party"—a group of businessmen and politicians in southeastern Pennsylvania including Congressmen Samuel D. Ingham of Bucks County and Thomas J. Rogers of Easton, Philadelphia financier George M. Dallas, and Richard Bache, who published the Philadelphia *Franklin Gazette*. All were related by marriage, and all had connections and interests in other parts of the state. More than in most states, however, leadership in Pennsylvania required sensitivity to public attitudes and moods, for election results depended heavily on what segments of the mass electorate happened at any given moment to take an interest in politics.

Initially, Pennsylvania had been considered Crawford's. Both Rush and Gallatin were in his camp, and the same was assumed to be true of the "Family Party." Even as late as December 1821, one of Crawford's managers in Washington listed Pennsylvania as a certain Crawford state.[50]

The turn from 1821 to 1822 brought a sudden change in the prospect. In the autumn of the preceding year, Calhoun had toured Pennsylvania and talked with a number of politicians there. In late December, Ingham, Rogers, and some other congressmen called on him in Washington and offered to support him for the presidency. Of course, he accepted eagerly. The "Family Party" soon signaled its support of Calhoun by editorials in Bache's *Franklin Gazette*.[51]

Why the "Family Party" turned to Calhoun was a mystery at the time and remains such now. It was later rumored that Dallas, like Ninian Edwards of Illinois, wanted to be minister to

---

50. Adams diary, May 12, 1820; William Duane, *A Visit to Colombia in the Years 1822 and 1823* (Philadelphia: T. H. Palmer, 1826); Rush to Gallatin, April 17, 1823, Papers of Albert Gallatin, New-York Historical Society; Crawford to Gallatin, May 26, 1823, Gallatin Papers; Jesse B. Thomas to Gallatin, Jan. 5, 1824, Gallatin Papers; Lewis Williams to Ruffin, Dec. 22, 1821, Ruffin, *Papers*, I, 258.

51. Calhoun to Maxcy, Dec. 31, 1821, Jan. 13, March 18, 1822, Calhoun, *Papers*, VI 595-597, 620-621, 751-752; Philadelphia *Franklin Gazette*, March 12, 15, 1822; Washington *National Intelligencer*, Jan. 1, 1823; Robert A. Garnett to Swift, Feb. 13, 1823, Swift Papers; Thomas J. Rogers to Maxcy, April 13, 1823, Galloway-Maxcy-Markoe Papers. See Klein, *Pennsylvania Politics*, pp. 125-130, and Wiltse, *Calhoun*, pp. 231-233.

Mexico and believed Calhoun could get him the appointment. It was also rumored that Calhoun had promised, if President, to appoint a "Family Party" henchman to the collectorship of the port of Philadelphia, a patronage post with fees worth a fortune and with jobs and contracts worth a great deal in political influence. Yet another theory was that the "Family Party" had been brought around by rich Carolinians who resided in Philadelphia, including Langdon Cheves, at one time president of the Bank of the United States.[52] Possibly, all these factors entered in and, in addition, the fingertips of politicians in the "Family Party" told them that they would have a hard time getting people to county conventions or to the polls for familiar candidates such as Crawford, Adams, or Clay and that they therefore needed a new name. Whatever the case, it was their sudden endorsement that made Calhoun a real presidential candidate.

The other candidates did not immediately concede the state. Crawford still had the backing of Rush and Gallatin, and his friends continued to believe that Pennsylvania might be won if Gallatin were taken on as the vice-presidential candidate or, even without that, if Crawford were nominated by the congressional caucus in such a way as to seem *the* Republican candidate.[53] Adams kept hearing that he was popular in northern and western Pennsylvania and especially among the state's Federalists.[54] Clay, too, received occasional encouraging reports, even though

52. Klein, *Pennsylvania Politics*, pp. 129-130; Washington *National Intelligencer*, Jan. 13, 1824; Louisa Catherine Adams to Adams, Aug. 23, 1822, Adams Papers.

53. Robert Walsh to Adams, Aug. 19, 1822, Adams Papers; Calhoun to Wheaton, Aug. 4, 1823, Calhoun, *Papers*, VIII, 207-208; Calhoun to Southard, Aug. 17, 1823, Calhoun, *Papers*, VIII, 233-234; Eph Bateman to Southard, Aug. 12, 1823, Southard Papers; J. Conard to Swift, Sept. 18, 1823, Swift Papers; Jesse B. Thomas to Gallatin, Jan. 5, 1824, Gallatin Papers; Rufus King to Charles A. King, Feb. 1, 1824, Rufus King Papers (New-York Historical Society).

54. Nathaniel Shaler to Adams, Jan. 13, 1822, Adams Papers; Joel Lewis to Adams, Feb. 12, March 4, 1822, ibid.; Degrand to Adams, July 17, 1822, ibid.; James Otis Morse to Adams, Aug. 5, 1822, ibid.; Calhoun to Maxcy, Dec. 15, 1822, Calhoun, *Papers*, VII, 387; Archibald Bard to Adams, Dec. 21, 1822, Adams Papers; Joseph Hopkinson to Adams, Jan. 1, 1823, Adams Papers; Degrand to Adams, April 22, 1823, Adams Papers; William Montgomery to Adams, July 1, 1823, Adams Papers; Washinton *National Journal*, Nov. 26, 1823; Rufus King to Charles A. King, Nov. 28, 1823, Rufus King Papers (New-York Historical Society); Richard B. Jones to Bailey, Dec. 4, 1823, Bailey Papers.

he himself estimated his prospects in Pennsylvania as nil.[55]

All candidates had to reckon on the possibility of another dramatic change. Should Calhoun fail to gather backing elsewhere, the "Family Party" might decide his cause was hopeless and turn to someone else. Alternatively, they might find Calhoun not to be saleable, for many Quakers had already indicated that they would find it hard to vote for a slaveholder, and mass meetings in the latter part of 1823 revealed surprisingly strong sentiment for Jackson. The "Family Party" could not even get a pro-Calhoun resolution from the Republican state convention of 1823 because so many delegates wanted to declare Jackson their first choice. Though one of Calhoun's managers dismissed the Jackson movement as a product of "the grog-shop politicians of villages & the rabble of Philadelphia and Pittsburgh," insisting that "the substantial yeomanry of the Country are for Calhoun," Calhoun himself estimated by September 1823 that he and Jackson were tied in Pennsylvania.[56] Thus, while Calhoun led in Pennsylvania, Adams seemed a possible heir if his candidacy were to falter; and Jackson had some prospect of capturing the state outright.

New York was the most coveted conquest of all.[57] Its

---

55. Clay to Porter, Feb. 2, 1823, Papers of Peter B. Porter, Buffalo and Erie County Historical Society; Louisville *Public Advertiser*, May 7, 1823; Clay to Josiah S. Johnston, June 25, 1824, James F. Hopkins, ed., *The Papers of Henry Clay*, 4 vols. in progress (Lexington, Ky.: University of Kentucky Press, 1959-1963), III, 785.

56. Baltimore *Weekly Register*, Nov. 9, 1822; John H. Eaton to Jackson, Jan. 11, 1823, Jackson Papers; McDuffie to ?, Jan. 13, 1823, Newsome, "Correspondence" (see 4 above), pp. 486-487; H. W. Peterson to Jackson, Feb. 3, 1823, Newsome, "Correspondence," pp. 486-487, George M. Dallas to Maxcy, March 8, 1823, Galloway-Maxcy-Markoe Papers; Washington *National Intelligencer*, May 13, 1823; Louisville *Public Advertiser*, May 10, 14, July 9, 1823; S. Simpson to Jackson, July 5, 1823, Jackson Papers; Washington *Republican*, Aug. 19, 1823; Louisa Catherine Adams diary, Sept. 1-2, 1823, Adams Papers; Calhoun to Ninian Edwards, Sept. 23, 1823, Calhoun, *Papers*, VIII, 281; Benjamin Chew to Maxcy, Oct. 3, 1823, Galloway-Maxcy-Markoe Papers; Hailperin, "Pro-Jackson Sentiment," pp. 193-206; Klein, *Pennsylvania Politics*, pp. 118-125. The quotation is from McDuffie's letter.

57. See David Stanwood Alexander, *A Political History of the State of New York, 1774-1882*, 3 vols. (New York: Henry Holt and Co., 1906-1909), I, 315-337; Jabez D. Hammond, *The History of Political Parties in the State of New York*, 2 vols. (Cooperstown, N.Y.: H. and E. Phinney, 1846), II, 125-205; Alvin Kass, *Politics in New York State, 1800-1830* (Syracuse: Syracuse University Press, 1965), passim; and C. H. Rammelkamp, "The Campaign of 1824 in New York," *Annual Report* of the American Historical Association (1904), pp. 177-201.

thirty-six votes were more than one-fourth of all those needed for a majority in the electoral college. As New York law stood in 1823, these votes would be cast by the state legislature, and the 160 members of the Senate and Assembly could choose either to cast all thirty-six votes as a bloc or to divide them among two or more candidates.

If the political situation in some other states was puzzling, that in New York was bewildering. Supreme Court Justice Joseph Story wrote to a New Yorker in September 1823: "the political state of things in New York, is to me a strange riddle, which I cannot fathom or comprehend. You seem broken up into parties so various, and so little defined by any great leading doctrines, that I attempt in vain even to master your vocabulary of names."[58]

Federalists and Republicans were only two of New York's parties, and divisions in the state seldom ran along Republican-Federalist lines. As of the early 1820s the principal groupings were Clintonians and Bucktails. The former included many old Republicans who had followed the Clinton family when it allied with Jefferson in the 1790s. It also included many people in areas west of the Hudson who identified with De Witt Clinton in his advocacy of the Erie Canal and many present and former Federalists who had turned to De Witt Clinton as a possible alternative to Madison in the presidential election of 1812. The Bucktails were originally a loose confederation of those who opposed the Clintonians. Their ranks sometimes took in onetime followers of Aaron Burr and other Republicans active in the Tammany Society of New York City. Their allies included the so-called "high-minded Federalists" who refused to back De Witt Clinton. Recently, the Bucktails had become a more cohesive group by virtue of election victories which gave them control of much of the state patronage, and leadership among them had gravitated to a so-called Albany Regency in which the most prominent figure was Van Buren.

---

58. Story to Ezekiel Bacon, Sept. 21, 1823, William W. Story, ed., *Life and Letters of Joseph Story* (Boston: Charles C. Little and James Brown, 1851), pp. 426-427.

Both in the electorate and in the legislature, significant numbers identified neither with the Clintonians nor with the Bucktails. No one could predict with confidence the combination likely to produce a majority in the legislature.

As of 1821, politicians were altogether in the dark as to how New York might go in the presidential election. One with excellent sources of information said that Adams had a good chance of being supported by the Bucktails. Adams himself thought it more likely that the Bucktails would support someone else and that the Clintonians would be for him.[59] Forecasts were all the more clouded because of uncertainty about Clinton himself. Recent illness had left him limited in movement and grossly fat. Nevertheless, it was possible that he might become a presidential candidate. No one knew whether or not he would. No one could predict whether, if he did, he would carry his own state.

In 1822 prospects in New York began to become somewhat clearer. Although Clinton flirted with a possible candidacy and encouraged potential supporters in Pennsylvania and Ohio as well as New York, politicians began more and more to discount him. The legislative session in the winter of 1821-1822 gave rise to an impression that Van Buren and the Albany Regency commanded a much stronger coalition than any which might form against it, and Van Buren began to indicate that his support would go to Crawford. He made a vehement attack on the Monroe administration for appointing a known Federalist as postmaster at Albany. In fact, the man had endorsements from almost all the New York delegation in the House of Representatives, including at least eleven Bucktails; but Van Buren chose publicly to charge Monroe and his advisers with compromising Republican principles.[60] Since Crawford was known to be at odds with the rest of the administration, this action made Van Buren seem an ally of Crawford. Shortly afterward came Van Buren's trip to Virginia and attendant rumors that

---

59. William Plumer, Jr., to William Plumer, Sr., Dec. 30, 1821, Jan. 3, 1822, Brown, *Missouri Compromise*, pp. 69-70, 74.

60. Adams diary, Jan. 5, 1822; R. J. Meigs to Adams, Feb. 19, 1822, Adams Papers.

he had made a pact with Spencer Roane and others of the Richmond Junto to revive the New York–Virginia coalition and give its backing to Crawford. Thereafter, for the remainder of 1822, most politicians surmised that Van Buren and his allies would do their utmost to put New York in Crawford's column.

In 1823, the Albany Regency gave its support to Crawford more and more openly. Its organs, the New York *National Advocate* and the Albany *Argus*, explicitly endorsed him. And in April 1823, after it had become clear that Crawford was the only candidate likely to be nominated by a congressional caucus, the Regency demonstrated both its inclinations and its power by convening Republican members of the New York legislature and securing from them a vote in principle in favor of such a caucus.[61]

Nevertheless, hope revived among the other candidates. Several of Adams's friends assured him that he was much the most popular man in western counties of New York, where emigrants from New England were plentiful. One New York legislator, who happened himself to be for Clay, judged that "a majority of the democratic party were at heart for Mr. Adams." Thurlow Weed, a struggling young newspaper publisher at Rochester, opened a vigorous campaign for Adams even though he had never set eyes on the secretary of state nor knew anyone who had. A newspaper at Poughkeepsie also came out for

61. Calhoun to Ninian Edwards, Aug. 20, 1822, Calhoun, *Papers*, VII, 247, 249; Robert Walsh to Adams, Aug. 19, 1822, Adams Papers; Clinton to Henry Post, Aug. 21, 1822, John Bigelow, "DeWitt Clinton as a Politician," *Harper's* 50 (Feb. 1875), 415; John Elliott to General Blackshear, Sept. 4, 1822, Shipp, *Giant Days*, pp. 171-173; Johnston Verplanck to Van Buren, Dec. 13, 1822, Papers of Martin Van Buren, Library of Congress; ? to Taylor, Jan. 6, 1823, Papers of John W. Taylor, New-York Historical Society; Alexander Hamilton to Taylor, Jan. 25, 1823, Taylor Papers; Rufus King to Charles A. King, Feb. 22, 1823, Rufus King Papers (New-York Historical Society); James Otis Morse to Adams, March 15, 1823, Adams Papers; John Armstrong to Christopher Van Deventer, Van Deventer Collection, William L. Clements Library, University of Michigan; Albany *Argus*, quoted in Washington *National Intelligencer*, April 4, 1823; New York *American*, April 3, 1823; John W. Taylor to Adams, April 8, 1823, Adams Papers; Peter J. Clark to Southard, April 17, 1823, Southard Papers; New York *National Advocate*, quoted in Washington *National Intelligencer*, April 19, 1823; Ambrose Spencer to Brown, May 5, 1823, Papers of Jacob Brown, William L. Clements Library, University of Michigan.

Adams. Although Senator Rufus King remained neutral regarding the presidency and advised his family to do likewise,
his son, Charles King, undertook to organize a pro-Adams
contingent in the legislature and converted his New York *American*
into an Adams organ. Friends of Adams also established the
Albany *Independent* as a voice to counter the Regency's Albany
Argus.[62]

Adams supporters and pro-Adams newspapers in New
York attacked the whole notion of congressional caucus dictation to the states. Going farther, they attacked the provision of
the New York constitution that gave the legislature power to
choose presidential electors. They called for a prompt change so
that the people could vote for electors in 1824. This proposed
reform began to be widely debated. In elections for the state
legislature in the autumn of 1823, many candidates ran as opponents of a congressional caucus and proponents of popular election of electors. Many won—so many, in fact, that the returns
were interpreted as adverse to Crawford, and the *Argus* had to
publish an editorial claiming that Federalists had voted for the
reformers in order to foment dissension among Republicans.[63]
It seemed possible that the new legislature might not be so obe-
dient to the Albany Regency. Even if the constitution remained
unchanged, the legislature might not vote for Crawford. If the
constitution were amended and the people made the decision,
New York's electoral votes would almost certainly be denied
the Georgian, for even warm supporters of his conceded that

62. Degrand to Adams, Oct. 7, 1821, Adams Papers; James Otis Morse to Adams, Aug.
5, 1822, ibid.; D. B. Stockholm to Adams, Jan. 10, 1823, ibid.; Jonathan A. Fisk to
Taylor, Jan. 14, 1823, Taylor Papers; Rufus King to Charles A. King, Jan. 31, 1823,
Rufus King Papers (New-York Historical Society); Rufus King to Edward King, Feb.
4, 1823, Papers of Rufus King, Cincinnati Historical Society; John A. King to Van
Buren, Feb. 23, 1823, Van Buren Papers; Seth Hunt to William B. Lee, April 1, July
31, 1823, Adams Papers; James Otis Morse to ?, April 10, 1823, Adams Papers;
Christopher Hughes to Adams, June 10, 1823, Adams Papers; Solomon Southwick
to Adams, July 9, 1823, Adams Papers; John W. Taylor to Adams, Aug. 2, 1823 (two
letters), Adams Papers; New York *American*, Oct. 18, 21, 24, 28, Nov. 8, 1823; Washington *National Journal*, Dec. 13, 1823; Hammond, *Political Parties*, II, 127; Harriet A. Weed,
ed., *Autobiography of Thurlow Weed* (Boston: Houghton Mifflin, 1883), pp. 104-108.

63. Albany *Argus*, quoted in Washington *National Intelligencer*, Nov. 20, 1823.

he had little popular following in New York. Adams thus had reason to believe that New York's votes might come to him.

Calhoun was equally encouraged. When Ingham, Rogers, and the other Pennsylvania congressmen came to offer him their support, they may have been accompanied by some New Yorkers. In any case, Calhoun immediately began to dream of winning the electoral votes of both Pennsylvania and New York, and he paid court indiscriminately to any New Yorker who might help him. Meeting James A. Hamilton, the son of Alexander Hamilton and a prominent New York Lawyer, Calhoun took him aside to speak in praise of his father and to say that Alexander Hamilton's "is the only true policy for the country." At the same time, Calhoun was doing his utmost to convince Van Buren of the purity of his Republicanism.[64]

Even though Federalists such as Hamilton and Rufus King refused to commit themselves and Van Buren backed Crawford, Calhoun succeeded in building up a group of followers in New York. Among them were General Joseph G. Swift, who had once been head of the Army Corps of Engineers; Samuel L. Gouverneur, a lawyer and President Monroe's son-in-law; and Henry Wheaton, another lawyer justly famous for his reports of U.S. Supreme Court proceedings. Even in the period when Van Buren was demonstrating his power in Albany, these men sent cheerful reports to Calhoun. They succeeded in launching the New York *Patriot* as a newspaper which would oppose Crawford and, by doing so, assist Calhoun. The *Patriot* then had a loud part in the campaign for popular election of electors. Calhoun therefore interpreted the reformers' successes in the autumn of 1823 as victories for him no less than for Adams.[65]

---

64. William Plumer, Jr., to William Plumer Sr., Jan. 3, 1822, Brown, *Missouri Compromise*, pp. 74-75, speaks of a New York-Pennsylvania approach to Calhoun; Calhoun to Maxcy, Dec. 31, 1821, Calhoun, *Papers*, VI, 595-597; Charles G. Haines to Van Deventer, Jan. 1, 1823, Van Deventer Collection; Charles Gardner to Van Deventer, April 8, 1823, Van Deventer Collection; Winfield Scott to Gouverneur, April 8, 1823, Gouverneur Papers; Calhoun to Southard, April 9, 1823, Calhoun, *Papers*, VIII, 11-12; James A. Hamilton, *Reminiscences* (New York: Charles Scribner and Co., (1869), p. 62; Remini, *Van Buren*, pp. 17, 27-28.

65. Calhoun to Wheaton, May 8, 1823, Calhoun, *Papers*, VIII, 53-56; Washington *National Intelligencer*, June 4, 1823; Calhoun to Micah Sterling, July 20, 1823, Calhoun,

Nor was Clay out of the race in New York. As a champion of internal improvements, he could hope to win some of Clinton's following if Clinton were not himself a candidate. Moreover, Clay had friends in New York prepared to back him even against Clinton. One was Peter B. Porter, who had been a Warhawk congressman in 1812 and a general during the war. He had been fighting Clinton to get the terminus of the Erie Canal at Black Rock instead of Buffalo, and he had a following among other western legislators resentful of decisions by Clinton. In May 1823 Porter said that, if the legislature voted then, it would divide evenly for Crawford, Adams, and Clay.[66] While his estimate may have been overoptimistic, there was no doubt that Clay had a base of support which might well expand.

As of the autumn of 1823, Crawford still seemed the leader in New York. The elections at the beginning of November shook the hold on the legislature of Crawford's partisans. They created a distinct possibility that New York would go over to popular election. If so, or even if not, Adams, Calhoun, or Clay might win some or all of the state's large bloc of electors.

Papers, VIII, 172-173; Joseph Kent to Southard, July 31, 1823, Southard Papers; Washington *Republican*, Aug. 16, Nov. 11, 1823; Calhoun to Ninian Edwards, Sept. 23, 1823, Calhoun, *Papers*, VIII, 281; Calhoun to Gouverneur, Nov. 9, 1823, Calhoun, *Papers*, VIII, 354-355; Calhoun to Charles G. Haines, Nov. 9, 1823, Calhoun, *Papers*, VIII, 355-356; Wiltse, *Calhoun*, pp. 273-275.

66. Dorothie Bobbé, *DeWitt Clinton* (New York: Minton, Balch, and Co., 1933), pp. 252-253; Robert A. Garnett to Swift, Feb, 13, 1823, Swift Papers, estimated that Clay led Adams; Rufus King to ?, Feb. 26, 1823, Rufus King Papers (New-York Historical Society), judged the legislature to be divided evenly between Adams and Clay; John Armstrong to Christopher Van Deventer, March 29, 1823, Van Deventer Collection, said that the politicians were evenly divided between Crawford and Clay; Porter to Clay, May 24, 1823, Porter Papers, spoke optimistically of Clay's prospects in the legislature; on the other hand, John W. Taylor to Adams, May 28, 1823, Adams Papers, reported Porter as saying that there was a three-way split in the legislature, with Clay the fourth-man-out; Henry Wheaton to Maxcy, June 18, 1823, Galloway-Maxcy-Markoe Papers, expressed fear that the anti-Federalists would all go over to Clay; Jasper Lynch to O'Connor, Sept. ?, 1823, Papers of John M. O'Connor, William L. Clements Library, University of Michigan, appraised the legislature as evenly divided for Crawford, Clay, and Adams; Porter to Clay, Sept. 6, 1823, Porter Papers, said it would split between Clay and Adams; H. Ripley to Force, Nov. 6, 1823, Papers of Peter Force, Library of Congress, described the western counties as for Clay rather than Adams; Lynch to O'Connor, Nov. 16, 1823, O'Connor Papers, said the large majority of legislators were now for Crawford. The extent of disagreement among politicians on the question of how 160 legislators would vote illustrates the uncertainty that prevailed.

Electoral College Prospects: In late October 1823, Calhoun's confidant in Maryland, Virgil Maxcy, wrote down projections of the probable electoral vote. A month later, the *National Journal*, Adams's organ in Washington, published its estimates. Early in 1824 the pro-Crawford Richmond *Enquirer* did likewise, and a Clay supporter, writing under the pen name, "Member of Congress," set forth his forecast in a letter to the Washington *National Intelligencer*.[67] Each of these tallies was biased, of course, and those put in print were intended to be persuasive as well as informative. Since they appeared at different times during a fast-moving campaign, they could not be perfectly comparable even if all were examples of cool analysis. Even so, these tabulations, together with other evidence, permit one to visualize how the various candidates and their supporters probably saw the electoral scene at the time when the pressing foreign policy issues were under debate. Table 2 offers a graphic representation.

Election by the House: If no candidate won a majority in the country, the election would be decided by the House of Representatives. The fates of the candidates would be in the hands of many of the same people upon whom thought focused when the question was a possible caucus nomination. But the mix would be wholly different. In the first place, the voting would not include senators; in the second place, Federalists and anticaucus Republicans would take part; in the third place, each state would have only one vote. The last was the most important difference. If the election went to the House, the four representatives from Delaware, Illinois, Mississippi, and Missouri would have as much power as the ninety-six from New York, Pennsylvania, Virginia, and Ohio.

Largely from the same data that indicated the probable line-up in a caucus, the various candidates could guess at likely first-ballot outcomes in the House. According to the Constitu-

---

67. Document filed between Oct. 24 and 25, 1823, Galloway-Maxcy-Markoe Papers; Washington *National Journal*, Nov. 26, 1823; Richmond *Enquirer*, Feb. 2, 1824; Washington *National Intelligencer*, Feb. 27, 1824.

TABLE 2: How well-informed contemporaries probably estimated
the 1824 electoral vote as of the winter of 1823-1824

■ Probable victor ▨ Possible victor

State	Elec. vote	Adams	Calhoun	Clay	Crawford	Jackson
N.Y.	36					
Pa.	28					
Va.	24					
Ohio	16					
Mass.	15					
N.C.	15					
Ky.	14					
Md.[a]	11					
S.C.	11					
Tenn.	11					
Ga.	9					
Me.	9					
Conn.	8					
N.H.	8					
N.J.	8					
Vt.	7					
Ala.	5					
Ind.	5					
La.	5					
R.I.	4					
Del.	3					
Ill.	3					
Miss.	3					
Mo.	3					
Total	261					
Min.		65	39	43	36	11
Max.		107	99	96	93	62

(Needed for victory: 131)

[a] Maryland chose electors by districts, and it seemed probable that its votes
would scatter among several candidates.

tion, the House could vote only on the three front-runners. In the autumn of 1823 it seemed probable that Adams and Crawford would be among the finalists. The open question appeared to be whether Clay or Calhoun would be the third. Probably, the candidates and their managers foresaw the results illustrated in table 3.

It thus seemed imaginable but unlikely that Adams could be a first-ballot victor. What appeared more probable was that a decision would come at a later point, after members of the House decided that one of the three candidates could not win and that a choice had to be made between the other two. On the basis of evidence available in the autumn of 1823, an odds-maker would probably have reckoned that, if the three were Adams, Clay, and Crawford, Clay would win, for a westerner would be more acceptable than a southerner to Adams men and more acceptable than a New Englander to Crawford men. Moreover, as the former speaker, he would have more personal friends in the House. If the three were Adams, Calhoun, and Crawford, victory might go to any one of the three, for Adams and Calhoun supporters could conceivably unite behind either man, or, alternatively, Calhoun supporters in slave state delegations could turn to Crawford.

Although the candidates doubtless gave some thought to the contingency of an election by the House, they could hardly devote much effort to planning or preparing for it. The nominating caucus and the general election were nearer at hand, and common sense suggested concentration on these events; for the election might not go to the House if one candidate developed enough momentum so that others became discouraged and dropped out of the race. In any event, the members of the House were likely to be more influenced by the voting returns in their states than by anything else. Hence the possibility of an election in the House affected the candidate's sets of mind chiefly by making them more concerned than they otherwise might have been about carrying states with small numbers of electoral votes.

TABLE 3: How well-informed contemporaries probably estimated, as of the winter of 1823-1824, the outcome if the House of Representatives chose a President in 1824

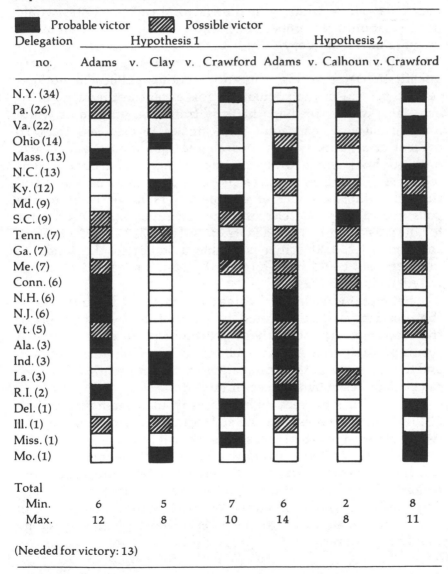

| | Adams v. Clay v. Crawford | | | Adams v. Calhoun v. Crawford | | |

■ Probable victor   ▨ Possible victor

Delegation no.	Hypothesis 1			Hypothesis 2		
	Adams v.	Clay v.	Crawford	Adams v.	Calhoun v.	Crawford
N.Y. (34)						
Pa. (26)						
Va. (22)						
Ohio (14)						
Mass. (13)						
N.C. (13)						
Ky. (12)						
Md. (9)						
S.C. (9)						
Tenn. (7)						
Ga. (7)						
Me. (7)						
Conn. (6)						
N.H. (6)						
N.J. (6)						
Vt. (5)						
Ala. (3)						
Ind. (3)						
La. (3)						
R.I. (2)						
Del. (1)						
Ill. (1)						
Miss. (1)						
Mo. (1)						

Total						
Min.	6	5	7	6	2	8
Max.	12	8	10	14	8	11

(Needed for victory: 13)

Source: For supporting data, see Appendix A.

THE VOTING PUBLIC

As of the autumn and winter of 1823-1824, no candidate had to despair of winning in the electoral college. Votes would not be cast until November 1824, and by then the line-up might be quite different. Very little had to change in order to transform the picture. Although only a few states retained property qualifications for voting, the entire voting public did not exceed 15 percent of the population, for, except in the rare northern states where freedmen had the franchise, only adult white males could vote, and adult white males formed less than 18 percent of a nation which was almost half female and nearly one-fifth black and in which the median age was around seventeen. In fact, since legislatures chose electors in some states and since the whole number of eligible voters never went to the polls in any state, the electorate which preoccupied candidates for the presidency consisted in its entirety of 723 state legislators and about 1,250,000 citizens. Table 4 indicates the kinds of numbers that could have formed the basis for politicians' computations in 1823-1824.

Because it was electoral votes that mattered, the outcome of the presidential election could be determined by a fraction of this electorate. Although there is little or no direct evidence, it seems probable that Adams, Calhoun, Clay, Crawford, Jackson, and the managers of their campaigns carried in their heads rough calculations resembling those in table 5.

Even if turnout were high, Adams would need no more than 201,000 popular votes plus the support of 189 legislators in the twelve states in which his prospects seemed best. If turnout were relatively low (as it was actually to be in 1824), he might need as few as 80,000 votes, plus the 189 legislators, to secure an absolute majority. None of the others had to have even that many votes. Any candidate who could induce only a few thousand people to switch to him or to go to the polls instead of staying home could become President.

STRATEGIES

Awareness of the small number of vote changes necessary for victory affected the candidates. Especially after Monroe's second term commenced, Clay asserted himself as a spokesman for the interests of segments of the population which seemed likely to be more numerous in 1824 than in 1816 or 1820. He called on the federal government to sponsor canals and roads which would contribute to economic development in the interior of the country. He advocated higher tariffs to help industry, and he talked of expanding foreign trade to benefit not only manufacturers but also merchants and shippers in eastern ports. On these subjects, his positions contrasted with those of Crawford and the states-rights' Republicans identified with him and known as "Radicals." They did not, however, set him off from Calhoun or necessarily from Adams, whose opinions on domestic issues remained indistinct.

Increasingly, therefore, Clay emphasized differences between himself and all members of the administration by attacking foreign policies with which Calhoun and Adams were necessarily identified and for which Crawford, too, carried some responsibility. At an early point, Clay championed recognition of the new Latin American republics. Time and again, he condemned Monroe's cabinet for indifference to "our neighbors, our brethren occupying a portion of the same continent, imitating our example and participating of the same sympathies with ourselves."[68] To the argument that the threat of recognition was an important bargaining chip in negotiations with Spain for peaceful cession of Florida and territory north of Texas, Clay responded that the Americans did not need King Ferdinand's permission to take land on their own borders. Appealing to the Anglophobia not only of Americans who remembered the Revolution and the War of 1812 but of Irishmen and other non-English immigrants, Clay charged that the true cause of the administration's timidity was fear of offending the British government, which might be resent-

---

68. Speech of Jan. 24, 1817, Clay, *Papers*, II, 291.

TABLE 4: Votes needed to win the presidency in 1824 (by state)

State	Electoral vote	Method of choosing electors[a]	Approximate no. of eligible voters in 1824[b]	Highest recent turnout[c] (percent)	Needed for absolute majority	
					If turnout = highest recent percentage	If turnout = 1824 actual
N.Y.	36	L	160 legislators	—	81 legislators	
Pa.	28	S-WB	215,200	66.6	71,700	23,400
Va.	24	S-WB	64,500	36.0	11,700	7,500
Ohio	16	S-WB	171,400	47.0	40,300	25,100
Mass.	15	S-WB	114,900	67.4	38,800	18,700
N.C.	15	S-WB	80,700	74.0	29,900	18,100
Ky.	14	S-WB	95,000	75.0	27,700	16,900
Md.	11	DB	57,000	77.2	22,000	16,700
S.C.	11	L	169 legislators	—	85 legislators	
Tenn.	9	DB	74,600	82.0	30,600	10,400
Ga.	9	L	86 legislators	—	44 legislators	
Me.	9	S-WB & DB	65,300	40.0	13,100	6,400
Conn.	8	S-WB	61,300	42.0	12,900	5,700
N.H.	8	S-WB	56,600	80.6	21,900	5,100
N.J.	8	S-WB	54,100	75.0	20,200	10,700
Vt.	7	L	214 legislators	—	108 legislators	
Ala.	5	S-WB	32,400	97.0	15,800	6,900
Ind.	5	S-WB	34,100	75.6	12,900	7,900
La.	5	L	64 legislators	—	33 legislators	
R.I.	4	S-WB	12,000	50.0	3,000	1,200
Del.	3	L	30 legislators	—	16 legislators	
Ill.	3	DB	25,300	49.0	6,200	2,400
Miss.	3	S-WB	11,600	80.0	4,700	2,600
Mo.	3	S-WB	24,100	61.2	7,400	1,400

a L: by legislature; S-W B: statewide ballot; DB: district ballot.

b Other than for Maryland and Indiana, estimates are based on the 1820 census. From that census, I have taken the total number of white males and deducted all under 16 years of age and one-half of those between 16 and 26. I have then extrapolated the increase of this adult white population in each state by assuming a rate of growth in the years 1820-1824 as equal to the average rate of growth in the same cohort between the census years 1810 and 1820. This does not correspond to the actual rate of growth between 1820 and 1830, and it produces some distortions. For example, it assumes a 15.6 percent annual increase in the population of Ohio, whereas the actual 1820-1830 increase averaged only 5.9 percent. But, since politicians making calculations in 1823 would have had only the 1810-1820 averages, they seem more appropriate to this table. From the totals thus derived, I have subtracted aliens, calculating their number as the total reported in the 1820 census plus a growth factor corresponding to that applied to the adult white population. For Alabama I have had to calculate growth from 1820 to 1824 on the basis of average growth for 1820 to 1830 because there was no census total prior to 1820. Accepting the calculations in George D. Luetscher, *Early Political Machinery in the United States* (Philadelphia: University of Pennsylvania Press, 1903), pp. 13 and 20, I have further assumed that in most states with some taxpaying qualifications for voting (Me., Mass., Conn., N.J., Pa., Md., N.C., Ohio, Ind., Miss., and Ill.), the electorate constituted only 95 percent of white males over 21 and that in Rhode Island, which had a property qualification, it constituted only 66.6 percent. On the basis of data in J. R. Pole, "Representation and Authority in Virginia from the Revolution to Reform," *Journal of Southern History*, 24 (Feb. 1958), 16-50, it can be calculated that in Virginia, which also had a property qualification, fewer than 30 percent of adult white males could vote. I have assumed, however, that politicians of the time would not have known these data and would probably have relied instead on the estimate in Jefferson's *Notes on Virginia* that Virginia's laws disfranchised only half of those potentially eligible. For Indiana, I have not used census figures but instead the state's official figures on eligible voters as given in Jacob Piatt Dunn, *Indiana and Indianans*, vol. I (Chicago: American Historical Society, 1919), 366. For Maryland, I have extrapolated from an estimate of eligible voters appearing in the *Baltimore Weekly Register*, 23 (Feb. 15, 1823), 370.

c For the most part, these figures are taken from Richard P. McCormick, *The Second American Party System: Party Formation in the Jacksonian Era* (Chapel Hill: University of North Carolina Press, 1966). Exceptions are New Hampshire, Maryland, Indiana, Illinois, Missouri, in which the calculations are my own, based on census data calculated as above, except with 1821-1824 populations calculated on the basis of average rates of growth for 1820-1830, and election data from A. J. Coolidge and J. J. B. Mansfield, *History and Description of New England: New Hampshire* (Boston: Austin J. Coolidge, 1860); *Baltimore Weekly Register*, 19 (Oct. 14, 1820), 111; Logan Esarey, *History of Indiana*, vol. I (Indianapolis: W. K. Stewart and Co., 1923), 222; Theodore C. Pease, *The Frontier State, 1818-1840* (Chicago: A. K. McClurg and Co., 1919), p. 89; and Walter Bickford Davis and Daniel S. Durrie, *An Illustrated History of Missouri* (St. Louis: A. J. Hall and Co., 1876), p. 72.

TABLE 5: Votes needed to win the presidency in 1824 (by candidate)

Candidate	State	Elec. vote	Absolute majority if turnout=highest recent[a]	Actual votes received[b] Elec.	Pop./L	Needed for victory if vote 1824 actual[c] Minimum[d]	Increment	Shift
Adams	Mass.	15	38,800	15	30,687	6,700	0	0
	N.H.	8	21,900	8	9,389	700	0	0
	Vt.	7	108L	7	108L	108L	0	0
	Md.	11	22,000	3	14,632	16,700	4,000	2,100
	Me.	9	13,100	9	10,289	2,400	0	0
	Conn.	8	12,900	8	9,261	2,000	0	0
	N.J.	8	20,200	0	9,110	10,700	3,100	1,600
	Ala.	5	15,800	0	2,416	6,900	8,800	4,400
	R.I.	4	3,000	4	2,145	300	0	0
	N.Y.	36	81L	26	57L	81L	24L	24L
	Ohio	16	40,300	0	12,280	25,100	25,500	12,800
	Ind.	5	12,900	0	3,095	7,900	9,600	4,900
	Other			4	5,436			
	Total	132	200,900 & 189L	84	108,740 & 165L	80,400 & 189L	51,000 & 24L	25,800 & 24L
Calhoun	S.C.	11	85L	0	0	85L		
	Pa.	28	71,700	0	0	23,400		
	Ill.	3	6,200	0	0	2,400		
	N.Y.	36	81L	0	0	81L		

	State							
	Md.	11	22,000	0	16,700	0	0	0
	Conn.	8	12,900	0	5,700	0	33L	33L
	N.J.	8	20,200	0	10,700	0	0	0
	Va.	24	11,700	0	7,500	0	0	0
	Del.	3	16L	0	16L	0		
	Total	*132*	*144,700 & 182L*	*0*	*61,400 & 182L*			
Clay	Ky.	14	27,700	14	17,331	7,000	0	0
	La.	5	64L	0	64L	33L	33L	33L
	Mo.	3	7,400	3	0	1,000	0	0
	Ohio	16	40,300	16	19,255	19,000	0	0
	Ind.	5	12,900	0	5,315	7,900	5,200	2,600
	N.Y.	36	81L	4	39L	81L	42L	42L
	Tenn.	9	30,600	0	0	10,400	21,000	10,400
	N.J.	8	20,200	0	0	10,700	22,000	10,700
	Ala.	5	15,800	0	67	6,900	13,600	13,500
	Ill.	3	6,200	0	1,047	2,400	2,700	1,400
	Miss.	3	4,700	0	0	2,600 5,100		
	Va.	24	11,700	0	416	7,500	14,200	7,100
	Other			0	3,705			
	Total	*131*	*177,500 & 145L*	*37*	*47,136 & 103L*	*75,400 & 114L*	*83,800 & 75L*	*48,300 & 75L*

(continued)

TABLE 5: (continued)

Candidate	State	Elec. vote	Absolute majority if turnout=highest recent	Actual votes received		Needed for victory if vote 1824 actual		
				Elec.	Pop./L	Minimum	Increment	Shift
Crawford	Va.	24	11,700	24	8,489	3,200	0	0
	Ga.	9	44L	9	N.K.ᵉ	44L	0	0
	N.Y.	36	81L	5	60L	81L	21L	21L
	N.C.	15	29,900	0	15,621	20,500	4,800	2,500
	Del.	3	16L	2	N.K.	16L	N.K.	N.K.
	Md.	11	22,000	1	3,364	16,700	26,500	13,300
	Me.	9	13,100	0	2,336	6,400	8,000	2,100
	N.H.	8	21,900	0	643	5,100	9,800	4,500
	R.I.	3	3,000	0	200	1,200	2,000	1,000
	Ala.	5	15,800	0	1,680	6,900	10,300	5,300
	Conn.	8	12,900	0	1,978	5,700	7,300	3,800
	Other				12,307			
	Total	131	130,300 & 141L	41	46,618 & 120L	65,700 & 141L	68,700 & 97L	32,500 & 21L
Jackson	Tenn.	11	30,600	11	20,197	400	0	0
	Pa.	28	71,700	28	36,100	6,000	0	0

Ala.	5	15,800	5	9,443	2,500	0	0
Ohio	16	40,300	0	18,489	19,300	900	450
N.C.	15	29,900	15	20,415	15,700	0	0
Md.	11	22,000	7	14,523	16,700	2,200	1,100
Miss.	3	4,700	3	3,234	1,700	0	0
N.J.	8	20,200	8	10,985	9,200	0	0
Ky.	14	27,700	0	6,455	10,900	10,900	4,500
Mo.	3	7,400	0	987	1,400	500	250
Ind.	5	12,900	5	7,343	5,400	0	0
Ill.	3	6,200	3	1,901	1,600	0	0
S.C.	11	85L	11	N.K.	85L	0	0
Other			3	3,472			
Total	133	289,400 & 85L	99	153,544 & L	90,800 & 85L	14,500	6,300

[a] From table 4 above.
[b] From Svend Petersen, *A Statistical History of American Presidential Elections* (New York: Frederick Ungar, 1963).
[c] L: by legislature.
[d] Minimum = smallest number of votes needed to lead the field; increment = additional votes needed to win if other candidates received the votes they actually received in 1824; shift = number of votes that would have yielded victory if cast for the candidate instead of for his rivals.
[e] N.K.: not known.

ful if Americans got an advantage in trade relations with the Latin Americans.[69]

In the spring of 1821 Clay set forth his foreign policy platform. He did so in a speech in Lexington, Kentucky, which was then reprinted in newspapers around the country.[70] In it, Clay reiterated a demand for recognition of and aid to the Latin American republics, again stressing that it was America's moral duty to countenance their cause and that the entire country stood to benefit from the resultant trade. Second, Clay declared that the United States had a larger duty—to give "tone, and hope, and confidence to the friends of liberty throughout the world." Third, Clay contended "that a sort of counterpoise to the Holy Alliance should be formed in the two Americas, in favor of National Independence and Liberty, to operate by the force of example and by moral influence."

With these generalities, Clay obviously hoped to appeal to citizens who might otherwise be attracted to Adams or Calhoun. The secretary of state had admitted to him that, with the Spanish treaty now ratified, recognition of some Latin American republics was probably not far off.[71] Clay wanted voters to remember that it was he who had pressed for such a step. Beyond that, he hoped to highlight the difference between his own posture and the cold neutrality that the administration would necessarily continue to profess. In advocating encouragement to "friends of liberty" everywhere and the formation of a hemisphere alliance, he traced a vision which he hoped many people would see as nobler and bolder than any presented to them by any members of the Monroe cabinet.

Between 1821 and 1823 Clay reiterated the themes of his Lexington speech. He did not change them. When the President announced in 1822 that he was prepared to recognize some Latin American states, Clay did in fact claim the credit. He lauded the revolutions in Naples and Spain and the independence movement

---

69. Clay to Jonathan Russell, Jan. 29, March 24, 1820, Clay, Papers, II, pp. 771, 787-788; speech of April 3, 1820, ibid., pp. 803-815; speech of May 10, 1820, ibid., pp. 853-859.
70. Speech of May 19, 1821, ibid., III, 79-82.
71. Adams diary, March 9, 1821.

in Greece and took the administration to task for failing to show adequate sympathy with these movements. He continued to attack the Holy Alliance and to call for an "American system" as a counterpoise.[72]

Throughout, Clay's chief target was Adams. In the summer of 1822, probably with Clay's knowledge if not connivance, a document was issued that accused Adams of having truckled to the British during the peace negotiations at Ghent and having shown a willingness to sacrifice the interests of westerners to those of New England fishermen. The author was Jonathan Russell of Rhode Island who, along with Clay and Adams, had been a member of the delegation at Ghent. All the while, newspapers supporting Clay emphasized Adams's Federalist past, his possible pro-British inclinations, and the likelihood that he represented narrow sectional interests.[73]

The logic of this campaign was self-evident. If Clay could make it appear that he alone was the nationalist candidate, he might rally to himself western and northern Republicans whose concern was to prevent the election of Crawford, the triumph of the Radicals, and the preservation of a southern dynasty.

Adams's strategy was partly dictated by these attacks from Clay, some of which were echoed by supporters of Crawford and Calhoun. He had the advantage of being the only prominent candidate who was not a slaveholder. He thus had some chance of capitalizing on the antislavery sentiment that had manifested itself in the North, parts of the West, and even parts of the South during the controversy of 1819-1820 over the admission of Missouri as a state. He had the disadvantages of being his father's son, a former Federalist, and a citizen of a state that was viewed as having interests adverse to those of many other states. Adams needed to establish his credentials as a Republican, a patriot, and a man with a national and not just sectional perspective.

---

72. Baltimore *Weekly Register*, Sept. 21, 1822; speech of March 29, 1823, Clay, *Papers*, III, 403-405.

73. Samuel Flagg Bemis, *John Quincy Adams and the Foundations of American Foreign Policy* (New York: Alfred A. Knopf, 1950), pp. 498-509; Adams to Louisa Catherine Adams, Aug. 1, 1822, Adams Papers.

During his early years as secretary of state, Adams helped himself as a presidential candidate by his negotiations with Spain. To be sure, some men argued that the United States should simply take Florida and the trans-Mississippi West. On the other hand, no one could doubt that the object of Adams's diplomacy was to gain territory that would enlarge and strengthen the South and West. When, in the midst of his negotiations, Jackson marched into Florida in pursuit of Seminole warriors, entrenched himself there, and hanged two Englishmen who had been supplying the Indians, Adams not only defended Jackson in the cabinet but let the fact of his doing so be advertised.[74]

After concluding the treaty with Spain, Adams withdrew his opposition to recognizing Latin American republics. Still having doubts about their viability, he did so on the ground that the public favored recognition.[75] Though he did not note the point in his diary, he must have perceived that the action would deprive Clay of a talking point.

In the meantime, Adams was acting in the cabinet the part of an ardent Republican and nationalist. Time and again, he drafted diplomatic notes which Monroe felt obliged to tone down. After the revolution in Spain, for example, Adams proposed sending congratulations and presented a text which Monroe felt sure would give offense to the Holy Alliance. To the instructions that Adams drew up for envoys to the newly recognized Latin American states, Monroe made the same objection. In negotiating with the French about commercial issues, Adams presented drafts which Crawford advised the Prsident would be certain to produce a rupture.[76]

Adams was particularly hard on the British. There were in progress negotiations looking toward policing of the Atlantic to halt trade in slaves, now illegal under both British and American

74. Washington *National Intelligencer*, Feb. 1, 1819; Baltimore *Weekly Register*, Feb. 3, 1819.
75. Adams diary, March 9, 1821.
76. Monroe to Adams, April 15, 17, 1820, July 23, 24, 27, Aug. 17, 1821, May 29, 1823, Adams Papers; Adams diary, May 18, 1820; Crawford to Monroe, July 20, 1821, Papers of James Monroe, Library of Congress; Adams to Monroe, July 25, 1821, Monroe Papers; Crawford to Barbour, July 25, 1821, Papers of James Barbour, New York Public Library.

law. Since most of the policing would necessarily be done by the Royal Navy, the British asked for limited authority to search American ships. Adams would not concede it. Again, he made sure that the public learned of the stand he had taken. To a political leader in Baltimore, he wrote: "both the last and the present Administrations have been willing to *concede* more to the British . . . than I have individually."[77]

Like Clay, Adams set forth a foreign policy platform. He did so in 1821 in a Fourth of July speech delivered in Washington and subsequently published not only in pro-Adams newspapers but as a pamphlet.[78] Much of his speech simply attacked Britain. Poletica, then the Russian minister to the United States, characterized it as "from one end to the other nothing but a violent diatribe against England, intermingled with republican exaggerations."[79] Also, however, the speech included a prophecy that colonialism would not survive anywhere. Giving more than an intimation of the forthcoming administration decision to recognize some of the Latin American republics, these passages answered Clay's implied accusation that Adams lacked sympathy for people struggling for independence. Also, Adams's speech countered Clay's appeal for a counterpoise to the Holy Alliance by calling in strident language for America to avoid involvement in European politics and to guard above all her own security and peace. "Wherever the standard of freedom or independence has been or shall be unfurled, there will her heart, her benedictions, and her prayers be," said Adams in the lines best to be remembered later. "But she goes not abroad in search of monsters to destroy. She is the well-wisher to the freedom and independence of all. She is the champion and vindicator only of her own."

Characterizing his speech variously as a direct reply to Clay's Lexington speech and as an address "to and for *man*, as

---

77. Bemis, *Adams and the Foundations*, pp. 423-435; Adams to S. Smith, May 30, 1823, Adams Papers.

78. Adams, *An Address delivered at the Request of a Commission of the Citizens of Washington* (Washington, D.C.: Davis and Force, 1821).

79. Poletica to Nesselrode, July 12, 1821, "Correspondence of Russian Ministers in Washington, 1818-1825," *American Historical Review*, 18 (Jan. 1913), 325-326.

well as to and for my country," Adams emphasized to various correspondents how plainly it demonstrated his hostility to the British. To a friendly Philadelphia editor, he wrote that he had meant to warn the British against yielding to their "malignant passions." To another prominent Philadelphian, he explained, "I thought it was high time that we should be asking ourselves, where we were in our relations with that country."[80] Adams manifestly hoped that his Fourth of July oration would put to rest any suspicion that he was an Anglophile.

In the following year, when there appeared Jonathan Russell's indictment of his conduct at Ghent, Adams set aside all but the most imperative business and employed the better part of his summer composing a book-length answer. Being diligent enough and lucky enough to find the originals of some documents that Russell had misquoted and misused, Adams succeeded in demolishing Russell's case.[81] The episode, had, however, demonstrated that the charge of partiality to Britain was a hydra he would have to fight as long as he remained a candidate, and thereafter he continually hacked at it. The *National Journal*, a newspaper started in Washington in November 1823 as a personal organ for Adams, asserted that independence of Britain and the rest of the Old World would remain the chord of its editorial policy.[82]

In campaigning for the presidency, Adams faced problems that did not face Clay, for he was responsible for what happened as well as for what was said. Apparently, he felt that mere rhetoric would have little practical effect on the policies of other governments toward the United States. Otherwise he would not have drafted the notes and dispatches which Crawford criticized and Monroe fretfully modified nor would he have assailed Great Britain in a public speech. On the other hand, he showed keen

80. Adams to Robert L. Walsh, July 10, 27, 1821, Worthington C. Ford, ed., *The Writings of John Quincy Adams*, 7 vols. (New York: Macmillan, 1913-1917), VII, 115, 136; Adams to C. J. Ingersoll, July 23, 1821, ibid., p. 122.

81. Bemis, *Adams and the Foundations*, pp. 498-509.

82. "The announcement for the *National Journal* appears in the front of the first bound volume in the Library of Congress; there is also a copy in the Force Papers.

concern lest the Monroe administration *do* something that would provoke anger or reprisals abroad. After recognition of the Latin American republics, he counseled Monroe to postpone actually sending envoys until reactions had been reported from London and the continental capitals. He fought in the cabinet against any encouragement of an independence movement in Cuba. The prospect that independence might be followed by American annexation, he argued, could lead the British to take preemptive action and seize the island. Similarly, though publicly declaring himself sympathetic with the Greeks, Adams was emphatic in cabinet in opposing any official encouragement. He protested even the proposal that a fact-finding commission be dispatched, as had been done early on for some of the Latin American states. Both the British and the Holy Allies, he warned, could take offense.[83]

The contrast between the boldness of Adams's language and the cautiousness of his actions was due in part, of course, to differences between his role as candidate and his role as responsible statesman. But Adams's efforts to avoid actual trouble with England or the continental powers also served his interests as a candidate. In the first place, he had to be aware that any real trouble with a foreign nation would be blamed on him. If the trouble were with England, the result could be fatally to weaken Adams's base of support in the sea-dependent New England states and among Anglophiles and former Federalists who, while they were sure to deplore his campaign oratory, might nevertheless vote for him as a lesser evil. In the second place, Adams could not ignore the fact that, if war began to seem imminent, public attention would shift away from the accomplishments for which he could claim credit, such as the annexation of Florida, and focus instead on the probable demands of the conflict to come. Notice, publicity, and interest would go to Calhoun, the secretary of war, who had been a clamorous advocate of preparedness, or perhaps to the military hero, Jackson. Reasons of politics as

---

83. Adams diary, Nov. 16, 27, 1822.

well as reasons of state could have led Adams to the positions he took within the cabinet.

Adams's optimum strategy thus involved preserving relative tranquility in the nation's international relations while at the same time persuading the doubtful that he was as patriotic and anti-British as any dyed-in-the-wool Jeffersonian and as much a nationalist and as much a partisan of the frontiersmen as was Clay. It was not a strategy easily pursued, especially by a man who felt compelled to explain to a diary the highmindedness of his every action.

Calhoun's task was simpler despite the fact that he, too, held a responsible office. The basis for his campaign was an assumption that none of the other candidates could win. He discounted Clay on the ground that no westerner could receive the votes of the North and South. Crawford would fail, he believed, because his Georgia base and Virginian support would arouse hostility in northern states where electors were chosen by popular ballot and because his advocacy of states rights would alienate people who wanted federal aid for canals, roads, and manufacturing establishments. Adams's disabilities were his identification with New England, his Federalist past, and his lack of experience on domestic issues. Calhoun thought that his own championing of internal improvements, a protective tariff, and frontier defense would capture some of Clay's constituents; his South Carolina background would bring him support in the South; and his nationalistic policies plus his Connecticut ties would allow him to win over some of Adams's partisans.[84]

Calhoun's strategy thus involved out-Claying Clay on internal issues while seeking to chop away at Adams's credibility as a candidate. Through his Federalist allies, the newspapers established by his friends, and Pennsylvania organs controlled by the

---

84. Calhoun to Moses Waddell, Sept. 25, 1821, Calhoun, *Papers*, VI 387-388; Calhoun to Lewis Cass, Dec. 9, 1821, ibid., pp. 560-561; Calhoun to Maxcy, Dec. 31, 1821, ibid., pp. 595-597; Calhoun to William D. Williamson, May 2, 1822, ibid., VII, 91; Calhoun to Ninian Edwards, June 12, 1822, ibid., pp. 159-161; Calhoun to Samuel D. Ingham, Nov. 2, 1822, ibid., pp. 327-328; Calhoun to Micah Sterling, March 27, 1823, ibid., p. 547; Calhoun to Jacob Brown, Aug. 8, 1823, ibid., VIII, 215.

"Family Party," Calhoun advertised his positions and sounded the refrain that, if neither Clay nor Adams could win, then all opponents of Crawford and the Radicals should rally in his camp. At first, this campaign avoided direct attacks on either Clay or Adams. By 1823, however, Calhoun had become more confident. Late that summer, he directed a change in policy, writing confidentially to his lieutenants that they and the pro-Calhoun press should begin to emphasize policy differences with Adams and to call attention to the fact that Adams's onetime Federalism so compromised him that he would never win the votes of true Republicans outside New England and might even fail to win their votes there.[85] Calhoun's strategy was thus in part complementary to Clay's. It aimed at discrediting Adams and driving him out of the race.

Crawford, too, had a simpler problem that Adams. He had to take blame or credit for what he did as secretary of the treasury, and he and his friends had continually to fight unfounded charges of misuse of funds or patronage. At least by 1823, however, he had less answerability for other activities of the administration, for it has become notorious that he opposed not only Adams and Calhoun but also Monroe on almost every domestic issue.[86]

Crawford campaigned as, in effect, the leader of an old Jeffersonian party whose principles had been deserted by the Monroe administration. His managers branded all other candidates as actual or potential tools of the Federalists. They contended that the whole Missouri question had been gotten up by Federalists as a device for disrupting Republican unity, and they labeled the domestic programs espoused by Clay and Calhoun as Hamilton's programs in new disguise. They said and for the most part believed that, in any case, these two renegade Republicans would eventually drop out. The ultimate contest would be between Crawford and

85. Calhoun to Wheaton, Sept. 26, 1823, ibid., pp. 286-287; Calhoun to Charles G. Haines, Nov. 9, 1823, ibid., pp. 355-356.
86. Joseph W. Story to Mason, Feb. 21, 1822, George S. Hilliard, ed., *Memoir and Correspondence of Jeremiah Mason* (Cambridge, Mass.: Riverside Press, 1873), p. 264; Calhoun to Maxcy, April 22, 1822, Calhoun, *Papers*, VI, 61; Joel R. Poinsett to Monroe, May 10, 1822, Monroe Papers; Tench Coxe to Southard, March 25, 1823, Southard Papers.

Adams. Hence they persistently voiced the theme that Adams, the ex-Federalist, was in fact the Federalist candidate.[87]

Until late in 1823, there was no Jackson strategy, for Jackson himself was not yet committed to running, and the men urging him to do so took no action except to disparage other candidates and stimulate signs of the general's personal popularity.

As of the autumn of 1823, Adams was therefore the central figure in the presidential campaign. Clay, Calhoun, and Crawford were all concentrating on undermining him, and he was battling their efforts to tar him as a lukewarm friend of liberty, an Anglophile, a Federalist, and a candidate with a hopelessly narrow electoral base. In view of the small numbers of legislators and voters whose shifts in opinion could transform the prospects for 1824, the contest was carried on relentlessly by all parties.

Knowing the stakes and strategies of the candidates, a detached observer aware of the pressing foreign policy issues might well have made the following predictions:

—That Adams would oppose acceptance of the proffered informal alliance with England. Likely to get most of the credit or blame for anything the administration did in foreign affairs, he would be held to have been its author. Those voters disposed to worry about his possible Federalist or Anglophile proclivities might feel that their fears had been confirmed. Furthermore, Adams would be open to fresh attack from Clay for failing to maintain America's independence. The result would be to cost him important marginal votes in the West, erode his support in the Middle States, and perhaps even lose him influential backers in Vermont, New Hampshire, and Maine. Adams's political interests would be best served if the British offer were spurned.

---

87. For example: Crawford to Gallatin, May 13, 1822, Henry Adams, ed., *The Writings of Albert Gallatin*, 3 vols. (Philadelphia: J. B. Lippincott, 1879), II, 241-244; Van Buren to Johnston Verplanck, Dec. 22, 1822, Van Buren Papers; Tench Coxe to Jefferson and Madison, Jan. 31, 1823, Papers of James Madison, Library of Congress; William Henry Harrison to James Barbour, April 18, 1824, Barbour Papers. The view was most strongly stated by Jefferson in letters to Gallatin of Oct. 20, 1822, Gallatin, *Writings*, II, 258-259, and Aug. 2, 1823, Gallatin Papers, and to Warden, Oct. 31, 1823, Papers of David Bailie Warden, Maryland Historical Society.

—That Adams would also oppose actual recognition of Greece. In the first place, he was likely to fear trouble with the continental powers, producing the domestic effects that he had tried to avert by counseling Monroe to be forceful in language but cautious in deed. In the second place, he had to anticipate embarrassment from the fact that the logical person to be envoy or commissioner to Greece was Edward Everett of Harvard, who had composed the pro-Greek manifesto in the *North American Review*, made no secret of his desire to have the job, and expected Adams's help in getting it. Since Everett was a Federalist, Adams had reason to expect that the appointment would fuel Republican prejudices. On the other hand, to deny Everett the post would be to offend Federalists in New England and elsewhere who might otherwise go to the polls for Adams and who seemed almost certain to do so if Calhoun fell out of the race. It was in Adams's interest as a candidate that any change in American posture toward Greece be postponed until after the election.

—That Crawford and Calhoun and their adherents would favor both alliance with England and recognition of Greece if Adams could be made to seem the sponsor of these acts because of the harm they might work on his election prospects.

—That Calhoun would advocate these steps with special vehemence because they promised him the added benefit of arousing public concern about a possible war and hence turning public attention to his department and to the preparedness measures which he had all along been advocating.

The test of what was and what was not in the personal political interest of the various candidates would have yielded much more specific predictions than any test based on suppositions about their ideological positions or about conditions in the politics of other countries. Moreover, most of these predictions would have been right on the nose.

5

Policy Choices

THE FIRST ROUND OF DEBATE

Canning's proposal that the United States and Britain join in opposing European interference in Latin America was first discussed by Monroe's cabinet on October 11, 1823. Adams had just completed a rain-drenched trip from Massachusetts. Calling at the White House, he was ushered into the cavernous room that the President used as an office, its high windows looking out southward across meadowland to the yellowing and reddening oaks and maples dipping up from the banks of the Potomac. Amid the Louis XVI furnishings he had brought back from France in the 1790s, the President sat next to a low escritoire. Calhoun already occupied one of the plush-covered, oval-back chairs near him. Adams took another. Before long, Attorney General William Wirt joined them, and the four men conversed briefly about the dispatches from Rush received two days earlier.[1]

Unfortunately, none of the four made a record of what was said. Adams customarily made notes on each day's events. When he had time, he entered detailed memoranda in a diary. During his first weeks back in Washington, he was too busy or preoccupied to write anything. The others present seldom kept notes

---

1. Louisa Catherine Adams to Mary Hellen Adams, Oct. 18, 1823, Adams Family Papers, Massachusetts Historical Society (hereafter, Adams Papers); Adams desk calendar, Oct. 11, 1823, ibid.

of any kind. We know almost nothing therefore of initial reactions by the President and his advisers.

Monroe plainly did not feel that a decision had to be made right away. He let Adams take the originals of Rush's letters but asked him for copies. On the next day he left Washington for his farm in Virginia. Once there, he sent the copies of Rush's dispatches to Jefferson and Madison, asking their advice.[2]

Since Monroe customarily shared information with the two and sought their counsel, there was nothing unusual in this. It would have been surprising if he had acted otherwise, for in this instance perhaps more than any other he had need of them. On his own, he could blunder as in France in 1794 or in Britain in 1806. If backed by Jefferson and Madison, he would at least have proof for posterity that any error was not his alone. One indication that he wanted a record of their advice as well as the advice itself was that he wrote to Jefferson when he was just about to ride within three miles of Monticello and could easily have detoured to put his question in person.

In writing to the former Presidents, Monroe conceded that the central issue was whether the United States should risk entanglement in European politics and wars and that he was "sensible . . . of the extent & difficulty of the question." Even so, he disclosed that his own inclination was "to meet the proposal of the British govt." Having written thus, he waited for their replies and for his own return to the capital.

In Washington Calhoun and Adams worked in their departments, making ready for late November, when Congress would begin to assemble. The newspapers which they read and letters which came to them dealt mainly with politics at home. In all probability, both men gave less thought to what they would advise the President than to rumors that Crawford was seriously

2. Monroe to Adams, Oct. 11, 1823, ibid.; Monroe to Jefferson, Oct. 17, 1823, Worthington C. Ford, "Some Original Documents on the Genesis of the Monroe Doctrine," *Proceedings* of the Massachusetts Historical Society, Second Series, 15 (1902) (hereafter, Ford, "Genesis"), 684-685. Monroe asked Jefferson to pass Rush's dispatches on to Madison, but he also wrote to Madison: Monroe to Madison, Oct. 17, 1823, William C. Rives Collection, Library of Congress.

ill, debate about the prospective nominating caucus in Congress, and forecasts and reports concerning elections in Tennessee, Pennsylvania, and New York that might offer some clues as to their respective prospects for the presidency. Their correspondence and that of members of their families were full of these subjects. It is difficult to believe that rumination on the issue posed by Rush's dispatches was wholly walled off from these other preoccupations.

Calhoun could surely see that if the administration accepted Canning's offer, there would be some outcry. In many parts of the country, the old animosity toward England survived. Among Irishmen in northeastern cities it was stronger still. New York, Pennsylvania, and Ohio papers damned the English for failing to defend Spain and accused them of designs on Cuba and the trade of South America, and Washington and Baltimore papers reprinted or excerpted such comments.[3] It was a near certainty that many editors would denounce an Anglo-American concert, even if they approved its objectives. It was equally sure that some would put the blame on Adams and say that he had shown his Federalist colors. This was precisely what Calhoun desired.

Doubtless, Calhoun saw considerations of policy as well as of politics that argued for accepting Canning's offer. For years he had been asking for coast fortifications and a system of military roads which would permit rapid movement of troops across the interior in case an enemy staged coastal raids comparable to the British attack on Washington in 1814 or secured a beachhead as a base for naval operations. Denied funds by Crawford's friends in Congress, Calhoun feared what might happen in a war. Writing

---

3. Richmond *Enquirer*, Feb. 15, 1823; Washington *National Intelligencer*, March 18, May 7, 22, June 13, July 16, Aug. 1, Nov. 17, 1823; Baltimore *Weekly Register*, July 12, Sept. 6, 27, 1823; Louisville *Public Advertiser*, Sept. 29, 1823; Baltimore *American*, Oct. 4, 1823; New York *American*, Nov. 21,. 1823; Walter R. Fee, *The Transition from Aristocracy to Democracy in New Jersey, 1789-1829* (Somerville, Mass.: Somerville Press, 1933), pp. 232-234; Herman Hailperin, "Pro-Jackson Sentiment in Pennsylvania, 1820-1828," *Pennsylvania Magazine of History and Biography*, 50 (July 1926), 204-206; Jarvis Means Morse, *A Neglected Period of Connecticut's History, 1881-1850* (New Haven: Yale University Press, 1933), pp. 64-73; Eugene H. Rosebloom, "Ohio in the Presidential Election of 1824," *Ohio Archeological and Historical Quarterly*, 26 (April 1917), 206.

to Secretary of the Navy Samuel Southard about Canning's overture, he evidenced relief that in a war over Latin America the United States would have some prospect of receiving protection and aid from England.[4] Also, perhaps, Calhoun hoped that public furor might shock the Congress into at last voting money for preparedness. There is no reason to suppose that he sat in his office or in his palatial home on E Street, rubbing his hands together and thinking of concert with Britain solely in terms of possible effects on the presidential campaign. On the other hand, he can hardly have been blind to the harm it might do to Adam's candidacy.

Adams, too, must have revolved in his mind arguments that had to do with the national interest. To be sure, he had spoken in the late spring to Addington, the British minister, of the "coincidence of principles" between their governments and the possibility that they might "compare their ideas and purposes together, with a view to the accommodation of great interests upon which they had hitherto differed."[5] But he had probably not envisioned any accommodation which the world and the American public might interpret as a de facto alliance, and, though he did not comment on the fact, even in his diary, he almost certainly perceived that if such an alliance materialized, his enemies would cry "Federalist," his seemingly narrow margins of support in Maine, Vermont, New York, New Jersey, and the Old Northwest might shrink, and his supporters elsewhere might give up his cause as hopeless. Acceptance of Canning's offer could doom Adams's hopes of becoming President. This perception would have stimulated a mental search for reasons why the offer should be rejected if not for stratagems by which its rejection might be effected. By the time of the President's return, Adams was to have made such a search and to have prepared defenses.

---

4. Calhoun to Southard, Oct. 12, 1823, W. Edwin Hemphill, ed., *The Papers of John C. Calhoun*, 8 vols. in progress (Columbia, S.C.: University of South Carolina Press, 1959——) (hereafter, Calhoun, *Papers*), VIII, 307.

5. Stratford Canning to George Canning, June 6, 1823, C. K. Webster, ed., *Britain and the Independence of Latin America: Select Documents from the Foreign Office Archives*; 2 vols. (London: Oxford University Press, 1938), II, 495-496; Adams diary, June 20, 1823.

Apart from working up arguments and gambits, there was not much for Adams to do before the President returned. Regarding Calhoun as wholly unscrupulous, he could hardly try to reason with him. To do so would be merely to give him warning of arguments he might meet at the cabinet table. Even if Crawford had not been convalescing in the country, Adams would have had similar grounds for not approaching him. Southard, the new secretary of the navy, was known to be close to Calhoun. In any case, neither he nor Attorney General William Wirt could be expected to carry much weight in the policy debate.

Adams could watch for fresh dispatches from Rush or other news from across the Atlantic. In fact, during the President's absence he did receive Rush's accounts of further meetings with Canning. In each, the foreign secretary seemed to show more and more alarm about what the continental powers might do and more and more eagerness for Anglo-American action. Rush had gone so far as to agree to issuance of a joint declaration if Britain first recognized the Latin American states. Fortunately, from Adam's standpoint, Canning had replied that he could not yet meet the condition.[6] Adams must have worried, however, lest the pouch soon bring a report that the British cabinet had relented on this point.

There was no way for Adams to get additional information. Addington, the British chargé, appeared to know little. The French minister was out of town. The Prussian minister was unlikely to be helpful. There was no Austrian minister. The only foreign representative with whom Adams could profitably talk was the Russian, Baron de Tuyll von Serooskerken, and Adams had to recognize that reports to Tuyll from St. Petersburg were slow in arriving and that, in any case, the tsar would not necessarily keep his minister in Washington abreast of developments in Europe.

Adams nevertheless had a meeting with Tuyll on October 16. The Russian came in to report that his government had rejected

---

6. Rush to Adams, Sept. 19, 1823, Stanislaus Murray Hamilton, ed., *The Writings of James Monroe*, 7 vols. (New York: G. P. Putnam's Sons, 1888-1903) (hereafter, Monroe, *Writings*), VII, 377-386.

overtures to recognize the regency in Colombia. The tsar had declared, he said, that, "faithful to the principles of policy which he follows in concert with his allies, he could not in any case receive an agent of any character, whether from the Regency of Colombia or from any other de facto governments, which owed their existence to the events of which the New World had in recent years been the theater." Tuyll went on to assure Adams that the tsar had no complaint against the United States for following a different policy. After learning in 1822 of American recognition of five of the new republics, said Tuyll, the tsar had merely expressed gratification that the United States would remain neutral in the conflict between these states and Spain and said he hoped that decision would not change.

Tuyll's words apparently gave Adams an idea. According to the Russian's account, the secretary of state responded that the United States would remain neutral as long as European powers did so. If that condition changed, the American cabinet would have to have "new deliberations." Writing some weeks later, Adams recalled having said to Tuyll also that he would tell the President of the conversation and that Tuyll could expect a formal reply.[7] Either at the time or afterward, it apparently entered Adams's mind that the problem posed by Canning might be finessed. The American government might issue a declaration such as Canning proposed, but do so on its own.

From Adams's standpoint, the idea had obvious merits. If the statement were made to Russia, it could be bolder than if made to France, for Adams knew from his own years in St. Petersburg of the tsar's curious affection and tolerance for the American republic. Since mail reached London long before it reached Russia, the English cabinet would have time to react. Quite possibly, it would issue a parallel declaration. If so, the United States would get the benefit of an association with England

---

7. Tuyll to Adams, Oct. 16, 1823, Worthington C. Ford, "John Quincy Adams and the Monroe Doctrine," *American Historical Review*, 7 (July 1902) (hereafter, Ford, "Adams"), 686; Tuyll to Nesselrode, Oct. 27, 1823, Ford, "Genesis," pp. 400-401; memorandum by Adams, n.d. (ca. Nov. 27, 1823), Ford, "Genesis," pp. 394-395.

with neither Adams nor the administration risking the charge of toadying to the mother country.

While awaiting Monroe's return, expected in the last week of October, Adams had several conversations with the Russian minister. He went out of his way to be cordial. When Tuyll showed him a draft report of their earlier meeting, Adams asked that the final paragraph be expanded so that it would record Adams's pleasure at having "new proof of the current, generous, and wholly moderate views which characterize the policy of the Emperor." Concerned by newspaper stories saying that the Holy Alliance intended to aid Spain in South America, Tuyll suggested that something about their actual exchanges be published in the semiauthoritative Washington *National Intelligencer*. Adams demurred. According to his own later recollection, he told Tuyll that it would be preferable for any statement to be part of the annual message which the President would soon present to Congress. Texts of notes between them could be appended to the message. Adams thus had already begun to think of the President's message as a vehicle for a unilateral declaration of policy.

Monroe's return was delayed by his wife's illness. He did not finally ride in from Virginia until November 5. Adams then walked over to the White House. The two exchanged a few words about the pending question of how to answer Canning. Adams, however, turned the conversation to the new subject of what should be said or written to Tuyll. While Monroe probably recognized that nothing in Tuyll's presentation to Adams necessitated a formal reply, Adams had committed the administration by telling Tuyll that one would be forthcoming. In effect, Adams had created a supplementary issue which also had a forcing deadline.[8]

The cabinet met on the second day after the President's return. Crawford did not come. Though still at a friend's home in Virginia, he was reported to be recuperating and likely to

---

8. Ford, "Genesis," pp. 395-397; Tuyll to Nesselrode, Oct. 27, 1823, ibid., pp. 400-401; Monroe to Calhoun, Nov. 3, 1823, Calhoun, *Papers*, VIII, 348; memorandum by Adams, n.d. (ca. Nov. 27, 1823), Ford, "Genesis," pp. 397-398.

arrive any day. Actually, he was temporarily paralyzed and unable to see or speak, owing either to a stroke or to an overdose of medicine taken as a cure for erysipelas, but his true condition was a well-kept secret.[9] The attorney general was also absent. Hence, Monroe, Adams, Calhoun, and Southard were the only men at the table.[10]

The question of how to answer Canning took precedence. By this time, Monroe had comments from both Jefferson and Madison.[11]

Jefferson emphatically recommended acceptance of the British overture. Though asserting that Americans should never become entangled in European broils and never "suffer Europe to intermeddle with cis-Atlantic affairs," Jefferson reasoned that Britain was more dangerous than any other power; that the United States would be completely secure if Britain were on its side; that "nothing would tend more to knit our affections than to be fighting once more side by side"; and that a war for South America, if it developed, would be a war primarily in America's interest. He predicted that, in any case, the joint Anglo-American declaration would probably prevent the war. The only drawback noted by Jefferson was that an accord with England would block annexation of Cuba; but he accounted this a small price to pay, especially since he intimated that it would not necessarily foreclose acceptance into the union of a free Cuba that voluntarily applied for admission as a state.

Madison, too, advised that an alliance with Britain would be advantageous. "There ought not to be any backwardness," he wrote, "in meeting her in the way she has proposed." Going farther, Madison urged that the United States and Britain not only combine to protect the Western Hemisphere but also join in supporting the Greeks.

---

9. Chase C. Mooney, *William H. Crawford, 1772-1834* (Lexington, Ky: The University Press of Kentucky, 1974), p. 241, discusses Crawford's illness.

10. The account of the cabinet meeting given below is based entirely on the Adams diary, Nov. 7, 1823.

11. Jefferson to Monroe, Oct. 24, 1823, Monroe, *Writings*, VII, 391-393; Madison to Monroe, Oct. 30, 1823, ibid., pp. 394-395.

These two letters undoubtedly encouraged Monroe to believe that his instinctive reaction had been right. That from Jefferson was doubly encouraging, for Jefferson was known to favor Crawford for the presidency and was known moreover to be venerated by many of Crawford's supporters.[12] His letter thus represented a virtual guarantee that a decision to accept Canning's offer would not be attacked by Crawford or by his friends in Congress. Of course, Monroe knew Jefferson and Madison to be astute politicians, and he may have suspected that their advice was influenced by awareness of the probable predicament for Adams. For him, however, the important fact was that the two former Presidents were on record as supporting the course of action toward which he himself leaned.

For the time being, Monroe nevertheless kept his opinion to himself. At any rate, he did not voice it in Adams's hearing, nor for the moment did he let Adams know of the letters from Jefferson and Madison. Quite possibly, he had already made some private disclosures to Calhoun, for Calhoun was his favorite among the cabinet and probably among the presidential candidates. In the formal cabinet meeting, Monroe merely issued a neutral invitation for discussion of the British offer and asked Calhoun to speak first, perhaps knowing that Calhoun would argue a case for accepting the offer.

Since the only record of the meeting is that composed by Adams, we know a good deal less about the points made by Calhoun than about those scored against him by Adams. It appears, however, that Calhoun presented theses similar to those in the letters from Jefferson and Madison: the United States would gain safety by being allied with the only power that could do it harm; the alliance would protect Latin American independence; it was perhaps the best means of deterring aid to Spain by the Holy Allies. Despite what he had earlier written to Southard, Calhoun

---

12. Jefferson to Gallatin, Aug. 2, 1823, Papers of Albert Gallatin, New-York Historical Society; Jefferson to Warden, Oct. 31, 1823, Papers of David Bailie Warden, Maryland Historical Society; Margaret Bayard Smith to Mrs. Boyd, Dec. 19, 1823, Gaillard Hunt, ed., *The First Forty Years of Washington Society in the Family Letters of Margaret Bayard Smith* (New York: Frederick Ungar, 1906), pp. 162-163.

prophesied that England would not oppose the Holy Allies unless sure of American cooperation. She would not risk throwing the trade of Europe into American hands.

Adams's diary entry indicates that he did not meet these arguments head-on. Instead, he asked Calhoun whether he would willingly forfeit a claim not only to Cuba but also to Texas. That would be the consequence of agreeing to all of Canning's points, he asserted, for the United States would thereby promise to take *no* territory in the former Spanish empire. This was an adroit thrust, for it reminded both Calhoun and Monroe of a line of criticism likely to be pursued by Clay and by some supporters of Andrew Jackson. Calhoun's response was that England could take these lands more easily, and the proposed agreement would guarantee that she did not do so.

Adams also pointed out the danger that the United States would seem to be making herself subordinate to England. According to his notes, everyone agreed that the administration should avoid giving such an impression. Monroe suggested that this might be accomplished if, instead of merely authorizing Rush to act, the government were to send a special envoy to Europe for the sole purpose of proclaiming American concurrence in opposing intervention in Latin America by the Holy Allies.

Before discussion reached a point of decision, Adams shifted the subject matter:

> I remarked that the communications recently received from the Russian Minister, Baron Tuyl [sic], afforded, as I thought, a very suitable and convenient opportunity for us to take our stand against the Holy Alliance, and at the same time to decline the overture of Great Britain. It would be more candid, as well as more dignified to avow our principles explicitly to Russia and France, than to come in as a cockboat in the wake of the British man-of-war.

Since Adams had not prepared drafts of possible responses to Rush, he could be sure that the cabinet meeting would yield no definitive decision on answering Canning. At worst, he could force a second or third round of debate on the specific language to be used. Adams did, however, have ready in his pocket a draft note to the Russian minister. In careful language, it reproached the tsar for refusing to recognize Latin American nations, and it asserted that these nations were "irrevocably independent of Spain."[13] As Adams doubtless hoped and expected, the rest of the cabinet meeting was consumed by argument about the note's wording and about what he should say orally in answer to Tuyll's question about the continued neutrality of the United States. By late afternoon, Calhoun had to leave. Adams could thus record with satisfaction that "the meeting broke up without coming to any conclusion."

Adams stayed behind to talk privately with the President. Either because he had sensed Monroe's attitude or because he did not want to dispute Calhoun's arguments in Calhoun's absence, he refrained from elaborating the case against allying with Britain. Instead, he concentrated on the prospective exchanges with Tuyll. He did urge the President, however, to think of those exchanges and the reply to Canning as somehow "parts of a combined system of policy and adapted to each other." To this vague proposition, the President could hardly dissent.

ADAMS ON THE DEFENSIVE

More than a week went by before the cabinet returned to Canning's proposition. Thus far, while Monroe and his advisers had regarded the issue as of the highest importance, they had felt that there was time for careful meditation. Canning had not disclosed to Rush any intelligence showing that a decision was urgent. Even Calhoun expressed puzzlement as to why he had not done so and why Rush had not pressed him on the subject. It was reasonable to assume that the continental powers would not make a final decision about the Spanish empire until the French subdued the revolutionaries in Spain proper, and dispatches from Gibraltar described the rebels as in control of

---

13. Adams to Tuyll (draft), Ford, "Adams," p. 692.

Cadiz and its environs, prepared to withstand a long siege, and confident of their eventual resurgence.[14]

The week between the two cabinet meetings brought the dismaying news that Cadiz had fallen and that the French were in control of all Spain. Reportedly, moreover, a French fleet was already preparing to transport across the Atlantic a large contingent of the Spanish troops that had fought for Ferdinand in Spain.[15] The American government, it appeared, no longer had leisure for a long debate.

Monroe seemed on the verge of decision. During the week, he repeatedly summoned Adams to the White House. He said that the fall of Cadiz alarmed him and that he feared all the South American states might be reconquered. Just before the cabinet was to meet, he showed Adams the letters from Jefferson and Madison.[16]

Adams wrote in his diary that he thought the President to be still undecided.[17] Probably, Monroe was exerting himself to get Adams's concurrence in a decision to accept Canning's terms, for he must have recognized that Adams would see the potential political costs to himself, and, if he had not known it before, he had learned from Adams's recent published exchanges with Jonathan Russell about the Ghent negotiations that it was the secretary of state's habit to keep detailed records useful for defending himself in controversies. Monroe could foresee at least a slight possibility that Adams would dissent from a decision to ally with England, make his dissent known through newspapers supporting him and through friends such as Rufus King, the chairman of the Senate Foreign Relations Committee, or perhaps even resign

14. Baltimore *Weekly Register*, Sept. 6, 20, Oct. 25, Nov. 8, 1823; New York *National Advocate*, quoted ibid., Nov. 1, 1823; Washington *Republican*, Nov. 3, 1823; Washington *National Journal*, Nov. 8, 1823; Richmond *Enquirer*, Nov. 9, 1823.

15. Baltimore *Patriot and Mercantile Advertiser*, Nov. 12, 1823; Washington *National Intelligencer*, Nov. 13, 15, 1823. The news seemed sufficiently important to be noted in the diary of a Maine man who otherwise paid little notice to national or international affairs: entry of Nov. 10, 1823, *The Journals of Hezekiah Prince, Jr., 1822-1828* (New York: Crown Publishers, 1965), p. 99.

16. Adams diary, Nov. 15, 1823.

17. Ibid.

and speak out against the administration. If so, the charge of courting Federalists would be leveled against Calhoun, and Monroe himself might come under attack, losing his cherished position as President of the whole nation and a figure above politics. The whole purpose of accepting Canning's offer might then be undone by a domestic debate which persuaded both the English and the continental powers that Americans were too divided to act effectively.

Adams's ability to use his leverage depended, of course, on the case he could make for casting a dissenting vote or resigning. Even to himself, he could hardly justify such action simply on the ground that he could not afford to be charged with pro-English or pro-Federalist leanings, and thus far the objections he had been able to frame were insufficient. Having opposed efforts to acquire Cuba and Texas, he could not break with the President solely on ground that a compact with England would prevent the United States from expanding. Indeed, when making the point in the earlier cabinet meeting, he had to take the jesuitical line that the United States should not make it impossible for Cubans and Texans to secure independence and then ask voluntarily for admission to the union.[18] Nor could Adams build a critical issue out of his phrase about a cock boat in the wake of a man-of-war, for Monroe was plainly prepared to arrange the formalities in such a way that the United States would seem to act as England's equal.

Nothing in the week between the two cabinet meetings strengthened Adams's position. Obviously, the news from Spain did not. A conversation with the British chargé was unencouraging, for Addington professed to understand Canning's motives no better than Adams. The Russian gambit seemed to have played out. Adams had worked out with Tuyll a dispatch in which the Russian reported the President to have confirmed Adams's pledge that the United States would remain neutral so long as European powers did so. In addition, a note was handed

---

18. Adams diary, Nov. 7, 1823. For Adams's earlier statements on Texas and Cuba, see ibid., April 13, 1820, Sept. 27, 30, Oct. 1, 1822.

to the Russian commenting on the tsar's refusal to recognize Colombia. Partially rewritten by Monroe, it merely expressed regret that the tsar's principles prevented him from acting as the United States had.[19] None of these communications took the place of a reply to Canning, and this being the case, Adams could not compose a commentary about them for the President's annual message which would serve such a purpose. The paragraphs he had drafted did not answer the urgent question posed by Canning's overture.[20]

When the cabinet met on November 18, it was once again an assembly of four—Monroe, Adams, Calhoun, and Southard. The President had a note saying that Crawford was still indisposed but would arrive in a few days. The attorney general was absent in Baltimore.[21]

Calhoun restated the case for acceptance of the British proposal. Answering one objection in advance, he suggested that Rush be authorized to act jointly with Canning if satisfied that circumstances required doing so. In other words, Canning would have to disclose his information about the emergency. Calhoun felt certain, however, that the emergency was real. Indeed, he gave Adams the impression of believing that the forces allegedly readying to sail from Spain might be sufficient in themselves to reconquer Mexico and South America.

Adams did not dispute Calhoun's estimate. He conceded that Spain, if backed by the Holy Alliance, might have some success. He voiced doubt, however, as to whether it could last. The urge for independence would continue, he argued; and in a few years the Latin Americans would once again break loose. If that were not so, they lacked spirit and resource, and the United States would err if it linked its fortunes with theirs.

---

19. Adams diary, Nov. 10, 1823; Tuyll to Nesselrode, Nov. 11, 1823, Ford, "Genesis," pp. 401-402; Adams to Tuyll (draft), Ford, "Adams," p. 692; Monroe to Adams, Nov. 10, 1823, enclosing a revision of the draft, Ford, "Adams," pp. 692-693, 695.

20. Adams to Monroe, Nov. 13 (17?), 1823, enclosing notes for the annual message, Nikolai N. Bolkhovitinov, "Russia and the Declaration of the Non-Colonization Principle: New Archival Evidence," *Oregon Historical Quarterly*, 72 (June 1971), 119.

21. Crawford to Monroe, Nov. 15, 1823, Papers of William H. Crawford, Duke University Library. The account of the cabinet meeting given here is based entirely on Adams diary, Nov. 18, 1823.

Again, the case that Adams could put together was not one which he could take to the public as adequate justification for a break with the rest of the administration. He would not win popularity by saying that he was ready to let Spain regain her empire for a few years. Having taken credit for extending recognition to the new republics, he could not consistently declare that they were unfit for American support. In Adams's arguments and in the testiness of his subsequent diary entry, one senses the approach of desperation.

The secretary of state still had the advantage, however, of operational control. Propriety prevented Calhoun from bringing to the meeting a draft dispatch to Rush. Even Monroe would have felt embarrassed about thus usurping Adams's function. Though he had tried to get Adams to prepare a draft, he had not succeeded. Adams had responded that he would draw one up once he knew the President's decision.[22] Hence the cabinet could only debate the principle. The extensive set of issues that would be posed by alternative wordings of a message to Rush remained for holding actions by the secretary of state.

On the principle involved, Adams elected not to make a determined fight. He wrote in his diary:

> After much discussion, I said I thought we should bring the whole answer to Mr. Canning's proposals to a test of right and wrong. Considering the South Americans as independent nations, they themselves, and no other nation, had the *right* to dispose of their condition. *We* have no right to dispose of them, either alone or in conjunction with other nations. Neither have any other nations the right of disposing of them without their consent. This principle will give us a clue to answer all Mr. Canning's questions with candor and confidence.

The passage is opaque. In this respect, it probably gives an accurate representation of what Adams said. He did not indicate what answers to Canning's questions his test of right or wrong would yield. Nor did he say that he would refuse to sign a

---

22. Adams diary, Nov. 13, 1823.

dispatch agreeing to Canning's proposals. And he left the cabinet meeting having at last promised to draft an instruction to Rush.

Adams gave one sign, furthermore, that he might reconcile himself to going along with the British proposal. For when the possibility of sending a special envoy came up again, Adams joined in putting forward names. When Monroe said that his own first choice would be Madison, Adams became positively enthusiastic. Though he had seen the letter in which Madison endorsed an English alliance and recommended joint action in Greece as well as Latin America, Adams probably recognized at least subconsciously that if it were Madison who signed the accord with England, critics would find it much harder to call it the work of a crypto-Federalist secretary of state. Perhaps this consideration was in Monroe's mind when he made the suggestion. During the meeting, Monroe also took occasion to announce that he would appoint James Brown of Louisiana minister to France. Since Brown was Clay's brother-in-law, the news served as a warning to Adams not to expect Clay's support for a contention that an English alliance would block American expansion. Monroe can be interpreted as trying to box in Adams so that he would have to go along with the rest of the cabinet. In any case, he, Calhoun, and Southard probably left the session feeling that a decision to accept Canning's offer had practically been made and that after one long go-around on the text of an instruction to Rush, Adams would give in to the majority.

THE SECOND ROUND OF DEBATE

Calhoun was already euphoric. The previous week had brought reports of elections in New York state. The People's Party organized during the summer to combat the Albany Regency had captured a number of seats in the state legislature. The legislative majority that had called for nomination of the Republican presidential candidate by a congressional caucus no longer existed. Since this majority had been assumed to be pro-Crawford, Calhoun interpreted the outcome as meaning also that Crawford would not get New York's votes in the general election. He was aware, of course, that many leaders in the People's Party were for Adams, but perhaps on the basis of expectation that an English alliance would kill Adams's candidacy, he discounted this fact. He wrote to one of his captains in New York, "if I mistake not, Mr. Adams will fall without a blow." After the second cabinet meeting on the Canning proposals, a congressman in close touch with Calhoun wrote that he knew as a certainty that Calhoun would soon inherit Adams's strength in New England.[23]

Since meetings of the cabinet ordinarily took place on Mondays, Adams had a week in which to prepare the promised draft. It started badly for him, for Wednesday's Washington newspapers carried a report that Britain was sending consuls to various Latin American posts, and Addington came by later in the day to confirm the report and add cheerily his own private opinion that British recognition of Latin American governments might occur any day. Though with misgivings, Adams had already backed up Rush by informing the British chargé that Rush had power to come to terms with Canning on condition that Britain did recognize some of those governments.[24] He undoubtedly feared that the condition would turn out to have been met and he would learn that Rush and Canning had issued their joint declaration, with his having no more voice in the matter.

On the other hand, fresh dispatches from Rush offered some reassurance. Dated October 2 and October 10 and received in Washington on November 16, they described Canning as having suddenly become less exigent. Indeed, the later of the two told of

---

23. Calhoun to Charles G. Haines, Nov. 9, 1823, Calhoun, *Papers*, VIII, 355-356; (cf. Calhoun to Joseph G. Swift, Nov. 9, 1823, ibid., p. 356, and Calhoun to Wheaton, Nov. 9, 1823, ibid., p. 357); George McDuffie to ?, Nov. 21, 1823, A. R. Newsome, ed., "Correspondence of John C. Calhoun, George McDuffie and Charles Fisher relating to the Presidential Campaign of 1824," *North Carolina Historical Review*, 7 (Oct. 1930), 489.

24. Washington *National Intelligencer*, Nov. 20, 1823; Washington *Republican*, Nov. 20, 1823; Adams diary, Nov. 20, 1823; Henry U. Addington to George Canning, Nov. 3, 1823, Bradford Perkins, "The Suppressed Dispatch of H. U. Addington: Washington, November 3, 1823," *Hispanic American Historical Review*, 38 (Nov. 1957), 480-485.

Canning's deliberately passing up opportunities to revive discussion of joint action concerning Latin America. In words gladdening to Adams, Rush wrote, "I therefore consider that all further discussion between us in relation to it is now at an end."[25] This information at least provided Adams with a new argument against accepting the earlier offer. It also supplied grounds for hope that no alliance would result, even if the American government said yes.

Equally heartening for Adams was reflection on a document delivered by Tuyll. On Sunday, the Russian had brought him a circular signed on August 30 by his foreign minister, Count Nesselrode. Obviously composed for a European audience, it congratulated the French on having driven into the confines of Barcelona and Cadiz "the manufacturers of Spain's maladies." It spoke of the unity and concord of the powers as having created a "new political system"—one in which limited police actions would suffice to protect legitimate regimes against men with wrongheaded theories or criminal aims. The defeat of revolution in Spain demonstrated that God smiled on the Holy Alliance, it went on, and the members of the Alliance would justify God's favor by taking no advantages for themselves from their success but rather by assuring that the restored monarch was sufficiently firmly seated to protect his country from error and misfortune without future help from outside. If prosperity for Spain were not an immediate result, it said, that fact would be a reproach to the Spanish king and to the Holy Allies. Though the document was merely an example of Russia's pious rhetoric, significant chiefly in indicating that the tsar would frown on France's seeking to compensate herself with a Spanish colony, it was potentially of great use for Adams. An " 'Io Triumphe' over the fallen cause of revolution, with sturdy promises to keep it down," it provided him with means for reviving his earlier stratagem.[26]

While meditating how best to exploit the intelligence from

25. Rush to Adams, Oct. 2, 10, 1823, Monroe, *Writings*, VII, 386-390.
26. Nesselrode to Tuyll, Aug. 30, 1823, Ford, "Genesis," pp. 402-405; Adams diary, Nov. 17, 1823.

London and the new opportunity offered by Tuyll, Adams made the most of his political advantage as the drafter of diplomatic correspondence. He prepared an instruction which would have authorized Rush to say that the United States concurred with Britain in all the five points upon which Canning had proposed a joint declaration.[27] The document would not, however, constitute a power of attorney for signing such a declaration. Instead, it would invite further discussion. With regard to the point that recognition of Latin American republics was a matter "of time and circumstances," it offered a barbed commentary, the purport of which was that the United States viewed recognition as right and Britain as having a moral obligation to extend it. With regard to Canning's point that Britain and the United States should not object to negotiated arrangements between the new nations and the mother country, the draft stipulated agreement on condition that such arrangements not include trade privileges for either. Finally, it asserted that accord on all other points turned on Britain's agreeing with the United States that the two "could not see with indifference any attempt by one or more powers of Europe to dispose of the Freedom or Independence of those States, without their consent, or against their will." Four paragraphs of elaboration implied that if a Latin American state chose voluntarily to relinquish its independence (and presumably to seek annexation by the United States), it would be immoral for either Britain or the United States to stand in the way. All in all, Adams's draft was so couched as to provoke prolonged and probably inconclusive negotiations via the trans-Atlantic mails.

Monroe received this document well in advance of the scheduled cabinet meeting. Whether he discussed it with Calhoun, Southard, or anyone else, we do not know. In any case, he returned it to Adams with proposals for extensive amendments.[28] On the critical final point, Monroe wanted Adams's language stricken altogether. In place of it, he proposed saying straight-

27. Adams to Rush (draft), Ford, "Genesis," pp. 385-387.
28. Ibid., pp. 387-388.

forwardly that the United States was not prepared to renounce Cuba forever. Although the event might be far off, if Cuba ever became independent, were recognized as independent by Spain, and then applied to enter the Union, the United States wished to remain free to consider its admission. At the same time Monroe wanted to say explicitly that if Britain accepted the American stipulations, the United States was prepared "to move in concert" with her.

Adams protested none of Monroe's amendments except this last. The question of what was to be said about Cuba and Texas was of relatively little importance to him. If there were to be a serious attack on Adams and the administration for not taking a firmer line, it would be led by Clay, and the Brown appointment presumably ensured that Clay would speak softly. The central problem for Adams remained, as from the beginning, the posture to be adopted toward Britain. The President's formula threatened to result in a joint declaration which some Americans would interpret as the handiwork of an England-lover. Hence Adams drew up a substitute paragraph saying that if the two governments reached an understanding, they should issue independent declarations.[29] If Rush judged that circumstances called for joint action, he should so report. The decision would then be made in Washington. It was, above all, the *appearance* of an alliance with England that Adams wanted to avoid.

When the cabinet met on November 21, the draft instructions to Rush led the agenda.[30] Calhoun's stand was surprising. According to Adams's diary, Calhoun supported him rather than the President on most points at issue. Like Adams, for example, Calhoun argued against any implication that the United States would acquiesce in special trade arrangements between Spain and her former colonies. Perhaps he was sensitive to constituents in Charleston and friends in Baltimore who were interested in South American trade. Perhaps he reasoned that the absence of a demand for most-favored-nation treatment would displease

---

29. Ibid., p. 388.
30. Again, the account of the cabinet meeting has to be based entirely on Adams diary, Nov. 21, 1823.

other merchants and shippers in east coast cities who were now supporters of Adams and who, if all went well, could soon be his supporters instead.

Also, Calhoun backed up Adams on the question of emergency powers for Rush. According to Adams's diary, Calhoun said he preferred Adams's substitute paragraph which authorized an independent declaration parallel to one by Canning but required that any joint declaration be referred back to Washington. Since Calhoun had earlier argued strongly for letting Rush act jointly with Canning, his reversal is not easily explained. It may be that he judged the difference between parallel declarations and a joint declaration negligible, in terms of their prospective effects on the European powers and on the American electorate. In any case, Calhoun's siding with Adams was sufficient to persuade the President to accept Adams's amendments. The cabinet thus agreed on a text which expressed substantial acceptance of Canning's points and authorized Rush to issue a statement to such effect if he judged it desirable.[31]

This instruction was designed to be read verbatim to Canning and perhaps eventually communicated to Congress and published. There was some discussion of a supplementary instruction for Rush's private guidance, but Adams did not yet have a complete draft to exhibit.

Adams also mentioned his most recent conversation with Tuyll. He had already described it to both Monroe and Calhoun. Now he said merely that he planned to prepare a paper stating disagreement with the tsar's principles, summarizing the principles of the United States, disclaiming any intention of imposing those principles on Europe, but asking the European powers to "abstain from the attempt to spread their principles in the American hemisphere, or to subjugate by force any part of these continents." Clearly, Adams again had in mind using correspondence with Russia as a means of stating American policy in such a way as to make it seem wholly dissociated from Britain's. Since he had nothing more specific to present and since the afternoon

---

31. Adams to Rush, Nov. 29, 1823, Monroe, *Writings*, pp. 405-408.

was wearing on, his colleagues did not at this time raise questions about the tactic. Monroe said that Adams should go ahead and draw up a text.

THE DRAFT PRESIDENTIAL MESSAGE

At this point, the President spread on the table a draft of the annual message which he would have to deliver to Congress eleven days thence. He had already collected from each cabinet member proposals as to what it should say about their business. The paragraphs drawn up by Adams included a report on American recognition of Latin American republics and expressions of confidence about their future but said nothing about a possible concert between the United States and Britain. In effect, Adams recommended that the President repeat points in his previous annual messages, introducing only one new theme—a declaration that there should be no future European colonization in the Western Hemisphere.[32]

Adams had developed this idea during the preceding summer. The stimulus was the controversy with Russia and Britain over the northern Pacific Ocean and the northwest coast of North America. Not only had the tsar issued a ukaz claiming sovereignty over the north Pacific but a Russian trading post had been set up at Bodega Bay in California. Meanwhile, British and American traders were quarreling about their respective rights at the mouth of the Columbia River. The chief American claimant was John Jacob Astor, whose fur-buyers had operated there but had been dispossessed by the British during the War of 1812. Congressmen who were friends of Astor had introduced resolutions calling on the administration to assert American rights in the region; but they had not been able to muster the votes to pass them. Debates in the winter of 1822-1823 had then suggested that the question might figure in the presidential campaign; for the friend of Astor who took the lead was a Virginian prom-

---

32. Adams to Monroe, Nov. 13 (17?), 1823, Bolkhovitinov, "Russia," p. 119.

inent among Crawfordites; a seconding speech was made by Francis Baylies, an anti-Adams man from Massachusetts, who argued that control of the northwest coast was a need of New England whalers; and other supporting speeches came from partisans of Clay. Friends of Adams in the House elected to oppose the measure chiefly on the ground that discretion should be left to the President.[33] Although the resolution was shelved, Adams must have recognized that he might hear more of the matter later.

Sometime in the spring, Monroe passed on to Adams a letter from James Lloyd, a newly elected senator from Massachusetts.[34] At great length, Lloyd argued the importance of resisting Russian pretensions in the Pacific. He cited the opinions of Boston fur merchants, from some of whom Adams had already heard, to the effect that furbearing sea otters had to be hunted in the waters claimed by the tsar and that the future of the northwest coast had a direct bearing on the prosperity of New England. Since Lloyd was counted as a probable but not certain supporter of Adams for the presidency, his opinion was one to which the secretary of state had to pay close attention. Almost at the same time, Adams was urged by Charles Jared Ingersoll, a well-connected Philadelphia politician, to take a bold stand on the northwest coast question.[35]

Whatever conclusion Adams had drawn from the debates in the House, he clearly felt that he needed to give satisfaction to men such as Lloyd and Ingersoll. The latter had advocated resisting the tsar by force. "What a glorious diversion it would be for the Greeks and Spaniards," he had written, "if the only republic were to take that father of mischief . . . by the beard and crush his power by sea." Somewhat disingenuously, Adams responded to Ingersoll that his sentiments on this point were "spirited and rational. I would call them wise, had not my own

---

33. 17th Congress, 2d session, *Annals of Congress* (Dec. 17-18, 1822, Jan. 24-25, Feb. 17, 1823), pp. 250-251, 397-406, 413-423, 679-686, 691-695.

34. Lloyd to Monroe, May 16, 1823, Monroe Papers, partially reproduced in Bolkhovitinov, "Russia," p. 116.

35. Ingersoll to Adams, May 10, 1823, Adams Papers.

entirely coincided with them." His actual misgivings he confided to his diary: "I find proof enough to put down the Russian argument; but how shall we answer the Russian cannon?"[36]

Adams obtained consent from Monroe and the cabinet to a formula which offered hope of at least postponing any conflict. It was to propose to St. Petersburg and London that the area of actual mutual interest—the waters and coast south of 55° north latitude—remain open to all parties for a period of years.[37] Apparently, it occurred to Adams that, if the practical solution to the pressing problem were on its way to acceptance, he and the administration might strike a posture which would be popular at home and perhaps be useful eventually as a point of reference in later diplomatic negotiations. He first articulated it as a letter to Senator Lloyd. "What right has Russia to *any* colonial footing on the *Continent* of North America? Has she any that we are bound to recognize?—And is it not time for the American *Nations* to inform the Sovereigns of Europe that the American continents are no longer open to the Settlement of *new* European colonies?"[38]

Although there is no evidence on the point, it seems probable that Adams showed these lines to Monroe. He was responding, after all, to a letter originally addressed to the President. If so, Monroe must have registered no objection to Adams's sentiments, for Adams soon spoke in a like sense to Tuyll. Afterward, the Russian reported that the American government was likely to press "the general principle that all foreign powers should renounce definitely and forever the establishment of new colonies in either of the Americas." After review of the text by Monroe, statements to this effect were included in instructions to the American ministers in London and St. Petersburg.[39] Adams

---

36. Adams to Ingersoll, June 19, 1823, Worthington C. Ford, ed., *The Writings of John Quincy Adams*, 7 vols. (New York: Macmillan, 1913-1917) (hereafter, Adams, *Writings*), VII, 488; Adams diary, July 1, 1823.

37. Ibid., June 28, 1823.

38. Adams to Lloyd, July 15, 1823, Bolkhovitinov, "Russia," p. 117.

39. Tuyll to Nesselrode, July 24, 1823, ibid., p. 118; Adams diary, July 17, 1823; Adams to Rush, July 22, 1823, William R. Manning, ed., *Diplomatic Correspondence of the United States: Canadian Relations 1784-1860*, 3 vols. in progress (Washington, D.C.: Carnegie

had thus prepared a record which could, if necessary, be exhibited to Congress and the public.

All this had occurred during the summer. Since then, Adams had heard no protests from Russia or Britain or their representatives in Washington. Moreover, he had received information that the Russian-American Company, which acted for the Russian government in the north Pacific, was now without power in St. Petersburg, and he had been told that Canning believed the Russians to have renounced "all their extravagant claims and pretensions."[40] Preparing paragraphs for the President's annual message, Adams had therefore decided to include a sentence saying that the northwest coast negotiations have provided "occasion . . . for asserting, as a principle in which the rights and interests of the United States are involved, that the American continents, by the free and independent condition which they have assumed and maintain, are henceforth not to be considered as subjects for future colonization by any European powers."

In his draft, Monroe retained Adams's language. He also included Adams's summaries of various negotiations in progress. He had added, however, an introduction which warned that republicanism was under attack in the world and that Americans might find themselves once again compelled to go to war to defend their principles. Further, Monroe had penned a denunciation of France and the Holy Alliance for forcibly putting down liberalism in Spain, and he had introduced a passage declaring Greece to be rightly independent and recommending that Congress agree to dispatch an American minister.[41]

Adams took exception to all of these additions. As he summarized his argument when recording the debate in his diary:

Endowment, 1940——), II, 55-65; Adams to Henry Middleton, July 22, 1823, 59th Congress, 2d session, Senate Document No. 162, "Proceedings of the Alaskan Boundary Tribunal," II, 47-51.

40. Middleton to Adams, Aug. 8, 1822, "Proceedings of the Alaskan Boundary Tribunal," II, 42-46; Christopher Hughes to Adams, Aug. 27, 1823, Bolkhovitinov, "Russia," p. 122.

41. Adams diary, Nov. 21, 1823. Unfortunately, Monroe's original draft has not been located. One is dependent therefore on Adams's recollected summary.

"This message would be a summons to arms—to arms against all Europe, and for objects of policy exclusively European— Greece and Spain."[42] Spain, France, and Russia, he predicted, would sever relations. An administration that could pride itself on achieving greater peace and security than any of its predecessors would enter its last year rousing the nation for war. In veiled allusion to the possibility of dissent like that in the period of the Napoleonic wars, Adams pleaded, "Let us use all possible means to carry the opinion of the nation with us."

Calhoun came to the President's support. There *was* peril, he said; republicanism was menaced as never before, and the nation should know it. The invasion of Spain had been the most direct attack ever on the principle of popular rule. The cause of Greece was just. In any case, if the administration did not lead, Clay would mobilize Congress and force recognition.

Calhoun's enthusiasm was understandable. If a sense of crisis produced reproach, it would fall on Adams. The secretary of war, who had regularly been appealing for military preparedness, would very likely be seen as more farsighted than Adams and certainly more farsighted than Crawford. In the forthcoming session of Congress, the business of the War and Navy departments would take precedence over that of the others. The publicity would benefit Calhoun, and, if the requested appropriations came, he would have a fresh armory of contracts and commissions. The recognition of Greece would not only deprive Clay of a talking point but also create a dilemma for Adams, for Adams would either have to sponsor the appointment of the Massachusetts Federalist Edward Everett, which would outrage Republicans, or refuse to sponsor him, thus alienating him and his friends and perhaps pushing more New England Federalists into Calhoun's camp.

Although Monroe defended his own text, he was not unbending. Whether or not he saw merit in Adams's arguments, he could not help being impressed with the passion behind them. Possibly, too, he heard Adam's reference to the danger

---

42. My description continues to be based on Adams diary, Nov. 21, 1823.

of a disunited public as warning that the secretary of state himself might mobilize opposition if his opinions were ignored. In any event, Monroe closed the meeting by saying that he would work up an alternative draft.

On the following day, Monroe received a visit from Adams.[43] Ostensibly, the secretary of state came to deliver a finished draft of a supplementary instruction to Rush. Actually, Adams did not regard it as complete. He planned to draw up yet another supplementary instruction to Rush. But it was enough of a unit to be sent by itself, and it gave Adams a pretext for reopening some of the previous day's questions, for it included three points which had been agreed upon in cabinet meetings: (1) British recognition of the Latin American states was indispensable for joint action; (2) Rush should not press too hard for recognition but should let the British act on their own; and (3) he should refuse to attend a European conference about Latin America unless Latin American governments were also represented.[44] The document was faithful to the compromises in the cabinet in that it expressed eagerness for "united ends and Councils" and "a harmonious concert of measures" but stopped short of promising that the United States would act jointly with England.

After handing the document to the President, Adams began to talk of the annual message. He wrote in his diary, "I said there were considerations of weight which I could not even easily mention at a Cabinet meeting." By his own account, he went on to argue again that Monroe should not conclude his presidency by talking of the peril of war. Instead, he should deliver the government to his successor "at peace and in amity with all the world." Picking up the previous day's discussion of Greece, Adams predicted that Clay would not want outright recognition because he might become President and would not want to take office "encumbered with a quarrel with all Europe." Touching Monroe's most sensitive spot, Adams argued that such a finish to his presidency would put a cloud on all the rest. Men might

---

43. Adams diary, Nov. 22, 1823.
44. Adams to Rush, Nov. 30, 1823, Ford, 'Genesis," pp. 389-392.

say, for example, that he had made a mistake in recognizing the Latin American states if the consequence were war. Adams said that he would have no objection to general expressions of sympathy for Spain and Greece, such as had appeared in the 1822 annual message, but he begged the President "to avoid anything which may be construed as hostility to the allies."

Monroe also had advice from others. He discussed the message with Albert Gallatin, who had just completed seven years as United States minister to France. Subsequently, Gallatin led Adams to believe that he had made comments similar to Adams's except with regard to Greece. On that point, he favored not only recognition but dispatch of a naval squadron to the Mediterranean. Characteristically, Adams detected nothing but wisdom in Gallatin's apparent concurrence with him, but on the one point of dissent he saw a self-interested motive—an irresponsible desire by Gallatin for popularity as "the great champion of Grecian liberty."[45] It may be, of course, that Gallatin exaggerated the extent to which he otherwise seconded Adams's counsel. If not, however, the fact probably made an impression on Monroe not only because Gallatin was a figure in the Republican Pantheon but also because he was a confidant and adviser of Crawford. What Gallatin said in the White House, Crawford might say in public, or at least have said for him by the *National Intelligencer*, the Richmond *Enquirer*, and friends in Congress. If Gallatin's report to Adams was accurate, then the President had to compose the alternative draft of his message in awareness that, if unchanged, it might be attacked by partisans of both Adams and Crawford and perhaps by the two secretaries themselves.

Whether Monroe was concerned only about Adams or about both Crawford and Adams, he did draw up an alternative which satisfied the secretary of state.[46] While the introduction retained a tone of foreboding, it became vague. The paragraphs

---

45. Adams diary, Nov. 24, 1823.
46. Ibid., Nov. 26, 1823; Annual Message from the President, Dec. 2, 1823, Monroe, *Writings*, VII, 325-342.

mentioning Spain were rewritten to emphasize that, while Americans might deplore events there, it was the policy of the United States not to take part in European wars and not to interfere in the internal concerns of European powers. The revised text expressed alarm only lest the Holy Alliance attempt to impose its political system in the Western Hemisphere. The United States would regard any such attempt, said Monroe, as "dangerous to our peace and safety." The American government could not "behold such interposition in any form with indifference." Monroe added, however, that neutrality with regard to conflict between Spain and the Latin American states remained "the true policy of the United States . . . , in the hope that other powers will pursue the same course." The passage on Greece was amended so as to express ardent hope for Greek independence without proposing recognition of a Greek government, let alone official aid in any tangible form. The new version fitted the prescription Adams had given Monroe in their private conversation—to make "earnest remonstrance against the interference of the European powers by force with South America, but to disclaim all interference on our part with Europe; to make an American cause, and adhere inflexibly to that."

Though the President's message was to be the scripture for most later exegeses of the Monroe Doctrine, in fact it settled neither of the critical policy issues. Monroe assumed that the United States might still enter into an alliance with Britain. He returned to Adams the supplementary instruction to Rush revised "so as not to refuse cooperating with Great Britain even if she should yet demur to the recognition of South American independence."[47] He and Adams had agreed that Congress might well command recognition of Greece. If so, it seemed likely that the President would not resist.[48] The twin questions of whether the United States would ally with a cisatlantic power and whether it would take an active role in cisatlantic politics both remained open.

---

47. Adams diary, Nov. 26, 1823. See Gale W. McGee, "The Monroe Doctrine: A Stopgap Measure," *Mississippi Valley Historical Review*, 38 (Sept. 1951), 233-250.
48. Adams diary, Nov. 22, 1823.

The Replies to Canning

Adams was well aware that the critical issues had not yet been settled. The passages in his diary concerning the President's message show him pleased with having won a battle but under no illusion that he had finished the war. He continued to work on a note to Tuyll, confessedly designed to be both a communication to the Russian government and "an unequivocal answer to the proposals made by Canning."[49]

The compromises embodied in the President's message helped Adams, for he could borrow or imitate language already agreed upon and thus avoid fresh debate. In the note to Russia, Adams wanted, however, to contrast the republics of the New World with monarchies of the Old World, saying that the former were guided by the principles of liberty, independence, and self-determination while the monarchies were led by entirely opposite principles. Though with many personal compliments to the tsar, he proposed to say that the United States hoped the Holy Alliance would not seek to impose its principles outside of Europe. The note would reiterate a promise that the United States would remain neutral as long as European powers did so, but it would conclude by declaring that the American government "could not see with indifference, the forcible interposition of any European Power, other than Spain, either to restore the dominion of Spain over her emancipated Colonies in America, or to establish Monarchical Governments in those Countries, or to transfer any of the possessions heretofore or yet subject to Spain in the American Hemisphere, to any other European Power."[50]

On November 25, when the cabinet first discussed this proposed new note to Tuyll, Calhoun evidenced understanding of what Adams was up to. He objected that the ardent republicanism of the note would be offensive to the British. Though expressing doubt whether any note at all was needed, he asked

---

49. Ibid., Nov. 25, 1823.
50. Adams's draft appears in Ford, "Genesis," pp. 405-408.

why Adams could not simply communicate to Tuyll parts of the President's message. Adams's rejoinder was that such a procedure would not satisfy protocol, and Calhoun had to accept that answer. Unable to take issue with Adams's expertise on matters of diplomatic form, he had to focus on what a note to Russia should say.

The debate ran over the better part of two days.[51] Wirt, who had theretofore been either absent or silent, insisted that the cabinet consider whether American interest in Latin America was really sufficient to justify utterances that might lead to war. He thus questioned not only Adams's proposed note to Tuyll but also the paragraphs previously agreed upon for inclusion in the President's message. A big man with wavy hair and a face which he liked to think resembled Goethe's, Wirt had the reputation for being brilliant but lazy. He had originally practiced law in Virginia and been close to Jefferson, Madison, and Monroe. Since becoming attorney general, he had shifted his base to Baltimore and practiced there part-time.[52] His circle therefore included lawyers and merchants in a city that had been a center of agitation for recognition of the Latin American republics. Yet he said that "he did not think this country would support the Government in a war for the independence of South America. There had never been much general excitement in their favor." He questioned whether the administration ought to strike a posture which it might then have to abandon because of lack of public and congressional support.

Originally, Adams had advanced a similar argument. Now, although he said that he remained uncertain about the real extent of American interest in Latin America, he did not join Wirt in advocating that the documents worked out during the preceding three weeks be reviewed afresh. Perhaps he had simply invested too much time and energy in making them better than he feared they might be. Hence, while urging the others

---

51. Adams diary, Nov. 25, 26, 1823.
52. See J. P. Kennedy, *Memoirs of the Life of William Wirt, Attorney-General of the United States*, 2 vols. (Philadelphia: Lea and Blanchard, 1849).

to listen to Wirt, he concentrated on trying to get their acceptance of his draft note to Russia.

Nor was Calhoun willing to see the game start all over. He
was sure, he said, that the Holy Allies planned to act against
Latin America. They were dedicated enemies of republicanism
and they "had an ultimate eye to us." If they enjoyed success in
Latin America, they would gain partisans in the United States,
and Americans themselves would divide into violent parties.
The people, he said, were wise enough to see their danger. It
was critical, therefore, that the Holy Allies be kept out of the
Americas, and the way to accomplish this was to persuade the
British to oppose them. Since the British would not oppose
them alone, the United States ought to seize the opportunity
offered by Canning. A common stand by the two maritime powers
would probably deter the Holy Allies. By taking a small risk
now, the United States could avoid having to take much greater
risks later. All efforts should be bent toward influencing the
British, said Calhoun, and the proposed note to Russia would
not serve that end.

Adams and Calhoun argued with passion and conviction.
Undoubtedly, they believed what they said. Nevertheless, there
was a certain fancifulness about their presentations. It is hard
to see what purpose was to be served by Adams's note to Tuyll
other than to make accord with England more difficult and to
establish a record which Adams could cite if charged at home
with being pro-British. Although Calhoun put together a more
coherent brief, he depended on far-fetched assumptions about
the future. He had clearly persuaded himself that an English
alliance was desirable, but it was not easy for him to explain
what the reasons were.

What Monroe made of the dispute is hard to tell. Though
he knew that Wirt had no political constituency, he may have
been impressed by Wirt's estimate that the public would not
support a bold policy. Whether from agreement with Calhoun's
arguments or from interest in Calhoun's candidacy, Monroe
clearly retained a disposition to form a concert with England.
He asked Adams if there were not a possibility that the British

would act on their own, stand forth as the protectors of Latin America, and, in effect, convert the new republics into dependencies. He did not seem satisfied by Adams's response that the point reinforced the case for prompt and wholly independent action by the United States. As the sun began to drop toward the now nearly leafless trees visible from the windows of his office, Monroe adjourned the meeting, saying that he would make a decision during the night.

On the next morning, Monroe had a messenger carry a letter to the State Department. It directed Adams to deliver the note to the Russian minister and to do so forthwith. It also directed him, however, to strike out all the passages that had been questioned during the preceding two days' debate. In particular, this meant that Adams was to take out the paragraph contrasting the principles of republics with those of monarchies. In terms of Adams's political objectives, this was the crucial text, for it was the part of the note which would give offense to the English and embarrass alliance negotiations. Adams therefore went to the White House to protest the President's decision. The paragraph, he argued grandly, was the heart of what promised to be "the most important paper that ever went from my hands." He asked Monroe to reconsider and promised to abide by the verdict and then returned to his office.[53]

Before Tuyll arrived at the State Department, Adams had Monroe's answer. The President had already commented that the paragraph in question did not seem to him a necessary part of a note to Russia. He said that he still disliked it and thought it would produce "an unfavorable effect." Nevertheless, he gave in. His consent was so grudging, however, that Adams voluntarily omitted the paragraph when he read the document to Tuyll. It ended up therefore as merely a communication to the tsar, amplifying what the President would shortly present to Congress.[54]

53. Monroe to Adams, Nov. 27, 1823, Ford, "Genesis," p. 409; Adams diary, Nov. 27, 1823.

54. Monroe to Adams, Nov. 27, 1823 (second letter), Ford, "Genesis," p. 409; Adams diary, Nov. 27, 1823; Adams to Tuyll, Nov. 27, 1823, Ford, "Genesis," pp. 405-408;

On December 2, at two in the afternoon, that message was delivered to the clerks of the House and Senate. Two instructions to Rush had already gone off to New York to be carried by packet to London. Tuyll had heard the note to his government, persuaded Adams to make some minor changes, received a text; and was preparing to transmit it to St. Petersburg. Still, however, the major issues remained unresolved.

In the President's mind, an alliance with Britain evidently remained an open option. In a letter to Jefferson, he described what he had done as affecting chiefly the form of that alliance. He had simply taken the first steps in Washington rather than in London. He did call to Jefferson's attention, however, the "unpleasant circumstance . . . that Mr. Canning's zeal, has much abated of late."[55] It is conceivable, of course, that Monroe merely wanted Jefferson to believe that he had not disregarded his advice and that he was hiding from him the extent to which he had given in to Adams and allowed Adams to protect himself, but that reading seems implausible, for only two days after the message to Congress, Monroe wrote urgently to Adams:

> The accounts which, I hear, are just rcd from England, make it important, that the instructions to Mr. Rush, should be forwarded immediately, and that he be instructed to state, that we will unite with the British govt, in measures, to prevent the interference of the allied powers, in the affairs of So. Am., and particularly in sending troops there. He should state also, that the attitude taken in the message, in regard to that object, was essentially founded, on the proposition made by Mr. Canning to him.

What had stirred Monroe was receipt of late October London newspapers prophesying that a Franco-Spanish expeditionary force would soon sail for South America. Adams, who saw him at the White House, found him "singularly disturbed."[56]

Tuyll to Nesselrode, Dec. 11, 1823, summarized in Nikolai N. Bolkhovitinov, *Doktrina Monro (Proiskhozhdenie i Kharakter)* (Moscow: Instituta mezhdunarodnykh otnoshenii, 1959), pp. 236-237.

55. Monroe to Jefferson, Dec. 4, ?, 1823, Monroe, *Writings*, VII, 342-345.

56. Monroe to Adams, Dec. 4, 1823, Adams Papers; Washington *National Intelligencer*, Dec. 1, 4, 1823; Adams diary, Dec. 4, 1823.

On December 5 Monroe convened a cabinet meeting. "The object is to confer," he wrote, "on the measures to be taken with Engld and the allied powers." Presumably, Adams brought to it the second supplementary instruction to Rush which he had begun to prepare earlier. That draft does not survive, nor does Adams's diary have an entry concerning the cabinet debate or subsequent conversations. All the evidence we have is the final instruction completed three days later, together with a diary note by Adams indicating that Monroe gave it close scrutiny before it went in the mails.[57]

We can guess that in the cabinet meeting Adams scoffed at the reports from London. He had done so from the outset. Perhaps at his instigation, the National Intelligencer also called them into question, suggesting that they had been planted to influence the London stock exchange.[58] Calhoun almost certainly took a contrary view and argued that it was urgent to act as the President wished. As to what Southard or Wirt may have said, we have not a clue.

The instruction sent to Rush on December 8 resembled what the President had asked for. Much of its phrasing, however, must have embodied concessions to Adams. Summarizing points made in the annual message and the note to Tuyll, it called attention to the "concurrence of these sentiments with those of the British Government." It asked that Britain now make similar declarations. Expressing Adams's view, the instruction continued: "It is hoped that nothing further will be necessary."

Against the possibility that the Holy Allies did have in view an expedition to South America, the instruction spoke of "a further concert of operations to counteract that design." What

---

57. Monroe to Adams, Dec. 5, 1823, Adams Papers; Adams to Rush, Dec. 8, 1823, Appendix 2 in Samuel Flagg Bemis, John Quincy Adams and the Foundations of American Foreign Policy (New York: Alfred A. Knopf, 1950), pp. 577-579; Adams diary, Dec. 4, 1823.
58. Washington National Intelligencer, Dec. 5, 1823. Despite the fact that the editors of the National Intelligencer supported Crawford, they were susceptible to influence from Adams, partly because they profited from the public printing, a privilege which Adams could (and later did) withdraw, and partly because they respected him. See Josephine Seaton, William Winston Seaton of the "National Intelligencer": A Biographical Study (Boston; James R. Osgood and Co., 1871), especially pp. 159-161.

authority Rush would have to effect such a concert was left un-
clear. He was told to "communicate freely and cautiously" with
Canning and try to ascertain "the *intentions* of Great Britain,
under all the contingent aspects, which the subject may assume."
The implication was that he should pass such information on to
Washington and allow decisions to be made there, but he was not
directed to do so.

The most striking sentence in the instruction read: "The
President is anxiously desirous, that the opening to a cordial
harmony, in the policy of the United States and of Britain, offered
on this occasion, may be extended to the general relations between the two Countries." Though styled by Adams to remain
equivocal, the instruction embodied a tentative offer to explore
possibilities of an entente and possibly an alliance.[59]

The decision to send this instruction represented a setback
for Adams. He had been attempting to consolidate the ground
he had won in the earlier disputes. As soon as the President's
message was out, he had taken occasion to talk with Clay. Judging
from the passage in his diary describing the conversation, he
went away satisfied that Clay understood the danger of letting
war fever develop. It could only help Calhoun. Adams also wrote
to Walsh of the Philadelphia *National Gazette*, urging him to
play up the noncolonization principle and by implication to play
down other subjects. Presumably at his direction, this line was
taken by his local organ, the Washington *National Journal*. And
even while the latest instruction to Rush was being drawn up,
Adams talked to Rufus King of the Senate Foreign Relations
Committee and told him that the President's message constituted an answer to an alliance overture from Britain.[60]

Now that the President had decided to answer Britain more

59. Adams to Rush, Dec. 8, 1823, Bemis, *Adams and the Foundations*, pp. 577-579.

60. Adams diary, Dec. 2, 1823; Adams to Walsh, Dec. 3, 1823, Adams Papers; Washington *National Journal*, Dec. 3, 5, 1823; memorandum by King, Charles R. King, ed.,
The Life and Correspondence of Rufus King, 6 vols. (New York: G. P. Putnam's Sons, 1894-
1900), VI, 534-536. The printed version of this memorandum and the original in
the Papers of Rufus King, New-York Historical Society, carry the date, Nov. 7, 1823,
but the text is clearly of later date, probably Dec. 7, 1823, for King was still in New
York on Nov. 7.

forthcomingly, it became Adams's chief concern to keep the fact from being known by the public. Conversely, it became the interest of his rivals to get the fact into the open. Hence, the pro-Calhoun dailies in Washington, Baltimore, and New York began to print paragraphs saying that passages in the President's message would be better understood when the people learned of the secret correspondence between Washington and London. The Crawfordite Richmond *Enquirer* took up the theme, and the Crawfordite organ in New York began to inveigh against quondam Federalists who would put the United States under "the protection of British cannon." Senator James Barbour of Virginia, one of Crawford's closest friends, gave consideration to proposing a congressional resolution which would ask that the administration pursue a concert with Britain. Madison encouraged him, but others apparently talked him out of it. On December 23 Rollin Mallary, a Vermonter not as yet surely identified with any candidate but suspected of being for Crawford, introduced in the House a resolution calling on the President to lay before Congress the correspondence relevant to affairs in South America.[61] Conceivably, Barbour accepted this motion as a substitute for the one he had had in mind.

Monroe informed Adams that he was inclined to comply with Mallary's request.[62] For some reason, however, he changed his mind. Perhaps Adams presented arguments against doing so. Perhaps the President was influenced by a dispatch from the American chargé in France which arrived at exactly this moment. Dated October 30, it reported the British ambassador in Paris as saying that South American affairs should be settled by trilateral negotiations among the French, British, and American governments. This report disturbed and puzzled Monroe. At the same time, however, newspapers carried rumors that elements

---

61. Washington *Republican*, Dec. 4, 1823; Baltimore *Morning Chronicle*, quoted ibid., Dec. 13 1823; New York *Patriot*, Dec. 6, 1823; Richmond *Enquirer*, Dec. 6, 1823; New York *Gazette*, quoted in Baltimore *Weekly Register*, Dec. 27, 1823; James Barbour to Madison, Dec. 2, 1823, Papers of James Madison, Library of Congress; Madison to Barbour, Dec. 5, 1823, Papers of James Barbour, New York Public Library; Washington *National Intelligencer*, Dec. 24, 1823.
62. Monroe to Adams, Dec. 25, 1823, Adams Papers.

of the British fleet were being equipped and manned for battle. This piece of intelligence may have led Monroe to suspect that the British were engaged in some intricate and delicate game. At any rate, he wrote Adams on Christmas day:

> The more I have reflected on the reply which ought to be given to the resolution . . . the better satisfied I have been, that we should be very guarded in the answer to it. There is much cause to suspect that hostile projects are entertained, by France, and even Russia, and the preparations imputed to the British govt, show, that it, is of opinion, that the demonstration of a determination to resist such attempts, is indispensable to their prevention, if indeed that can have the effect.[63]

In consequence of a cabinet meeting of which we have no record, Adams prepared a formal letter to Monroe saying simply that the State Department had "no information . . . either of any Determination of any Sovereign or Sovereigns to assist Spain [in reconquest of her empire] . . . or of any disposition or determination of any Government of Europe to oppose any such aid or assistance to Spain if it should be given." If there was further discussion in the cabinet, we have no evidence of it. Two weeks later the President notified the House that he had "no information on that subject not known to Congress which can be disclosed without injury to the public good."[64]

Although this response produced some complaints in Congress and in the press, it was accepted for the time being. Calhoun was not prepared to go behind the President's back to encourage a demand for information. Furthermore, he probably felt that the actual documents were less useful to him than unsubstantiated rumors. His organs in Washington and New York did their utmost to create belief that Adams wanted the

---

63. Daniel Sheldon to Adams, Oct. 30, 1823, William R. Manning, ed., *Diplomatic Correspondence of the United States concerning the Independence of the Latin American Nations*, 3 vols. (New York: Oxford University Press, 1925), II, 1399-1400; Baltimore *Patriot*, Dec. 23, 1823; Monroe to Adams, Dec. 25, 1823, Adams Papers.

64. Adams to Monroe, Dec. 26, 1823, Adams Papers; Monroe to the House of Representatives, Jan. 12, 1824, James D. Richardson, ed., *A Compilation of the Messages and Papers of the Presidents*, 9 vols. (n.p.: Bureau of National Literature and Art, 1903), II, 221.

United States to be a satellite of Britain or even of the Holy Alliance while Calhoun wanted his country to be the defender of liberty in the hemisphere.[65] Because Crawford had been absent from Washington, his friends did not know enough about what was in the documents to be certain that they should continue to press for their publication. Clay was in a like predicament.

America's actual or prospective relationship with Britain thus remained ill-defined both within the administration and in the mind of the public. The President's message to Congress, the note to Tuyll, and the initial instructions to Rush had outlined an independent American policy. The instructions to Rush, however, pointed out that this policy coincided with that of Canning, and the last instruction encouraged further discussion of an alliance if Canning were so disposed. What happened next depended in part on Canning, whose reaction the administration could not know before mid-February or even later. It also depended on the balance by that time among presidential candidates, for a number of elections, caucuses, and conventions of the first two months of 1824 could alter the relative influence of Adams, Calhoun, and the others.

Decision On Greece

In the meantime, the second fundamental issue took precedence. Although Monroe had been dissuaded from calling for recognition, his message had endorsed the Greek cause. It remained an open question whether there would follow recognition of or aid to the Greeks.

From Calhoun, Daniel Webster had obtained advance information about the message, and soon after it appeared, he introduced a resolution in the House calling for formal recognition of Greece and dispatch of an American commissioner. Webster

---

65. Washington *Republican*, Dec. 19, 26, 1823, Jan. 6, 1824; New York *Patriot*, Dec. 23, 26, 1823; Jan. 7, 11, 1824; Philadelphia *Franklin Gazette*, Dec. 23, 1823. Adams's organ, the Washington *National Journal*, Jan. 21, 1824, summarized the charges being made and attempted to rebut them.

said, however, that he did not want the resolution debated until later. Presumably, he wanted time not only to prepare a suitable oration but also to let public support appear. According to gossip that reached Adams, Southard as well as Calhoun was urging Webster on and Monroe himself had given Webster his blessing.[66]

During the six-week interval before the House held its debate, Greece commanded more newspaper space than South America and the Holy Alliance. A New Yorker wrote to Southard, "we are all mad for the Greeks." Similar reports came out of Boston and also out of interior cities such as Cincinnati and Louisville. A New York daily claimed at one point that Greece had displaced the presidential contest as a preoccupation of the public.[67] Whether this was true or not, the Greek question aroused interest in Washington in part because of its potential effect on that contest.

For well-informed politicians could perceive that the issue was embarrassing to Adams. Even those with no inside knowledge could infer from the President's message that the secretary of state was dubious about recognition. Those who discussed the subject with Calhoun or Southard or their close friends doubtless learned how energetically Adams had fought it. Votes for a resolution for recognition would thus be votes against the secretary of state. If numerous enough, they could indicate that his prospects were poor in a congressional caucus or in a presidential election by the House. The result might be to lead some of his supporters to defect to candidates with seemingly better chances of success.

If Adams's opposition to recognition could be brought into

---

66. Webster to Everett, Nov. 28, 1823, Papers of Edward Everett, Massachusetts Historical Society; Washington *National Intelligencer*, Dec. 5, 1823; Adams diary, Jan. 2, 1824.

67. Elbert Anderson to Southard, Dec. 21, 1823, Papers of Samuel L. Southard, Princeton University Library; George Washington Adams to Louisa Catherine Adams, Dec. 24, 1823, Adams Papers; Washington *National Intelligencer*, Dec. 29, 1823; Leverett Saltonstall to Webster, Jan. 9, 1824, Papers of Daniel Webster, Library of Congress; Louisville *Public Advertiser*, Jan. 14, 17, 1824; New York *Commercial Advertiser*, Jan. 6, 1824, cited in Myrtle A. Cline, *American Attitude toward the Greek War of Independence* (Atlanta, Ga.: Higgins-McArthur Co., 1930), p. 113.

the open, that fact in itself could cost him votes. In his home state of Massachusetts, Grecophiles were already denouncing merchants who traded with the Turks via Smyrna and who opposed recognition on the ground that it would hurt their trade. If led to believe that Adams was an enemy of the Greek cause, they would undoubtedly suspect him of siding with these merchants and putting crass material interests above higher values. Through Everett's *North American Review*, such a verdict on Adams would be broadcast and reach exactly the people likely to be Adams supporters in other states.

Even if Adams's opposition were not unmasked, passage of a recognition resolution would complicate his life. Everett had already written Adams that he wanted to be the first U.S. envoy to Greece, and Adams's managers in Massachusetts were insistent that the appointment of such a well-known Federalist could do him no end of harm.[68]

Nor was the problem in Massachusetts the only one which the recognition resolution posed for Adams, for there were also ardent Grecophiles in the pivotal state of New York, and some were men whose backing Adams needed. A pro-Greek committee had been formed in New York City in November 1823. It included several of the city's leading merchants, bankers, and lawyers. The cause was then taken up by several newspapers, including the *American*. Edited by Charles King, a son of Senator Rufus King, the *American* was the organ of the People's Party and had hitherto been regarded as pro-Adams. Elsewhere in the state, the most ardent partisans of Greece were likewise identified with the People's Party.[69] Since support from King's *American* and members of the People's Party was essential if Adams were to win New York's electoral votes, the recognition issue obviously endangered his prospects.

Adams's rivals were well aware of these facts. Calhoun understood them best and had most hope of profiting. On his behalf,

---

68. P. P. F. Degrand to Adams, Jan. 9, 1824, Adams Papers.
69. Cline, *American Attitude*, pp. 38-40; New York *American*, Dec. 11, 22, 1823; Glyndon G. Van Deusen, *Thurlow Weed, Wizard of the Lobby* (Boston: Little, Brown, 1947), p. 22.

Webster courted Everett, asking his help in preparing the oration, assuring him that no one else could even be considered as an envoy, and writing that Calhoun "desired me to say to you that he is as friendly to the Greeks as yourself." In New York, Calhoun's agent, General Joseph G. Swift, became active in the Greek agitation, making a special effort to cooperate with King, and the *Patriot*, which had previously feuded with the *American*, began to laud its stand on the Greek question.[70]

Meanwhile, Calhoun and his friends used such resources as they had to promote passage of a recognition resolution. With George M. Dallas and others of the "Family Party" exerting leadership, committees were formed and rallies were held in Philadelphia. Governor Shulze of Pennsylvania, who had been selected by the Family Party, included an appeal for recognition in his message to the legislature. In the other Calhoun stronghold, South Carolina, the governor and the legislature joined in petitioning Congress for recognition. The pro-Calhoun Federalists in Baltimore arranged a ball to raise money for Greece. In Washington, Calhoun's organ, the *Republican*, reported every manifestation of pro-Greek feeling and published almost daily some letter or editorial advocating recognition.[71]

While Clay may not have had as exact an appreciation of the situation as Calhoun, he too saw an opportunity to score at Adams's expense. At the very least, he saw that some members of the People's Party in New York might be won over by a candidate who identified himself with Greece. Having more freedom of action than Calhoun, he could speak out for Webster's resolution. As soon as he gave a signal that he would do so, there began to be additional pro-Greek demonstrations in the West. The Kentucky and Louisiana legislatures passed resolutions in favor of recognition, and newspapers supporting Clay called editorially for recognition and even for outright aid. The United States

---

70. Webster to Everett, Dec. 6, 1823, J. W. McIntyre, ed., *The Writings and Speeches of Daniel Webster*, 18 vols. (Boston: Little, Brown, 1903), XVII, 332-333; New York *American*, Nov. 23, 28, 1823; New York *Patriot*, Dec. 24, 1823.

71. Washington *National Intelligencer*, Dec. 16, 1823, Jan. 13, 1824; Philadelphia *National Gazette*, Dec. 10, 1823; Washington *Republican*, Dec. 18, 20, 21, 22, 24, 27, 29, 30, 1823, Jan. 1-9, 1824. See Cline, *American Attitude*, pp. 59-61.

should help Greece, they said, just as France had once helped the United States.[72]

Some Crawfordites joined in. The editor of the Boston *Statesman* did so, declaring that only base interest in the Turkish opium trade could explain anyone's opposing recognition. Benjamin F. Butler, Van Buren's law partner, figured in rallies for Greece in Albany. The governor of Virginia imitated the governors of Pennsylvania and South Carolina by including an appeal for Greece in an official message, and the Richmond *Enquirer* published an editorial likening the situation of the Greeks to that of Americans in 1776.[73]

The small group trying to build a movement for Jackson also saw potential benefit in the issue. They were already exploiting the sense of crisis created by rumors of possible European intervention in South America. In various parts of the West and in Pennsylvania, rallies ended with resolutions declaring that a time of peril called for a President with Jackson's background and gifts—a veteran of the Revolution, a soldier, and a patriot above politics. Pseudonymous letters to newspapers sounded the same theme. Some of the organizers of this campaign evidently felt that people who sympathized with Greece might respond to a similar appeal. At any rate, in both New York and Baltimore, balls were scheduled to honor Jackson and to raise money for the Greeks.[74]

Despite all these pressures, there is no evidence that Adams considered changing his position and acquiescing in recognition of Greece. It is possible though unlikely that he attached highest importance to avoiding the necessity of either supporting or opposing an appointment for Everett. Conceivably, he felt trapped, for he had stated his views to the cabinet with such clarity that it would be awkward to explain a reversal. More-

72. Lexington *Kentucky Gazette*, Jan. 9, 1824, Cline, *American Attitude*, p. 99; Louisville *Public Advertiser*, Jan. 14, 17, 1824; Washington *National Intelligencer*, Jan. 10, 27, 1824.

73. Boston *Statesman*, Jan. 1, 1824, cited in Cline, *American Attitude*, p. 85; Washington *Republican*, Dec. 20, 1823; Richmond *Enquirer*, Dec. 20, 1823, Jan. 5, 1824.

74. Baltimore *Weekly Register*, Jan. 3, 1824; Baltimore *American*, Jan. 21, 1824; Washington *National Intelligencer*, Jan. 23, 1824.

over, before significant public agitation developed, Adams had confided to one or two friendly congressmen his opposition to recognition, and he would have to offer some explanation to them.[75] Probably, however, one should assume simply that Adams had developed a conviction that involvement in European politics would be wrong and that, while his psychic mechanisms could and did tune convictions to interests, they were not engineered to keep the two in constant and perfect harmony.

With his conscience banning the option of retreat, Adams had no choice but to maneuver for the defeat of Webster's resolution and, while doing so, to keep himself behind the scenes. Early in January, Senator King wrote his son, Charles, the editor of the New York American, that expressions of sympathy for Greece were admirable but that official recognition might bring unwanted complications. Since he had just talked with Adams, it is not unlikely that Adams encouraged his writing so. The chief journal in Philadelphia supporting Adams, Walsh's National Gazette, made the same argument in an editorial. So, in due course, did the Boston Advertiser, which was controlled by Adams's managers in Massachusetts. The Washington National Journal whose editorials were thought to be dictated or even written by Adams himself, remained ambiguous and noncommittal.[76]

In the House, a member friendly to Adams introduced a resolution calling for correspondence between the government and Greek agents. Adams may have put him up to doing so. In any case, he complied gladly, for the correspondence included a message from him to the Greek representative in London which stated in strong terms a hope for Greek independence but explained that the United States could not intervene in an on-

75. Adams diary, Nov. 24, 28, 1823.
76. King to Charles A. King, Jan. 2, 1824, King, Life and Correspondence of Rufus King, VI, 545; Adams calendar, Jan. 1, 1824; Philadelphia National Gazette, Dec. 23, 1823; Boston Advertiser, Dec. 19, 29, 1823, Jan. 10, 1824, cited in Cline, American Attitude, pp. 77-80, 83-84, 86; Washington National Journal, Jan. 7, 1824. The editor of the Richmond Enquirer felt sure that Adams himself wrote many National Journal editorials: Thomas Ritchie to Gales and Seaton, Aug. 8, 1824, Papers of Joseph Gales and William Winston Seaton, Library of Congress.

going war and that recognition could not be extended until independence had become, as in South America, an accomplished fact.[77] This message served as a brief against recognition while at the same time giving Adams protection against a charge of lacking sympathy for Greek aspirations. It was not perfect protection. Mrs. Everett read the message as evidence of a "hard heart." The newspapers championing recognition were not able, however, to take it as a text for an assault on Adams. They had to say merely that the secretary's sentiments should be translated into policy.[78]

Samuel Breck, the one member of the House from Pennsylvania who was a friend and supporter of Adams, introduced a resolution asking for information about American trade with the Ottoman empire. It is quite likely that he did so at Adams's instigation, for Adams felt that the risk to trade was a strong argument against recognition, and his calendar discloses that he talked with Breck not long before the motion was presented. The result was publication of a document showing that in 1822 Americans had done almost $800,000 worth of business with the Turks.[79]

Adams tried some cautious lobbying with members of the House. He went to see Poinsett of South Carolina, the chairman of the House Foreign Relations Committee, and said to him mysteriously "that there was a person probably now at Constantinople upon an errand which might suffer by these movements in Congress." In fact, it was a special agent whom Adams had commissioned to explore the possibility of a commercial convention, but Adams did not say so. His own diary entry indicates that he gave Poinsett an impression that the administration was making a secret effort to aid the Greeks.[80]

---

77. 18th Congress, 1st session, *Annals of Congress* (Dec. 29, 1823), p. 843; Adams to Andreas Luriottis, Aug. 18, 1823, *American State Papers*, 5 (Washington, D.C.: Gales and Seaton, 1834), 257.

78. Mrs. Edward Everett to Everett, Jan. 10, 1824, Paul R. Frothingham, *Edward Everett, Orator and Statesman* (Boston: Little, Brown, 1925), p. 79; Washington *Republican*, Jan. 11, 1824.

79. 18th Congress, 1st session, *Annals of Congress* (Dec. 22, 1823), p. 849; Adams calendar, Dec. 16, 1823; 18th Congress, 1st session, House Executive Report No. 32.

80. Adams diary, Jan. 3, 1824. The agent was George B. English. See James A. Field,

A few days later, Adams went to the White House only to find Poinsett there, asking the President if he could tell the House that the administration opposed Webster's resolution. With Adams luckily present, Monroe refrained from answering, apparently saying that he would have to consult his cabinet. When the question was in fact put to the cabinet, Calhoun and Southard took the position that Poinsett should not be authorized to make any statement about the administration's views, and Adams was content to let that be the decision.[81]

Though Adams's diary gives no evidence, he must have had a subsequent conversation with Monroe, for Monroe was later to tell Poinsett that he did, in fact, oppose the Webster resolution, regarding it as an encroachment on executive prerogative.[82] This was exactly the line that Adams took with a trusted Massachusetts congressman:

> It was quite immaterial what the modification of the resolution might be, the objection to it, under whatever form it might assume, would be the same. It was the intermeddling of the Legislature with the duties of the Executive. It was the adoption of Clay's South American system, seizing upon the popular feeling of the moment to perplex and embarrass the Administration.[83]

If Adams spoke to Monroe with equal vehemence, he may have frightened him into backing him; or he may simply have persuaded him. In any case, he obtained help from the President in his defensive campaign.

Even so, Adams would probably have seen recognition voted by the House had he not suddenly found unexpected reinforcements. When debate opened, Webster felt sure that his motion would carry by a large majority. The oration which he had crafted was judged elegant, powerful, and moving even by men

Jr., *America and the Mediterranean World, 1776-1882* (Princeton: Princeton University Press, 1969), pp. 133-134.

81. Adams diary, Jan. 9, 10, 1824.

82. Poinsett to Daniel Webster, n.d., Webster Papers. (The letter is filed at the end of 1823, but internal evidence makes it almost certain that it was written sometime during the second or third week of January 1824.)

83. Adams diary, Jan. 17, 1824.

who disagreed with him or disliked him personally. Clay took the floor and argued the case with equal eloquence. There then followed speeches for the motion from a broad spectrum of the House—Francis Baylies of Massachusetts, a supporter of Crawford; Henry Dwight, also of Massachusetts, a presumptive Adams supporter but a passionate Grecophile; Patrick Farrelly, an Irishman from Pennsylvania and a Calhoun man; Daniel Pope Cook of Illinois, once close to Adams but now a backer of Clay; and Sam Houston of Tennessee, a man close to Jackson. It was a well-chosen array.[84]

Poinsett had proferred a substitute merely expressing hope that the President would recognize when he judged circumstances to warrant doing so, but there was little evidence of enthusiasm for his formula. Timothy Fuller of Massachusetts, the man to whom Adams had confided his uncompromising opposition, was the only member to speak for Poinsett's substitute.

But Crawfordites from the South took the floor to oppose both motions. First came old John Randolph of Roanoke. Independent and unpredictable, he could well have been speaking only for himself. Following him, however, came Alfred Cuthbert and George Cary. Since both were from Crawford's own state of Georgia and were conspicuous backers of the secretary of the treasury, their performances signaled a party line. After them came Ichabod Bartlett of New Hamsphire and Christopher Rankin of Mississippi, each of whom was a Crawfordite leader in his region. The final speech against Webster's motion was then made by Alexander Smyth of Virginia who not only was a Crawford backer but also had gained nationwide notoriety by an open letter to constituents explaining why he could never in conscience vote for Adams for President.[85] It could not have been made more clear that Crawford's sympathizers were being asked to stay out of the coalition against Adams. The message was understood. On a voice vote, the House tabled both the Webster and Poinsett

84. Webster to Everett, Dec. 9, 1823, Everett Papers; Rufus King to Charles A. King, Jan. 19, 1824, Rufus King Papers (New-York Historical Society); John E. Wright to Hammond, Jan. 21, 1824, Papers of Charles Hammond, Ohio Historical Society; 18th Congress, 1st session, *Annals of Congress* Jan. 19-24, 26, 1824), pp. 1086-1099, 1103-1214.
85. Washington *National Intelligencer*, Jan. 7, 1823.

resolutions. The majority almost certainly consisted of Adams and Crawford men voting together.

How is the behavior of the Crawfordites to be explained? Of course, one must assume that those who spoke believed some of what they said. They need not have thought that recognition would mean war with the Turks or the Holy Allies. None of them described this danger with much conviction. Probably, however, they did feel, as a matter of principle, that affairs in such a far-away place as Greece were not a proper concern of Americans. Crawford himself had voiced such an attitude when the cabinet discussed the Greek question in connection with Monroe's annual message of 1822.[86] Few of the Crawfordite congressmen can have believed, however, that defeat of the Webster resolution had anything like the importance of ensuring that Crawford became President. Nor can they have been blind to the fact that passage of the resolution would injure Adams, one of Crawford's principal rivals. Why then did they come to Adams's rescue?

As is so often the case with political or parliamentary maneuvers, written records supply no evidence. Tactical planning takes place in private conversations. Instructions or suggestions are passed on by word of mouth. Nothing survives except the fact of the outcome.

One can, however, see reasons why at that particular juncture Crawfordite leaders might have wanted to help Adams. Their hopes for New England were fading. In Maine, where chances had seemed best, a bellwether congressional race had just been won by a man sworn to oppose Crawford. The state legislative caucus had already endorsed Adams and seemed likely to do so again by an even larger majority. The two Maine senators, though still allies of Crawford, no longer held out hope. Reports from Massachusetts, Connecticut, and Rhode Island indicated that any waning in support for Adams would benefit Calhoun or perhaps Jackson, not Crawford.[87]

---

86. Adams diary, Nov. 27, 1822. In the summer of 1823, however, Adams thought Crawford, like Calhoun, to favor some involvement in Greek affairs: ibid., Aug. 15, 1823.

87. Washington *National Intelligencer*, Sept. 27, 1823; Baltimore *Weekly Register*, Nov. 22, 1823, Jan. 10, 1824 (the Maine legislature did, in fact, reendorse Adams: Wash-

The New York elections had been disappointing. Although Crawfordite organs such as the Albany *Argus* and the Richmond *Enquirer* tried to deny it, the People's Party victories plainly registered opposition to New York's voting for the nominee of a congressional caucus. Van Buren now doubted whether the Regency could prevent popular election of electors or even if they did, whether they could get a majority for Crawford in the legislature.[88] In these circumstances, it seemed advantageous that the opposition remain divided and that nothing send Adams supporters in New York scampering to Clay, Calhoun, or Jackson.

From North Carolina, which they regarded as pivotal for them, the Crawfordite leaders had just received the shocking news that the legislature had chosen an anti-Crawford speaker. Calhoun's organ in Washington made much of this fact and of evidence that most North Carolina newspapers were supporting Calhoun instead of Crawford. One pro-Crawford congressman from the state wrote a letter coupling mention of the Greek question with references to Calhoun's rising influence.[89] He and others may well have felt that if a vote on Greece weakened Adams, the benefit would all go to Calhoun.

At the time of the Greek debate, moreover, Crawfordite leaders were preoccupied with plans for the congressional caucus. They could be sure that Crawford would have more votes than any other candidate. The question was whether enough representatives and senators would attend so that the outcome would seem to represent the will of Republicans in Congress. Backers of Jackson, Calhoun, and Clay were advocating a boycott. They had contrived resolutions by the Tennessee, Pennsyl-

ington *National Intelligencer*, Jan. 24, 1824); William King to John Holmes, Jan. 15, 1824, Papers of John Holmes, Maine Historical Society; Richmond *Enquirer*, Jan. 15, 1824; Baltimore *Weekly Register*, Oct. 25, 1823; Washington *National Intelligencer*, Jan. 29, 1824.

88. Albany *Argus*, quoted in Washington *National Intelligencer*, Nov. 20, 1823; Richmond *Enquirer*, Nov. 25, 1823; Joseph Delafield to Bailey, Jan. 8, 1824, Papers of John Bailey, New-York Historical Society.

89. Baltimore *Weekly Register*, Nov. 29, 1823; Feb. 3, 1824; Washington *Republican*, Nov. 28, Dec. 2, 1823; letter of Dec. 31, 1823, A. R. Newsome, ed., "Letters of Romulus M. Saunders to Bartlett Yancey, 1821-1828," *North Carolina Historical Review*, 8 (Oct. 1931), 440.

vania, and Ohio legislatures condemning the caucus and recommending that representatives from these states not attend. In the Maryland legislature, Calhoun's Federalist allies had teamed up with Adams supporters to obtain a similar resolution.[90] Adams's backers were not as yet, however, committed to this strategy. From the Crawfordite standpoint, therefore, it must have seemed advantageous to woo the Adams congressmen rather than to alienate them by lining up with Calhoun and Clay on the Greek issue.

Probably, the Crawfordite leaders were encouraged to reach such a conclusion by maneuvers on the part of Adams men. When debate on Greece was about to begin, someone from the Adams camp led Senator William King of Maine to believe that Adams had decided he could not win and was prepared to accept a caucus nomination as Crawford's running mate. It seems clear that Adams himself did not conceive such a stratagem. His diary indicates that he was surprised when the rumor came back to him. On the other hand, he did not immediately send word to King that the report was untrue, nor did he rebuke a friendly New York congressman who told him of discussing with a Crawford leader the philosophical compatibility between Adams and Crawford. In fact, Adams gave the Crawfordites some encouragement. Appearing at the Columbian Institute, Adams gratuitously offered a public toast to Crawford, wishing him a speedy return to health. Only when the defeat of Webster's resolution was certain did he advise the leader of his partisans in Congress that he would not accept a caucus nomination for vice president and that he opposed the holding of a caucus.[91]

The tabling of Webster's resolution meant that at least for the moment it was the policy of the United States not to involve itself in European politics. Of course, had the resolution passed

90. Baltimore *Weekly Register*, Dec. 27, 1823, Jan. 10, 17, 1824.
91. Adams diary, Jan. 20, 23, 25, 1824; Baltimore *Patriot*, Jan. 4, 1824. A Virginia congressman close to both Calhoun men and Crawford men professed to see many signs of a nascent coalition between Crawford and Adams supporters: Robert A. Garnett to Swift, Jan. 9, 1824, Papers of Joseph G. Swift, United States Military Academy.

the House, it would still have needed action by the Senate. Senator Rufus King of New York felt that the Senate would not have approved. In view of what Webster termed "the unexampled burst of feeling which this cause has called forth from all classes of society," it is possible, however, that the Senate would have found it hard not to go along with the House.[92] But the vote in the House was decisive. Once that occurred, the issue was closed, at least for the time being.

American policy was by no means fixed. The outcome of the debate in Congress signified that the United States had decided not to thrust itself into European politics. To that extent, the principle of nonentanglement had been reaffirmed. It remained a question, however, whether the nation would deal with the Western Hemisphere as part of the European system or as in some sense a separate system. Although Adams had thus far succeeded in maintaining the latter tack, the secret instructions to Rush left open the possibility of entering into a concert with Britain. No final decision could come until Canning responded.

THE AFTERMATH ABROAD

Actually, however, Canning's choice had already been made back in the autumn of 1823 when the Monroe cabinet was beginning its debate. In view of Wellington's obstinate insistence that there was no real danger of France's sending forces across the Atlantic, Canning could not generate the sense of panic necessary to win cabinet approval of a public declaration such as he had outlined to Rush, let alone of formal recognition of Latin American republics, as the United States seemed to demand. The duke had permitted him to do no more than speak strongly to Prince Polignac and to demand that a memorandum recording what he had said be sent by Polignac to his superiors in Paris.

Canning clung for a while to the notion of a concert with the

---

92. Rufus King to Charles A. King, Jan. 30, 1824, Rufus King Papers (New York-Historical Society); 18th Congress 1st session, *Annals of Congress* (Jan. 19, 1824), p. 1097.

United States. He took the line that if a congress of powers were convened to discuss the future of the Spanish colonies, Britain should refuse to participate unless the American government were represented. But, since Wellington deemed such a condition preposterous, Canning had to retreat to the position that Britain should decline to take part on the ground that her interests in the Americas were much greater than those of the other powers and that she should not run the risk of having to compromise with them. For this position he found enough support elsewhere in the cabinet to stand firm against Wellington's contention that Britain was obligated to consult with her allies.[93]

In the meantime, reports coming to London from Paris made it more and more difficult for Canning to pretend that there was peril so portentous that extraordinary measures were required. Ambassador Stuart, who had earlier been hammering an alarm bell, now wrote from Paris that Canning's words to Polignac had made a deep impression. Both Villèle and Chateaubriand, he said, had assured him emphatically that they had no intention even to lend ships or troops to Spain and certainly would not send forces to the Americas on their own. Villèle had gone on to say that the independence of the Spanish colonies was inevitable and that France and Britain should cooperate in persuading Spain and the Holy Allies to recognize this fact.[94] After early November 1823, nothing in correspondence from Paris gave Canning reason or excuse to renew his overtures to Rush.

If Canning retained any thought of pursuing an alliance with the United States, he probably abandoned it after reading the text of Monroe's message to Congress. Because it led the Whigs to charge that the Liverpool cabinet had shown timidity and thus forfeited to the American government the leadership in opposing Europe, the message embarrassed Canning in his quest for con-

---

93. Wellington to Canning, Nov. 21, 1823, Duke of Wellington, ed., *Despatches, Correspondence and Memoranda of Field Marshal Arthur Duke of Wellington*, 8 vols. (London: John Murray, 1867-1880), II, 181; Canning to Wellington, Jan. 22, 1824, ibid., pp. 191-192; Wellington to Canning, Jan. 23, 1824, ibid., p. 192.

94. Sir Charles Stuart to Canning, Nov. 3, 18, 1823, Webster, *Britain and the Independence of Latin America*, II, 123-124, 129; Stuart to Canning, Nov. 24, Dec. 4, 8, 1823, Foreign Office Records, Public Record Office, Great Britain (hereafter, FO): France, CCCI.

The Department of State, 1820-1866

trol of the House of Commons. Because it came so close to saying exactly what all European courts now knew to have been said to Polignac, it also embarrassed Canning in his relations with foreign diplomats, for they inevitably asked whether there was or was not an understanding between Washington and London. Further, Monroe's message irritated Canning because, in addition to speaking of Latin America, it enunciated a general noncolonization principle which seemed to challenge British as well as Russian pretensions.[95]

After Monroe's message was published in England and on the continent, Canning had to spend his energies battling to release the Polignac memorandum so that he could prove to the Whigs and others that Britain had not been behindhand in moving to protect Latin America. Only by getting Liverpool's active aid did he succeed in overcoming Wellington's opposition. On the side, Canning had to keep pointing out to the Russian, Austrian, and French governments that there were major differences between Britain and the United States and that the continental autocrats should not jump to the assumption that they faced an Anglo-American combination supporting republicanism against monarchy.[96]

Canning succeeded in both endeavors. The release of the Polignac memorandum cut the ground from under his domestic critics. Meanwhile, the Holy Allies and France appeared to accept his reassurances. In any event, their foreign ministers and ambassadors continued to treat with him as if they still thought some common approach might be developed for mediating between Spain and her rebellious subjects. And in the end, Canning emerged with all he wanted. Eventually even Wellington had to acknowledge grudgingly that Canning's increased

95. Canning to Charles Bagot, Jan. 9, 1824, Josceline Bagot, *George Canning and his Friends*, 2 vols. (London: John Murray, 1909), II, 207-210.

96. Wellington to Liverpool, March 5, 1824, Wellington, *Despatches*, II, 228-229; Liverpool to Wellington, March ?, 1824, ibid., pp. 242-243; Charles Duke Yonge, *The Life and Administration of Robert Banks Jenkinson, Second Earl of Liverpool*, 3 vols. (London: Macmillan, 1868), III, 264-268; Canning to Charles Bagot, Jan. 22, 1824 (two letters), Bagot, *George Canning and his Friends*, II, 215-218, 221-222; Canning to Sir Henry Wellesley, Jan. 23, 1824, FO: Austria, CLXXXII; Canning to Stuart, Jan. 9, 1824, Webster, *Britain and the Independence of Latin America*, II, 133-134.

strength in the House made him irresistible in the cabinet. By the end of 1824, the duke was to feel impotent to prevent Britain's recognizing the Latin American republics and counsel his indignant king to acquiesce.[97] Upon Liverpool's retirement in the following year, the king would see no choice other than to name Canning as prime minister. Looking back on 1823-1824, Canning was then to voice his famous boast of having called the New World into existence to redress the balance of the Old. In the meantime, however, he had decided not again to try to make the United States a weight on Britain's side in that balance. When hearing from Rush of Monroe's possible interest in continuing the earlier negotiations, Canning said simply that conditions had changed and the time for concerted Anglo-American action had passed.[98]

As for France, the signals sent to London reflected faithfully the trend in policy. After seeing Polignac's memorandum, Villèle abandoned all thought of aiding Spain. In fact, he became preoccupied with fear that Canning's words hid some ulterior purpose. The coincidence of a slave uprising in Demerara which caused the British government to increase its army and send 5,000 soldiers and naval reinforcements to the West Indies led the French prime minister to fear that perhaps the British planned to recognize Latin American governments and interpose their forces to turn back those of Spain or possibly even to seize some Spanish colony for themselves. He could foresee that either event might arouse anger or panic in the eastern capitals and create a situation that might culminate in war. Throughout the winter and spring of 1823-1824, Villèle's chief concern was lest France find herself caught in the middle as earlier in the Spanish revolution, and he did what he could to persuade the eastern courts that the Spanish colonies were and would remain independent and at the same time to persuade the British that they should defer recognition until the Holy Allies

---

97. Letter of Dec. 4, 1824, Peter Quennell, ed., *The Private Letters of Princess Lieven to Prince Metternich, 1820-1826* (London: John Murray, 1937), pp. 338-339; memorandum by Wellington, Jan.?, 1825, Wellington, *Despatches*, II, 388-390.

98. Rush to Adams, Feb. 9, 1824, Manning, *Diplomatic Correspondence: Independence*, III, 1519-1522.

could accept it unprotestingly.[99] Villèle felt no hesitation about letting the Western Hemisphere drift off as a separate political system. In fact, he took steps to further such a development by pursuing secret negotiations which would result in France's abandoning her legal claim to Haiti and recognizing that nation as independent.[100]

Chateaubriand, too, was chastened by the Polignac memorandum. He could not, however, give up his vision of being the Frenchman to establish Bourbon monarchies in the New World. Long after Villèle had abandoned the notion as "visionary," Chateaubriand still talked as if it might become reality.[101] Having consorted mostly with right-wing Tories when ambassador in London, he found it easy to continue believing that Britain might support him. After seeing Monroe's message, he wrote to Ambassador Polignac:

> We think that temperate monarchies established in America, more or less allied with the mother Country, would be a good result for England and for us.
> Mr. Canning can have no more desire than I to favor military uprisings, the sovereignty of the people, and all the pretty things which Mr. Monroe says to us about the actual governments.[102]

Chateaubriand believed that he could ensure acquiescence if not cooperation by Britain if he persuaded Ferdinand to open

---

99. Stuart to Canning, Nov. 3, 1823, Webster, *Britain and the Independence of Latin America*, II, 122; Villèle to Prince Polignac, Nov. 1, 1823, Jan. 24, Feb. 10, 1824, Count de Villèle, *Mémoires et correspondance*, 6 vols. (Paris: Perrin et Cie., 1889), IV, 489-490, 529, 531-532.

100. William Spence Robertson, *France and the Independence of Latin America* (Baltimore: Johns Hopkins University Press, 1939), pp. 298-301.

101. Chateaubriand to Marquis de Talaru, Nov, 1, 12, 1823, Archives du ministere des affaires étrangères, Correspondance politique (hereafter, CP): Espagne, DCCXXIV; Chateaubriand to Count de la Ferronays, Nov. 1, 1823, Viscount de Chateaubriand, *Congrès de Vérone. Guerre d' Espagne. Negociations: colonies espagnoles*, 2 vols. (Paris: Béthune et Plon, 1838), II, 272-273; Chateaubriand to Polignac, Nov. 10, 17, 1823, Jan. 12, 26, May 13, 1824, Louis Thomas, ed., *Correspondance générale de Chateaubriand*, 5 vols. (Paris: Édouard Champion, 1912-1924) (hereafter, Chateaubriand, *Correspondance*), V, 70, 73, 126-130, 144-150, 218.

102. Chateaubriand to Polignac, Jan. 4, 1824, Chateaubriand, *Correspondance*, V, 114.

up trade with Spanish colonial ports.[103] This would give British merchants everything they might hope to gain from the colonies becoming independent. Their pressure on Canning would ease, and the Liverpool government would have no cause for opposing the establishment of autonomous monarchies. Reasoning thus, Chateaubriand exerted himself in every way to get the desired decree out of the king of Spain. The undertaking was not easy, for he had to work through a prickly and lazy French ambassador in Madrid, the Marquis de Talaru, who was not a friend of his and who, in any case, was preoccupied by desire to leave Spain because he had at home a wife who believed that her health suffered if she ever slept alone and was currently using her physician as bedmate.[104] Yet another complication was the presence in Madrid of Pozzo di Borgo, the Russian ambassador to France. In spite of the fact that French troops occupied Spain, the Spanish king and his advisers seemed to pay more attention to Pozzo than to Talaru, and reports to Paris indicated that Pozzo did not encourage them to make concessions of any kind. Nevertheless, Ferdinand eventually issued a decree authorizing foreign ships to trade with Spanish colonial ports. When Chateaubriand learned of it, he wrote with satisfaction that Canning's hands would thereafter be tied.[105]

It is not clear how Chateaubriand viewed the contingency that England might oppose his scheme even in light of this Spanish decree. In several letters he speculated gloomily on the possibility that Canning would not be deterred from recognizing Latin American republics and that Spain would then declare war.[106] Assuming that Russia would back Spain and feeling, as

---

103. Chateaubriand to Polignac, Feb. 16, 1824, ibid., pp. 166-167.

104. Chateaubriand to Talaru, Dec. 11, 31, 1823, Jan. 12, 26, Feb. 12, 14, 29, 1824, CP: Espagne, DCCXXV-DCCXXVI; Chateaubriand to Polignac, Dec. 22, 1823, Chateaubriand, *Correspondance*, V, 106; Maréchal de Castellane, *Journal, 1804-1862*, 6 vols. (Paris: Plon, 1895), II, 6-7.

105. Talaru to Chateaubriand, Nov. 21, 29, Dec. 6, 19, 1823, CP: Espagne, DCCXXIV-DCCXXV; Chateaubriand to Polignac, May 13, 1824, Chateaubriand, *Correspondance*, V, 218.

106. Chateaubriand to Polignac, Dec. 15, 1823, Jan. 5, March 22, 1824, Chateaubriand, *Correspondance*, V, 101, 119-120, 193-196; Chateaubriand to Count de Rayneval, Feb.

he had said earlier, that France's "true policy is a Russian policy," he could hardly help visualizing conflict between France and England. He even mused on the possibility that, in spite of everything, France might find herself acting in conjunction with her "natural ally," the United States.[107] Though Chateaubriand kept reassuring his ambassadors that war was not in prospect, he evidently attached so much importance to his project for Bourbon monarchies in the New World that he was not prepared to join Villèle in giving absolute priority to avoidance of an Anglo-French conflict.

Chateaubriand, however, did not long retain control of French diplomacy. Growing coolness between him and Villèle had been rumored for some time. In the winter of 1823-1824 Chateaubriand offended not only Villèle but some of Villèle's friends in the Chamber and the Tuileries by accepting a decoration which the tsar offered to him and not to the prime minister. He then became one target of maneuvers by Sosthènes de la Rochefoucauld, the intrigue-prone friend of Villèle, the king, and the king's mistress, for la Rochefoucauld perceived the feasibility of a cabinet reshuffle which would open up a place for his father, the Duc de Doudeauville. When Chateaubriand opposed Villèle's cherished plan for refunding the national debt, Louis XVIII brusquely dismissed him, naming the less imaginative and more tractable Baron de Damas as his successor.[108] Real or latent differences in approach to the problem of the Spanish colonies had nothing to do with this change. One result, however, was to ensure that Villèle's attitude would prevail.

In September 1824 Louis XVIII died. For a moment politicians in Paris and elsewhere wondered if the accession of Monsieur, the Comte de Artois, as Charles X would spell the end of Villèle's power and perhaps a turn by France toward policies

---

17, 1824, Chateaubriand, *Congrès de Vérone*, II 275; Chateaubriand to Count de Serre, March 16, 1824, Chateaubriand, *Congrès de Vérone*, II, 277.

107. Chateaubriand to Talaru, Dec. 11, 1823, Chateaubriand, *Congrès de Vérone*, II, 322; Chateaubriand to Polignac, March 15, 1824, Chateaubriand, *Correspondance*, V, 180-181.

108. Emmanuel Beau de Loménie, *La carrière politique de Chateaubriand de 1814 à 1830*, 2 vols. (Paris: Plon, 1929), II, 96-136.

more markedly like those of the Holy Allies. But the new king retained Villèle and supported him as firmly as had his predecesor. When Britain decided to recognize some of the new American states, the French government braved the displeasure of the eastern courts by informing them that it had no choice but to follow suit. At no point, even before Chateaubriand's departure from office, did France create occasion for either London or Washington to consider revival of conversations about a possible alliance.

This being the case, it hardly mattered what posture the Russian government adopted. In fact, that posture was variable and uncertain. Pozzo followed one line while Foreign Minister Nesselrode wavered, and the tsar remained relatively silent.

Following the victorious French army into Spain, Pozzo went to Madrid and took it upon himself to act, in effect, as proconsul for the Holy Alliance. He counseled Ferdinand not to appease revolutionaries either at home or in the colonies. Although he helped the French ambassador persuade Ferdinand to ask that the powers use their good offices between Spain and her colonies, he encouraged the king to believe that the result would be another European congress, from which would emerge a united appeal to the colonies to submit and, when they refused, support for Spain in subduing them. Maybe this is what he expected and wanted. Maybe he was just leading Ferdinand on. Maybe he had something else in mind, for one of his dispatches to St. Petersburg suggested that the outcome of a congress might be some pronouncement acknowledging that the colonies had cut their ties with the mother country but placing them somehow beyond the pale. Whatever was in his mind, Pozzo gave other diplomats in Madrid the impression that he favored European intervention in the Americas and that his position had the blessing of the tsar.[109]

---

109. Talaru to Chateaubriand, Nov, 29, Dec. 6, 1823, CP: Espagne, DCCXXIV; Adrien Maggiolo, *Corse, France et Russie: Pozzo di Borgo, 1764-1842* (Paris: Calmann Levy, 1890), pp. 277-281; Pozzo to Nesselrode, Jan. 30, 1824, partially quoted in Dexter Perkins, *The Monroe Doctrine, 1823-1826* (Cambridge, Mass.: Harvard University Press, 1932), pp. 176-177, and Bolkhovitinov, *Doktrina Monro*, pp. 268-269.

In St. Petersburg, Nesselrode was the recipient of reports from Pozzo and also of complaints from Vienna and Paris that Pozzo's intransigence jeopardized peace between the continental states and England. Not only liking and admiring Pozzo but knowing that the tsar felt likewise, Nesselrode hesitated to bridle the ambassador. At the same time, he had to feel concern about the complaints, for he was aware that the tsar might well cool toward him if Prince Metternich ceased to sing his praises or if Chateaubriand protested that Russian policy undermined his standing vis-à-vis Villèle.[110] In addition, Nesselrode had to cope with the people in his own department and elsewhere whose preoccupation was the future of the Russian-American Company.

In ordinary circumstances, Nesselrode might have reverted to being a mere clerk, leaving all significant decisions to the tsar. But Alexander fell ill in January 1824, was unable for several weeks to deal with business at all, and afterward limited the amount of time he spent with any visitors. Hence Nesselrode had to guess at the tsar's pleasure and handle Pozzo and the foreign governments largely by himself.

Prudently, Nesselrode chose to make few decisions. He did point out to Pozzo the importance which the tsar attached to keeping Chateaubriand in office. He also cautioned him once to bear in mind that Russia's interest in the Spanish colonies was abstract and that Russia herself was not likely to supply Spain with anything more than money. In the meantime, he led the Austrians to believe that he agreed with Metternich that the actual fate of the Spanish colonies was unimportant; that what was critical was for the continental powers and England to preserve a common front against revolutionary principles; and that compromise was therefore desirable, even if it involved offense

---

110. Count Lebzeltern to Prince Metternich, March 22, 1824 (two dispatches), Grand Duke Nicolas Mikhailovitch, ed., *Les rapports diplomatiques de Lebzeltern, Ministre d' Autriche à la Cour de Russie (1816-1826)* (St. Petersburg: Gosudarstvennie Bymag', 1913), pp. 131-132; La Ferronays to Minister of Foreign Affairs, Feb. 17, 1824, Grand Duke Nicolas Mikhailovitch, *L' empereur Alexandre Ier: Essai d' étude historique,* 2 vols. (St. Petersburg: Papiers de l' État, 1912), II, 507; Nesselrode to Countess Nesselrode, Jan. 9, 1821, Count A. de Nesselrode, ed., *Lettres et papiers du Chancelier Comte de Nesselrode, 1760-1850,* 12 vols. (Paris: A. Lehure, 1908), VI, 114.

to Spain. On the other hand, Nesselrode led the French to think that he sympathized with Pozzo. He even went so far as to speculate aloud before the French ambassador, La Ferronays, about the possibility of an international army's being sent to the Americas.[111]

If Nesselrode actually had an opinion of his own, it is impossible to decipher it. In dealing with matters affecting the Russian-American Company, however, he seemed to take it for granted that relations with the United States were going to remain amicable. Overriding the company's objections, he insisted on conclusion and ratification of an agreement limiting their operations to territory north of 54° 40′. The agreement, he told them, had the virtue of committing the United States to formal recognition of Russia's right to some land in North America. Also, he said vaguely, it served higher interests of the state.[112] All in all, the signals given out by Nesselrode suggested that the Russian government, while it would never countenance the revolutions in the Americas, felt that they did not menace order and piety as did revolutions in Europe and hence did not necessitate a crusade on the part of legitimate monarchies.

Insofar as the tsar's health permitted him to intervene, he did little to put Russian policy on a more settled course. To be sure, he defended Pozzo, urged the convening of a congress, and said on one occasion that he expected such a congress to result in some aid to Spain. But, like Metternich, he showed much less

---

111. Mikhailovitch, *Alexandre Ier*, I, 293; N. K. Shilder, *Imperator' Aleksandr Pervyi: Ego Zhizn i Tsarstvovanie*, 4 vols. (St. Petersburg: A. S. Suborin, 1905), IV, 307-310; Nesselrode to Pozzo, Jan. 22, 1824, Maggiolo, *Corse, France et Russie*, pp. 279-280; Lebzeltern to Metternich, Dec. 30, 1823, March 22, 1824, Mikhailovitch, *Rapports diplomatiques de Lebzeltern*, pp. 124, 131; La Ferronays to Minister of Foreign Affairs, March, 1, May 14, 1824, CP: Russie, CLXVI.

112. Count N. S. Mordvinov to Nesselrode, Jan. 8, 1824, S. B. Okun, *The Russian-American Company*, translated from the Russian (Cambridge, Mass.: Harvard University Press, 1951), p. 87; Mordvinov to Nesselrode, March 3, 1824, 59th Congress, 2d session, Senate Document No. 162, "Proceedings of the Alaskan Boundary Tribunal," II, 152-153; Middleton to Adams, April 19, 1824, ibid., pp. 69-80; Nesselrode to Mordvinov, April 23, 1824, ibid., pp. 166-169; Nesselrode to Mordvinov, April 30, 1824, V. A. Bil 'basov, ed., *Arkhiv Grafov' Mordvinovykh*, 6 vols. (St. Petersburg: I. N. Skorokhodova, 1902), V, 649-654; minutes of the Council of Ministers, Aug. 2, 1824, ibid., pp. 677-678.

concern about the Spanish colonies per se than about the preservation of solidarity among European monarchies. After the dismissal of Chateaubriand, he seemed worried chiefly lest the issue lead France to side with Britain against the Holy Allies. His interest in the Spanish colonies seemed to become more and more academic. Except for expressing displeasure when Britain recognized some of the republics and when France showed signs of following suit, he seemed to let the whole subject slip from his mind.[113]

Despite Pozzo's activities, the Russian government thus put little pressure on France to aid Spain in the Americas. Knowing that Britain would resist, Villèle in any case had decided to give no such aid. His resoluteness on this point was sufficiently evident to quiet apprehensions in London. The conditions on the continent and in England that had given rise to Canning's bid for an American alliance thus disappeared.

The Aftermath At Home

In the United States, the setting for foreign policy decisions meanwhile underwent rapid changes. On the evening of February 14, 1824, the congressional nominating caucus convened in the chamber of the House. Only a handful of senators or representatives leaning to Adams, Calhoun, Clay, or Jackson appeared. The final tally showed sixty-four votes for Crawford and four for other candidates. Though Crawfordite newspapers argued that the result should still be binding on Republicans, the smallness of the turnout made it clear to everyone that the caucus not only would not decide the election but would not even influence it significantly.[114]

---

113. Lebzeltern to Metternich, April 17, 1824, Mikhailovitch, *Rapports diplomatiques de Lebzeltern*, pp. 136-139; La Ferronays to Minister of Foreign Affairs, March 1, 1824, Feb. 22, 1825, Mikhailovitch, *Alexandre Ier*, II, 511, 517-519; La Ferronays to Minister of Foreign Affairs, May 14, Sept 11, 1824, CP: Russie, CLXVI-CLXVII.

114. Baltimore *Weekly Register*, Feb. 21, 28, 1824; Washington *National Intelligencer*, Feb. 16, March 10, 1824; Richmond *Enquirer*, Feb. 18, 1824; Daniel Webster to Jeremiah Mason, Feb. 15, 1824, Webster, *Writings*, IV, 80-81; Washington *Republican*, Feb. 24, 1824; Louisa Catherine Adams to Charles Francis Adams, March 7, 1824, Adams

A more startling development occurred later in February when a representative convention assembled in Philadelphia to make a presidential nomination, for the leaders of the Family Party found that they could not get enough Pennsylvania Republicans to support Calhoun. Switching sides abruptly, they joined in nominating Jackson, whose popularity had been soaring ever since the fall of Cadiz produced a sense of crisis among the public. For practical purposes, Calhoun ceased to be a contender. Without Pennsylvania, he had no realistic prospect of winning. He and his friends had to turn to thoughts of the vice-presidency.[115]

By the spring of 1824, Crawford was a weakened candidate, sure of carrying only Georgia and Virginia. Jackson now shared the West with Clay and had Pennsylvania besides. The Carolinas, Alabama, Mississippi, and all the middle states except Pennsylvania remained uncertain. All New England seemed Adams's. Within the administration, therefore, Adams was stronger than he had been a few months earlier. With his favorite, Calhoun, out of the running, the President had to contemplate being succeeded by Crawford, whom he detested; Clay, who had been his outspoken critic; Jackson, whose judgment he distrusted; or by Adams. In these circumstances, it was no longer open to Monroe to overrule his secretary of state on a matter that might affect his election prospects. Even if Rush had reported Canning as showing interest in renewed alliance talks, it is probable that he would have been directed not to pursue the subject.

Adams was able to base his appeal to the electorate on accomplishments in foreign affairs, chiefly the acquisition of title to Florida and the trans-Mississippi West. He had escaped the danger of having to defend himself against charges of being the man who had made the United States a satellite of England or the man who had either ignored the merits of Edward Everett

---

Papers; Rufus King to John A. King, March 10, 1824, Rufus King Papers (New-York Historical Society); Adams diary, March 13, 20, 31, 1824.

115. Philadelphia *Franklin Gazette*, Feb. 19, 1824; Calhoun to Maxcy, Feb. 27, 1824, Calhoun, *Papers*, VIII, 554-555. (Only a few weeks earlier, Calhoun had proclaimed Pennsylvania "firm as a rock": Calhoun to Swift, Jan. 25, 1824, Calhoun, *Papers*, VIII, 504.)

or sent a Federalist to Greece. For Adams and the other candidates, the effect of decisions associated with the Monroe Doctrine was to make foreign policy less a matter of controversy than it might otherwise have been. Even Clay found it advisable to minimize foreign affairs in his campaign documents.

The one other possible effect was to make Jackson a more appealing candidate. Popular support for him grew at precisely the period when newspapers were most full of reports that European powers might have designs on the Western Hemisphere, and it is striking how often resolutions adopted by assemblies in widely scattered places emphasized this peril as a reason for calling the general to the presidency.[116] Perhaps the alleged crisis contributed at least to the pace of the movement for him.

In any case, Jackson pulled ahead of the others, even though the sense of danger subsided. In November 1824, he polled over 150,000 votes as compared with less than 109,000 for Adams and less than 50,000 each for Crawford and Clay. Except for Kentucky, Missouri, and Ohio, Jackson carried all the West. He also won both Carolinas, New Jersey, and Pennsylvania, and he split Maryland with Adams and Crawford. Nevertheless, he failed to win a majority in the electoral college. The contest went to the House, with Jackson, Adams, and Crawford the three contenders. Clay, no longer in the running, urged his supporters to vote for Adams, and Adams won on the first ballot.

The explanation for this outcome is only partly to be found in the history recounted here. While the approach of the election had a great deal to do with the foreign policy decisions of the Monroe administration in the winter of 1823-1824, those decisions affected the election only in that they enabled Adams to remain a strong candidate. For the basic policies adopted by the administration, preserving isolation from European politics and limiting at least to the Western Hemisphere the area in which the United States would exert ideological leadership, were already policies tailored to satisfy the widest possible spectrum of the electorate.

---

116. Louisville *Public Advertiser*, March 22, June 25, July 9, 1823; Washington *National Intelligencer*, April 30, Nov. 5, 11, 14, 26, 1823; Washington *Republican*, Aug. 19, 1823; Baltimore *Weekly Register*, Nov. 8, 1823, Jan. 9, 23, 1824; Philadelphia *Franklin Gazette*,· Dec. 23, 1823.

6

Implications

In this reexamination of the origins of the Monroe Doctrine, I have developed two themes with implications beyond the particular episode. One has been explicit—that domestic politics may be a critical determinant of foreign policy. The other has been implicit, though it has probably not escaped the attentive reader. It is an argument for an unusual method of attempting to distinguish such determinants—that of placing oneself at a point in the past and asking: what kind of analysis would have produced the most accurate prediction of what was to occur? Each of these general themes deserves some elaboration.

Since foreign policy is nearly always debated and analyzed in terms of national interests, lofty moral purposes, and the like, it may seem perverse to contend that the actual decisions may be controlled by domestic political factors which the policymakers seldom mention, either at the time or in their later reconstructions. But the character of foreign policy debate is, in fact, indicative of the high uncertainty that shrouds it. National interest is almost as empty a concept as the good of mankind, and standards of right and wrong as applied to nations are equally vague. More specific discussion of issues tends to concern contingencies which are hard to predict and largely uncontrollable—the outcomes of political processes in other governmental systems. In these circumstances, it is not surprising that the positions which men take may be products of rationalization. Indeed, this is probably more likely to be the case with foreign policy than domestic policy, for on domestic issues the interests of specific groups of citizens may be more evident and the criteria for distinguishing right from wrong may be more clear.

In the instance of the Monroe Doctrine, the positions adopted by American policymakers seem to me to be best explained as functions of their domestic ambitions—Monroe's, to leave the presidency without being followed by recrimination and to be succeeded by someone who would not repudiate his policies; Adams's, Calhoun's, and Clay's, to become President; Jefferson's, Gallatin's, and perhaps Madison's, to see Crawford succeed. Consistently with their fundamental beliefs, any of these men could have taken different positions. Adams, for example, could have reasoned just as easily as Jefferson that concert with England would guarantee America's independence, security, and peace. He actually said as much not long before the specific issues materialized. The processes producing the actual foreign policy decisions are better understood as bargaining encounters among men with differing perspectives and ambitions than as debates about the merits of different policies. And the outcomes are most explicable as ones that equilibrated the competing or conflicting interests of men with differing political assets.

This conclusion may seem cynical. It is not meant to be. For it is in fact an affirmation that foreign policy can be determined less by the cleverness or wisdom of a few policymakers than by the political structure which determines their incentives.

Among the men who played roles in this history, the one with greatest freedom to pursue national interest as he perceived and defined it was the Russian tsar. Genuinely an absolute monarch, he had to pay little heed to the parochial interests of elements in Russian society. The chief limitations upon his choices of policy were those imposed by his conscience, his estimate of the coercive power at his disposal, and his perceptions of the international system: that is, by his calculations concerning the probable behavior of other governments.

Next to Alexander, Louis XVIII enjoyed the greatest latitude for determining foreign policy on the basis of his own estimate of what was best for the nation. Ruling a less powerful and less advantageously situated state, he did not have Alexander's freedom to maneuver within the international system, and at home he suffered limitations not felt by the tsar. In deciding what ought to be done, he had to consult not only his own conscience but the attitudes of his relatives, his court, his supporters in the legislative chambers, and, to a limited extent, larger public groups that might be affected. He felt compelled to listen to advice from Villèle which emphasized domestic interests, for he had to avoid a situation in which his only option was the post chaise. Even so, he could afford to base his decisions to a significant degree upon his own beliefs and perceptions.

Of no one in Britain could the same assertion be made. The king could influence policy, but he could not dictate it. Lord Liverpool had to give first priority to the maintenance of his majority at Westminster, and in the long run that meant choosing those foreign policies which would give least offense to elements within his heterogeneous coalition. Except momentarily, his own abstract conceptions of national interest could carry relatively little weight. The same was true for members of his government, including Canning. Indeed, Canning's position was so precarious that his recommendations could be little more than products of his estimates as to what his cabinet colleagues would permit that would be popular among the backbenchers who formed his own base of strength. For practical purposes, British foreign policy reflected the attitudes and interests of the two houses of parliament.

In the United States, the Constitution accorded the President discretion greater than that of the British prime minister but less than that of the French king. Monroe could have decided the issues before him by the light of his own conscience, constrained only by knowledge that he could be overruled by Congress. Even if Monroe had been temperamentally disposed to exercise his discretion, however, he would have had difficulty doing so because of the structure of his executive branch. He had around him cabinet members with independent support both in the Congress and in the country at large. Only at great cost could he have obeyed his instincts if they told him to disregard and break with all the men who headed executive departments. In practice, he judged that, being already at outs with Crawford, he could not afford a rupture with Adams. In all likelihood, he would have reached the same conclusion even if he had been a more forceful and determined man.

The power of cabinet members derived from their actual or potential constituencies. Like their counterparts in Britain, they had to tend these constituencies. But, given the structure of the American political system, that meant appealing to the interests and prejudices not only of legislators but of varieties of voters scattered among the various states. While Adams and Calhoun had some latitude for acting according to their private beliefs and their perceptions of what the international system required or would permit, the boundaries were narrow. On one side was need to win the President's assent; on the other, need to hold or increase their margins of congressional and public support. To a large extent, therefore, American foreign policy approximated whatever consensus obtained among a majority of the interested electorate.

I have argued here that the positions of American policymakers and the outcomes of their debates could have been more accurately predicted by analysis of their domestic political interests than by analysis of their private beliefs or of the options defined for them by apparent actions or intentions of other nations. The reason is that the structure of the American government was such as to give policymakers strong incentives for following what appeared to be effective public opinion. The same did not hold true at all for Russia, where the best prediction would have been based on knowledge of the beliefs and perceptions of the tsar. It was less true of France and even of Britain than of the United States, and it would not be equally valid for the United States in later periods, when cabinet members came to be chosen as servants of the President and complex bureaucracies grew to be important elements in the foreign policy process.

Nevertheless, I would suggest that the relationship between governmental structure and foreign policy should command more attention than it has from historians, political scientists, official analysts, and journalists who write about international affairs. For we all share an instinctive tendency to adopt a single model and to assume that all governments fit it—to take it for granted, for example, that if conceptions of strategic advantage govern the policy of one, they must govern the policies of all. With the nations of the 1820s as illustrations, I would contend that the controlling factors are likely to differ, depending on how the government is organized, how secure in office the policymakers are, and where they see the sources of and threats to their own tenure or advancement. As indicated, I would offer the hypothesis that autochthonous ideas of national interest, perceptions of external forces, and perceptions of internal forces will have an influence on policy that varies proportionally with the position of the government on a spectrum running from the purely authoritarian to the purely democratic. I would argue further that scholars, analysts, and policymakers should keep this hypothesis in mind when speculating not only on why governments have acted as they have but on how they may act in the future.

My second theme is sounded more for fellow historians than for others who may read this book, but it may have some immediate interest for those who make a habit of looking at what historians write and some potential interest for anyone who engages in political forecasting. For the logic usually used in historical reconstruction is that which mathematicians have formalized as regression analysis. Using such analysis, an economist can put into a computer all the data concerning trends preceding some given outcome. Then, by changing the data for a particular trend, he can make the computer tell him whether the outcome would have been significantly different. With regard to a recession, for example, he can ask whether an increase in the money supply some six or twelve months earlier would have made it less severe. In a crude way and usually without the assistance of computers, historians make similar calculations. To cite a well-known example, some writers on the Civil War have argued that if the southern economy had not developed as it did, the South would never have seceded. Others have said that if the abolitionists had been less hotheaded, no armed conflict could have occurred. Still others have contended that secession and war could have been averted only if the southerners had voluntarily abolished slavery. In each instance, retrospective judgment as to what was the most important cause of the event depends on an imaginative construction of what would have happened if a particular factor had been absent or different in character.

Historians employ such reasoning even though they refer to history as a seamless web and recognize that it is illogical to suppose that if one set of conditions had been different, all other conditions would have remained the same. When confronted with formal regression analyses executed by colleagues who have learned mathematics, they are apt to express indignation for precisely this reason. Nevertheless, they resort covertly to something like regression analysis because they see no better way of generalizing about causal forces.

I have tried in this book to use a form of analysis which is somewhat different. Lacking skill in formal logic, I am not prepared to specify all the assumptions which it involves, and I confess that it derives from the nonformal epistemology of Benedetto Croce and R. G. Collingwood, which emphasizes the historian's explaining the past by achieving empathy with the people who experienced it.

I have tried to ask here what predictions a well-informed observer would have made in 1823 on the basis of three different assumptions about what was likely to control decisions facing the United States government. I argue that the observer would not have been able to foretell the course of debate by reasoning from knowledge about the backgrounds and previous opinions of the men involved or from knowledge of the external world which they were presumably trying to influence. He would have been able to make an accurate forecast if he had assumed that the positions of the policymakers would match their domestic political interests. As indicated earlier, I would add the caution that this particular finding applied to Americans of 1823 and would not have applied equally to Europeans of that time and does not necessarily apply to Americans of any later time.

In any case, the point here is that the approach enables one to identify a set of critical determinants without having to resort to guesswork about what might have been. To conclude that domestic political factors were dominant does not require speculation on what posture Adams or Calhoun might have adopted if not candidates for the presidency or to replay the scenario with different characters in key roles. Instead, one takes the facts as they were, uses his imagination to situate himself at some moment before the fact, asks what factors might determine a then uncertain outcome, decides which weightings of these factors would have produced the most accurate forecasts of the actual outcome, and explains that outcome accordingly. While conceding that this approach still leaves room for differences in judgment due to differences in the selection and evaluation of evidence, I would argue that it has advantages over regression analysis. I would even suggest that a formalized version of it might prove more powerful if applied by economists and economic historians. I hope some of them will test this proposition.

In any case, I think that this approach yields better understanding of how the Monroe Doctrine took form, for it enables one to see for the first time how the character and structure of domestic politics shaped fundamental foreign policy choices. It is probably superfluous to remark in conclusion that the choices so shaped were wise ones. For more than a century, Americans were to find the consequences tolerable. Until the doctrine was given new connotations in the 1890s and afterward, most other people in the world were also to find the consequences unobjectionable. Very few foreign policy decisions have passed such tests. And the credit belongs not to Monroe or Adams or any other individual but to the pluralistic, relatively representative, and highly politicized system within which they worked. The Monroe Doctrine may be said to have epitomized the foreign policy of democracy.

Appendices
Index

Appendix A

Evidence Concerning Presidential Preferences of Members of the House and Senate in the Winter of 1823-1824

REPRESENTATIVES

Joel Abbot (Ga.)   Attended the caucus in 1824; hence probably for Crawford.

Parmenio Adams (N.Y.)   Reported to be for Adams: J. O. Morse to Adams, July 14, 1823, Adams Family Papers, Massachusetts Historical Society. (Not seated until Jan. 7, 1824).

Adam R. Alexander (Tenn.)   No information.

Mark Alexander (Va.)   Attended the caucus in 1824; hence probably for Crawford.

Robert Allen (Tenn.)   No information.

Samuel C. Allen (Mass.)   For Adams: Adams diary, May 1, 1824.

James Allison, Jr. (Pa.)   No information.

William S. Archer (Va.)   Attended the caucus in 1824; hence probably for Crawford.

John Bailey (Mass.)   Previously clerk of the State Department and a manager of the Adams campaign: Papers of John Bailey, New-York Historical Society.

William L. Ball (Va.)   For Crawford: Baltimore *Weekly Register*, Feb. 14, 1824.

Noyes Barber (Conn.)   For Crawford: Adams diary, Jan. 21, 1825.

John S. Barbour (Va.)   Attended the caucus in 1824; hence probably for Crawford.

Philip P. Barbour (Va.)   No information.

Ichabod Bartlett (N.H.)   For Crawford: Josiah Butler to Adams, July 25, 1823, Adams Papers; William Plumer, Jr., to William Plumer, Sr., Dec. 22, 1823, Everett S. Brown, ed., *The Missouri Compromise and Presidential Politics, 1820-1825, from the Letters of William Plumer, Jr.* (St. Louis: Missouri Historical

Society, 1926), pp. 90-91; Webster to Jeremiah Mason, Dec. 22, 1823, Papers of Daniel Webster, Library of Congress; William Plumer, Sr., to William Plumer, Jr., Jan. 5, 1824, Papers of William Plumer, Sr., Library of Congress.

Mordecai Bartley (O.)   No information.

Burwell Bassett (Va.)   Signed the caucus call and attended the caucus; hence almost certainly for Crawford.

Francis Baylies (Mass.)   For Crawford: Papers of Francis Baylies, Taunton Public Library, Taunton, Mass.; memo by Jonathan Russell, n.d., Papers of William H. Crawford, Duke University Library; Washington *National Intelligencer*, Aug. 16, 1823. One pro-Crawford congressman suspected him, however, of being for Clay: Lewis Williams to Virgil Maxcy, Sept. 15, 1823, Papers of the Galloway, Maxcy, and Markoe Families, Library of Congress.

Philemon Beecher (O.)   A Federalist: 81st Congress, 2d session, House Document No. 607, "A Biographical Directory of the American Congress, 1774-1949" (hereafter, *BDC*); no other information.

John Blair (Tenn.)   No information.

William C. Bradley (Vt.)   Probably for Crawford: Adams diary, Jan. 12, 1824.

Samuel Breck (Pa.)   A Federalist; said to have been the sole supporter of Adams in the Pennsylvania delegation: Allen Johnson and Dumas Malone, eds., *The Dictionary of American Biography*, 22 vols. (New York: Macmillan, 1928-1944) (hereafter, *DAB*).

William L. Brent (La.)   No information.

John Brown (Pa.)   No information.

James Buchanan (Pa.)   A Federalist; for Calhoun: Philip Shriver Klein, *President James Buchanan: A Biography* (University Park, Pa.: Pennsylvania State University Press, 1962), p. 44.

Daniel A. A. Buck (Vt.)   No information.

Richard A. Buckner (Ky.)   No information.

William Burleigh (Me.)   Probably for Adams: Baltimore *Weekly Register*, Nov. 22, 1823, Feb. 14, 1824.

Hutchins G. Burton (N.C.)   For Crawford: ibid., Feb. 14, 1824; William Plumer, Jr., to William Plumer, Sr., Feb. 16, 1824, Brown, *Missouri Compromise*, p. 100; Adams diary, March 24, 1824.

John W. Cady (N.Y.)   For Adams: John W. Taylor to Adams, Aug. 2, 1823, Adams Papers.

Churchill C. Cambreleng (N.Y.)   For Crawford: J. O. Morse to Adams, July 24, 1823, Adams Papers; Adams diary, Jan. 25, 1824.

John W. Campbell (O.)   Anti-Crawford: Baltimore *Weekly Register*, Jan. 25, 1823.

Robert B. Campbell (S.C.)   No information.

John Carter (S.C.)   Possibly for Adams: Adams diary, May 3, 1824.

George Cary (Ga.)   Attended the caucus; hence probably for Crawford.

George Cassedy (N.J.)   No information.

Lot Clark (N.Y.)   Attended the caucus; hence probably for Crawford.

Henry Clay (Ky.)   Presumably for Clay.

Thomas W. Cobb (Ga.)   For Crawford: Cobb to Crawford, Jan. 15, 1825, J. E. D. Shipp, *Giant Days, or the Life and Times of William H. Crawford* (Americus, Ga.: Southern Printers, 1909), pp. 179-180;· Washington *National Intelligencer*, April 10, 1823.

John Cocke (Tenn.)   No information.

Ela Collins (N.Y.)   For Adams: Morse to Adams, July 24, 1823, Adams Papers.

Lewis Condict (N.J.)   No information.

Henry W. Connor (N.C.)   For Crawford: Thomas W. Cobb to Tait, Feb. 2, 1824, Papers of Charles W. Tait, Alabama Department of Archives and History.

Daniel P. Cook (Ill.)   For Adams: Cook to Adams, July 30, 1821, Aug. 29, 1823, Adams Papers.

Samuel C. Crafts (Vt.)   No information.

Hector Craig (N.Y.)   No information.

Benjamin W. Crowninshield (Mass.)   Probably for Adams: P. P. F. Degrand to Adams, Jan. 23, 1822, Oct. 16, 1822, Adams Papers; memo by Jonathan Russell, n.d., Crawford Papers (Duke). But Adams himself had thought Crowninshield an ally of Crawford: Adams diary, March 26, 1818.

John Culpepper (N.C.)   For Crawford: Cobb to Tait, Feb. 2, 1824, Tait Papers.

Joshua Cushman (Me.)   For Adams: unsigned memorandum, Dec. 1, 1821, Adams Papers.

Alfred Cuthbert (Ga.)   For Crawford: Adams diary, May 25, 1824.

Rowland Day (N.Y.)   Attended the caucus; hence probably for Crawford.

Job Durfee (R.I.)   For Adams: Degrand to Adams, Dec. 10, 1823, Adams Papers.

Henry W. Dwight (Mass.)   For Adams: Adams diary, April 18, May 1, 1824.

Justin Dwinnell (N.Y.)   For Adams: Morse to Adams, July 24, 1823, Adams Papers.

Lewis Eaton (N.Y.)   For Adams: John W. Taylor to Adams, Aug. 2, 1823, Adams Papers.

Samuel Eddy (R.I.)   For Crawford: Degrand to Adams, Dec. 10, 1823, Adams Papers.

Samuel Edwards (Pa.)   A Federalist: *BDC*; no other information.

Weldon N. Edwards (N.C.)   Attended the caucus; hence probably for Crawford.

William Cox Ellis (Pa.)   A Federalist: *BDC*; no other information.

Patrick Farrelly (Pa.)   For Calhoun: Philadelphia *Franklin Gazette*, Jan. 10, 1824.

John Findlay (Pa.)   For Calhoun: ibid.

John Floyd (Va.)   For Crawford: Charles H. Ambler, *The Life and Diary of John Floyd* (Richmond: Richmond Press, 1918), p. 60.

Charles A. Foote (N.Y.)   For Adams: Morse to Adams, July 24, 1823, Adams
    Papers; Adams diary, Feb. 2, 1825.
Samuel A. Foote (Conn.)   No information.
John Forsyth (Ga.)   For Crawford: Adams diary, May 25, 1824.
Walter Forward (Pa.)   For Crawford: Adams diary, May 20, 1824.
Joel Frost (N.Y.)   Attended the caucus; hence probably for Crawford.
Timothy Fuller (Mass.)   For Adams: Adams to Fuller, July 31, 1823, Adams
    Papers; memorandum by Jonathan Russell, n.d., Crawford Papers (Duke).
Robert S. Garnett (Va.)   For Calhoun or Crawford: letters by him to Swift,
    Papers of Joseph G. Swift, United States Military Academy, indicate sup-
    port for Calhoun, but Cobb to Tait, Feb. 2, 1824, Tait Papers, lists him
    as pro-Crawford but resolved not to attend the caucus.
Daniel Garrison (N.J.)   No information.
Alfred M. Gatlin (N.C.)   Attended the caucus; hence probably for Crawford.
John W. Gazlay (O.)   For Crawford originally but by Feb. 1824 for Jackson:
    Harry R. Stevens, *The Early Jackson Party in Ohio* (Durham: Duke Univer-
    sity Press, 1957), pp. 45-47, 84-85.
Joseph Gist (S.C.)   For Crawford: Adams diary, May 3, 1824.
Andrew R. Govan (S.C.)   No information.
Henry H. Gurley (La.)   No information.
Thomas H. Hall (N.C.)   Attended the caucus; hence probably for Crawford.
James Hamilton, Jr. (S.C.)   Signed the anticaucus resolution; possibly for
    Adams: Adams diary, May 3, 1824.
Robert Harris (Pa.)   No information.
Matthew Harvey (N.H.)   No information.
Moses Hayden (N.Y.)   For Adams: Morse to Adams, July 24, 1823, Adams
    Papers.
Joseph Hemphill (Pa.)   A Federalist: *BDC*; no other information.
Robert P. Henry (Ky.)   No information.
John Herkimer (N.Y.)   For Adams: Morse to Adams, July 24, 1823, Adams
    Papers; John W. Taylor to Adams, Aug. 2, 1823, ibid.
Ebenezer Herrick (Me.)   For Adams: unsigned memorandum, Dec. 1, 1821,
    Adams Papers.
William Heyward (Md.)   Attended the caucus; hence probably for Craw-
    ford.
Aaron Hobart (Mass.)   Leaning to Crawford: memorandum by Jonathan
    Russell, n.d., Crawford Papers (Duke).
James L. Hogeboom (N.Y.)   Reported for Adams: Morse to Adams, July 24,
    1823, Adams Papers; but attended the caucus and hence probably for
    Crawford.
George Holcombe (N.J.)   Signed the anticaucus resolution; hence probably
    against Crawford; no other information.
Charles Hooks (N.C.)   Attended the caucus; hence probably for Crawford.
Samuel Houston (Tenn.)   For Jackson: Baltimore *Weekly Register*, Feb. 14,

1824; Houston to Robert Williams, Feb. 4, 1824, Papers of Andrew Jackson, Library of Congress.

Samuel D. Ingham (Pa.)   For Calhoun: Charles M. Wiltse, *John C. Calhoun, Nationalist, 1782-1828* (Indianapolis: Bobbs-Merrill Co., 1944), pp. 232, 272, 280.

Jacob C. Isacks (Tenn.)   For Jackson: Adams diary, April 12, 1824.

Lemuel Jenkins (N.Y.)   Attended the caucus; hence probably for Crawford.

Jonathan Jennings (Ind.)   Probably for Adams: Adams to Jennings, July 14, 1820, Adams Papers; signed the anticaucus resolution.

Francis Johnson (Ky.)   For Adams: BDC.

John T. Johnson (Ky.)   For Jackson: BDC.

Joseph Johnson (Va.)   No information.

Joseph Kent (Md.)   For Calhoun: Calhoun to Virgil Maxcy, Jan. 13, 1822, W. Edwin Hemphill, ed., *The Papers of John C. Calhoun*, 8 vols. in progress (Columbia, S.C.: University of South Carolina Press, 1959), VI, 620.

David Kidder (Me.)   No information.

George Kremer (Pa.)   For Calhoun: Philip S. Klein, *Pennsylvania Politics, 1817-1832: A Game without Rules* (Philadelphia: Historical Society of Pennsylvania, 1940), p. 97.

Samuel Lathrop (Mass.)   Probably for Adams: Adams diary, May 1, 1824.

Samuel Lawrence (N.Y.)   For Adams: Morse to Adams, July 24, 1823, Adams Papers.

John Lee (Md.)   No information.

Jabez Leftwich (Va.)   Attended the caucus; hence probably for Crawford.

Robert P. Letcher (Ky.)   For Clay: Adams diary, Dec. 23, 1824.

Enoch Lincoln (Me.)   Said to be personally for Adams but politically aligned with pro-Crawford elements in Maine: unsigned memo, Dec. 1, 1821, Adams Papers.

Elisha Litchfield (N.Y.)   For Crawford: Baltimore *Weekly Register*, Feb. 14, 1824.

Peter Little (Md.)   For Calhoun: Calhoun to Maxcy, Jan. 13, 1882, Calhoun, *Papers*, VI, 620-621.

Arthur Livermore (N.H.)   No information.

Edward Livingston (La.)   Probably for Jackson: there are several letters from Livingston in the Jackson Papers; while none makes a commitment about the caucus, they are all very friendly.

John Locke (Mass.)   No information.

John Long (N.C.)   Attended the caucus; hence probably for Crawford.

Stephen Longfellow (Me.)   A Federalist; no further information.

Rollin C. Mallary (Vt.)   No information.

Willie P. Mangum (N.C.)   For Crawford: Mangum to Ruffin, Jan. 20, 1824: J. G. de Roulhac Hamilton, ed., *The Papers of Thomas Ruffin*, 4 vols. (Raleigh, N.C.: Edwards and Broughton, 1918-1920), I, 287-288; Cobb to Tait, Feb. 2, 1824, Tait Papers.

Philip S. Markley (Pa.)   Attended the caucus; hence probably for Crawford.

Henry C. Martindale (N.Y.)   For Adams: Morse to Adams, July 24, 1823, Adams Papers; Hunt to Lee, July 31, 1824, ibid.; Taylor to Adams, Aug. 2, 1823, ibid.

Dudley Marvin (N.Y.)   Probably for Adams: *BDC*.

James Matlack (N.J.)   No information.

Aaron Matson (N.H.)   No information.

Duncan McArthur (O.)   No information.

William McCoy (Va.)   Attended the caucus; hence probably for Crawford.

George McDuffie (S.C.)   For Calhoun: Calhoun, *Papers*, passim.

Samuel McKean (Pa.)   For Calhoun: Klein, *Pennsylvania Politics*, p. 210.

John McKee (Ala.)   For Crawford: Gabriel Moore to Bailey, July 3, 1823, Bailey Papers; Cobb to Tait, Feb. 2, 1824, Tait Papers.

Isaac McKim (Md.)   For Crawford: Cobb to Tait, Feb. 2, 1824, Tait Papers.

Louis McLane (Del.)   For Crawford: Papers of Louis McLane, University of Delaware.

William McLean (O.)   For Calhoun: Eugene H. Rosebloom, "Ohio in the Presidential Election of 1824," *Ohio Archeological and Historical Quarterly*, 26 (April 1917), 178.

Charles F. Mercer (Va.)   A Federalist; no further information.

Thomas Metcalfe (Ky.)   Signed the anticaucus resolution; no further information.

Daniel H. Miller (Pa.)   No information.

George E. Mitchell (Md.)   No information.

James S. Mitchell (Pa.)   No information.

Gabriel Moore (Ala.)   For Adams: Moore to Bailey, July 3, 1823, Bailey Papers.

Thomas P. Moore (Ky.)   No information.

John J. Morgan (N.Y.)   Possibly for Adams: Morse to Adams, July 24, 1823, Adams Papers.

Raphael Neale (Md.)   No information.

Jeremiah Nelson (Mass.)   A Federalist; for Adams: Adams diary, May 1, 1824.

Thomas Newton, Jr. (Va.)   No information.

Jeremiah O'Brien (Me.)   No information.

George W. Owen (Ala.)   For Adams or Jackson: Moore to Bailey, July 3, 1823, Bailey Papers; J. G. Lynn to Jackson, Aug. 18, 1823, Jackson Papers.

John Patterson (O.)   No information.

Thomas Patterson (Pa.)   No information.

George Plumer (Pa.)   No information.

William Plumer, Jr. (N.H.)   For Adams: Brown, *Missouri Compromise*, passim.

Joel R. Poinsett (S.C.)   Probably for Adams: Adams diary, May 3, 1824.

William Prince (Ind.)   For Crawford: Anon. to Adams, Sept. 30, 1822, Adams Papers.

John Randolph (Va.)   For Crawford: Shipp, *Giant Days*, pp. 167-168.

Christopher Rankin (Miss.)   For Crawford: James Cornell to Adams, Sept. 2, 1823, Adams Papers.

John Reed (Mass.)   For Adams: Adams diary, May 1, 1824.

James B. Reynolds (Tenn.)   No information.

Charles Rich (Vt.)   No information.

John Richards (N.Y.)   Possibly for Adams: Morse to Adams, July 24, 1823, Adams Papers; Taylor to Adams, Aug. 2, 1823, ibid. But attended the caucus.

William C. Rives (Va.)   Attended the caucus; hence probably for Crawford.

Thomas J. Rogers (Pa.)   For Calhoun: Klein, *Pennsylvania Politics*, pp. 125ff.

Robert S. Rose (N.Y.)   No information.

Thomas R. Ross (O.)   No information.

James T. Sandford (Tenn.)   No information.

Romulus M. Saunders (N.C.)   For Crawford: A. R. Newsome, ed., "Letters of Romulus M. Saunders to Bartlett Yancey, 1821-1828," *North Carolina Historical Review*, 8 (Oct. 1931), 427-462.

John Scott (Mo.)   For Crawford or Clay: D. P. Cook to Adams, Aug. 29, 1822, Adams Papers; John B. C. Lucas to Adams, Jan. 24, 1823, ibid.

Peter Sharpe (N.Y.)   For Adams: Morse to Adams, July 24, 1823, ibid.

Jonas Sibley (Mass.)   On the fence between Adams and Crawford, memo by Jonathan Russell, undated, Crawford Papers (Duke).

John Sloane (O.)   No information.

Arthur Smith (Va.)   Attended the caucus; hence probably for Crawford.

William Smith (Va.)   For Crawford: Calhoun to J. E. Calhoun, May 14, 1822, Calhoun, *Papers*, VII, 111; attended the caucus.

Alexander Smyth (Va.)   For Crawford: Washington *National Intelligencer*, Jan. 7, 1823.

Richard D. Spaight (N.C.)   Attended the caucus; hence probably for Crawford.

John S. Spence (Md.)   No information.

James Standifer (Tenn.)   No information.

James Stephenson (Va.)   No information.

Ansel Sterling (Conn.)   For Calhoun: Adams diary, Jan. 21, 1825.

Andrew Stevenson (Va.)   Attended the caucus; hence probably for Crawford.

Andrew Stewart (Pa.)   Probably for Crawford: Walter Lowrie to Gallatin, Feb. 21, 1824, Papers of Albert Gallatin, New-York Historical Society.

Ebenezer Stoddard (Conn.)   For Crawford: Adams diary, Jan. 21, 1825; attended the caucus.

Henry R. Storrs (N.Y.)   A Federalist reportedly for Adams: Morse to Adams, July 24, 1823; Adams diary, April 18, May 15, 1824.

James Strong (N.Y.)   No information.

Samuel Swan (N.J.)   No information.

Edward F. Tattnall (Ga.)   For Crawford: Washington *National Intelligencer*, Feb. 14, 1824.

John W. Taylor (N.Y.)   For Adams: Taylor to Adams, Jan. 28, 1823, Adams Papers; Adams diary, Nov. 28, 1823.

Egbert Ten Eyck (N.Y.)   For either Adams or Crawford: reported to be for Adams: Morse to Adams, July 24, 1823, Adams Papers; but attended the caucus.

John Test (Ind.)   For Adams: Anon. to Adams, Sept. 30, 1822, Adams Papers.

Philip Thompson (Ky.)   No information.

Wiley Thompson (Ga.)   Attended the caucus; hence probably for Crawford.

John Tod (Pa.)   No information.

Gideon Tomlinson (Conn.)   For Adams: Adams diary, Feb. 2, 1825.

Albert H. Tracy (N.Y.)   For Adams: Adams diary, April 17, 1824.

David Trimble (Ky.)   For Clay: Adams diary, May 23, 1824.

George Tucker (Va.)   Attended the caucus; hence probably for Crawford.

Starling Tucker (S.C.)   For Crawford: Cobb to Tait, Feb. 2, 1824, Tait Papers.

Jacob Tyson (N.Y.)   Attended the caucus; hence probably for Crawford.

Daniel Udree (Pa.)   No information.

Stephen Van Rensselaer (N.Y.)   For Adams: Taylor to Adams, Aug. 2, 1823, Adams Papers.

William W. Van Wyck (N.Y.)   Probably for Adams: Morse to Adams, July 24, 1823, Adams Papers.

Joseph Vance (O.)   No information.

Robert B. Vance (N.C.   No information.

Samuel F. Vinton (O.)   No information.

Henry R. Warfield (Md.)   A Federalist for Clay: Warfield to Clay, Dec. 18, 1821, Clay, *Papers*, III, 149.

Isaac Wayne (Pa.)   A Federalist; no further information.

Daniel Webster (Mass.)   For Calhoun: see index under Webster.

Thomas Whipple (N.H.)   Probably for Crawford: Plumer, Jr., to Plumer, Sr., Dec. 22, 1823, Brown, *Missouri Compromise*, pp. 90-91.

David White (Ky.)   No information.

Lemuel Whitman (Conn.)   For Calhoun: Adams diary, Jan. 21, 1825.

Elisha Whittlesey (O.)   No information.

Charles A. Wickliffe (Ky.)   No information.

Isaac Williams, Jr. (N.Y.)   For Adams: Morse to Adams, July 24, 1823, Adams Papers; Taylor to Adams, Aug. 2, 1823, ibid.

Jared Williams (Va.)   Attended the caucus; hence probably for Crawford.

Lewis Williams (N.C.)   For Crawford: Williams to Ruffin, Dec. 22, 1821, Ruffin, *Papers*, I, 258.

Henry Wilson (Pa.)   No information.

Isaac Wilson (N.Y.)   No information.

James Wilson (Pa.)   No information.
John Wilson (S.C.)   For Crawford: Adams diary, May 3, 1824.
William Wilson (O.)   No information.
Silas Wood (N.Y.)   No information.
William Woods (N.Y.)   No information.
John C. Wright (O.)   For Clay: Wright to Hammond, Jan. 8, 1824, Papers of Charles Hammond, Ohio Historical Society.

SENATORS

James Barbour (Va.)   For Crawford: Ritchie to Barbour, May 21, 1823, Papers of James Barbour, New York Public Library; Van Buren to Barbour, Oct. 9, 1823, ibid.
David Barton (Mo.)   For Adams: Cook to Adams, Aug. 29, 1822, Adams Papers; Baltimore *American*, Feb. 9, 1824.
Samuel Bell (N.H.)   Reported to be for Crawford: Josiah Butler to Adams, Nov. 25, 1823, Adams Papers; Plumer, Jr., to Plumer, Sr., Nov. 22, 1823, Brown, *Missouri Compromise*, pp. 90-91 (but was for Adams later: Adams diary, May 27, 1824).
Thomas H. Benton (Mo.)   For Clay: see index under Benton.
Elijah Boardman (Conn.)   No information; died Oct. 8, 1823; replaced by H. W. Edwards.
John Branch (N.C.)   No information.
Ethan Allen Brown (O.)   No information.
James Brown (La.)   Clay's brother-in-law; hence presumably for Clay.
John Chandler (Me.)   For Crawford: see index under Chandler.
Thomas Clayton (Del.)   No information.
James De Wolf (R.I.)   Reported to be for Adams or Clay: Degrand to Adams, Dec. 2, 1823, Adams Papers; reported to be for Adams, Robert Fairchild to Adams, Dec. 10, 1823, ibid.; reported to be for Crawford, Adams diary, May 13, 1824.
Mahlon Dickerson (N.J.)   For Crawford: Papers of Mahlon Dickerson, New Jersey Historical Society.
John H. Eaton (Tenn.)   For Jackson: there are many letters from Eaton to Jackson in the Jackson Papers.
Henry W. Edwards (Conn.)   For Calhoun: Calhoun to Swift, Sept. 8, 1823, Calhoun, *Papers*, VIII, 261-262.
Ninian Edwards (Ill.)   For Calhoun: see index under Edwards.
John Elliott (Ga.)   For Crawford: Adams diary, May 22, 1824.
William Findlay (Pa.)   For Calhoun: Wiltse, *Calhoun*, p. 232.
John Gaillard (S.C.)   For Crawford: Adams diary, May 22, 1824.
Robert Y. Hayne (S.C.)   For Calhoun: Thomas D. Jervey, *Robert Y. Hayne and His Times* (New York: Macmillan, 1909), pp. 143-147.

David Holmes (Miss.)   No information.

John Holmes (Me.)   For Crawford: see index under Holmes.

Andrew Jackson (Tenn.)   Presumably for Jackson.

Henry Johnson (La.)   No information.

Richard M. Johnson (Ky.)   For Clay: Papers of Richard M. Johnson, Library of Congress; Adams diary, Jan. 28, 1824.

Josiah S. Johnston (La.)   Appointed to succeed James Brown, who resigned Dec. 10, 1823; for Clay: Clay to Johnston, June 25, 1824, James F. Hopkins, ed., *The Papers of Henry Clay*, 4 vols. in progress (Lexington, Ky.: University of Kentucky Press, 1959—), III, 785.

William Kelly (Ala.)   For Adams or Jackson: Moore to Bailey, July 23, 1823, Bailey Papers; J. G. Lyon to Jackson, Aug. 18, 1823, Jackson Papers.

Rufus King (N.Y.)   Probably for Adams: see index under King.

William R. King (Ala.)   For Jackson: Lyon to Jackson, Aug. 18, 1823, Jackson Papers.

Nehemiah R. Knight (R.I.)   For Crawford: Adams diary, May 12, 1824.

James Lanman (Conn.)   For Crawford: Morse to Adams, July 24, 1823, Adams Papers; Adams diary, Feb. 2, 1825.

Edward Lloyd (Md.)   For Crawford: Ingersoll diary, Feb. 9, 1823, William M. Meigs, *The Life of Charles Jared Ingersoll* (Philadelphia: J. B. Lippincott, 1897), pp. 114-115; signed the caucus call and attended the caucus.

James Lloyd (Mass.)   For Adams or Crawford: reported to be for Adams: Degrand to Adams, June 8, 1822, Adams Papers; but also reported to be Crawford: Isaac Munroe to Bailey, Nov. 19, 1821, Bailey Papers and assumed by Crawford to be a Crawford man: Crawford to Tait, Sept. 17, 1822, Shipp, *Giant Days*, pp. 234-235.

Walter Lowrie (Pa.)   For Crawford: Lowrie to Gallatin, Feb. 10, 21, 1824, Gallatin Papers.

Nathaniel Macon (N.C.)   For Crawford: William E. Dodd, *Life of Nathaniel Macon* (Raleigh, N.C.: Edwards and Broughton, 1903), pp. 333ff.

Joseph McIlvaine (N.J.)   No information.

Elijah H. Mills (Mass.)   For Adams: Henry Cabot Lodge, ed., "Extracts from the Familiar Correspondence of the Hon. E. H. Mills," *Proceedings* of the Massachusetts Historical Society, 19 (1881-1882), 37.

James Noble (Ind.)   Reported to be for Adams: Anon. to Adams, Sept. 30, 1822, Adams Papers; but attended the caucus and hence probably for Crawford.

William A. Palmer (Vt.)   No information.

John F. Parrott (N.H.)   For Adams: Parrott to Mason, Jan. 7, 1823, Papers of Jeremiah Mason, New Hampshire Historical Society.

Benjamin Ruggles (O.)   For Clay: Ruggles to Hammond, Jan. 1, March 10, 1824, Hammond Papers. (In the latter letter, Ruggles explained that he attended the caucus but voted for Clay; Adams, however, assumed him to be for Crawford: Adams diary, May 22, 1824.)

Horatio Seymour (Vt.)   For Adams: Adams diary, April 5, 1824.

Samuel Smith (Md.)   For Crawford: Frank A. Cassell, *Merchant Congressman in the Young Republic: Samuel Smith of Maryland* (Madison: University of Wisconsin Press, 1971), pp. 81-82; Adams diary, May 22, 1824.

Isham Talbot (Ky.)   No information.

John Taylor (Va.)   For Crawford, Calhoun, or Adams: reported to be for Crawford: Thomas Waggaman to Adams, Jan. 3, 1823, Adams Papers, and Cobb to Tait, Feb. 2, 1824, Tait Papers; thought by Calhoun to be in his camp: Calhoun to O. Edwards, May 2, 1823, Calhoun, *Papers*, VIII, 45; but later thought by Adams to be an Adams man: Adams diary, May 26, 1824.

Waller Taylor (Ind.)   No information.

Jesse B. Thomas (Ill.)   For Crawford: Papers of Jesse B. Thomas, Illinois State Historical Society.

Martin Van Buren (N.Y.)   For Crawford: see index under Van Buren.

Nicholas Van Dyke (Del.)   No information.

Nicholas Ware (Ga.)   For Crawford: Adams diary, May 22, 1824.

Thomas H. Williams (Miss.)   No information.

Appendix B
Sources and Studies

ARCHIVES AND MANUSCRIPTS

Adams Family Papers, Massachusetts Historical Society.

Bailey, John: New-York Historical Society.

Barbour Family Papers, University of Virginia Library.

Barbour, James: New York Public Library.

Barron, James: Earl Gregg Swem Library, College of William and Mary.

Baylies, Francis: Library of Congress and Old Colony Historical Society, Taunton, Mass.

Berrien, John MacPherson: Southern Historical Collection, University of North Carolina Library.

Brackenridge, Henry M.: University of Pittsburgh Libraries.

Brown, Jacob: Massachusetts Historical Society and William L. Clements Library, University of Michigan.

Brown, James: Department of Archives and Manuscripts, Louisiana State University.

Buchanan, Roberdeau: Historical Society of Pennsylvania.

Clay, Henry: Library of Congress.

Cook, Daniel Pope: Chicago Historical Society.

Coryell, Lewis S.: Historical Society of Pennsylvania.

Crawford, William H.: Duke University Library, Library of Congress, and Rice University Library.

Cuyler, Telemon Cruger Smith: University of Georgia Library.

Dallas Family Papers, Temple University Libraries.

Dickerson, Mahlon: New Jersey Historical Society.

Easton, Rufus: Missouri Historical Society.

Edwards, Ninian: Chicago Historical Society and Illinois Historical Survey Collections, University of Illinois, Champaign-Urbana.

Eustis, William: Library of Congress.

Everett, Edward: Massachusetts Historical Society.

Flagg, Azariah C.: New York Public Library.

Floyd, John: Library of Congress.

Force, Peter: Library of Congress and William L. Clements Library, University of Michigan.

France, Archives du ministère des affaires étrangères, Correspondance politique.

Gales, Joseph, and William Winston Seaton: Library of Congress.

Gallatin, Albert: New-York Historical Society.

Gilpin, Henry D. and family: Historical Society of Pennsylvania.

Gooch Family Papers, University of Virginia Library.

Goodhue Family Papers, New York Society Library.

Gouverneur, Samuel L.: New York Public Library.

Great Britain: Foreign Office Archives, Public Record Office.

Hammond, Charles: Ohio Historical Society Library and Ohio State Library.

Harper, Robert Goodloe: Maryland Historical Society and Library of Congress.

Hill, Isaac: New Hampshire Historical Society.

Holmes, John: Maine Historical Society and New York Public Library.

Hopkinson Family Papers, Historical Society of Pennsylvania.

Ingersoll, Charles Jared: Historical Society of Pennsylvania.

Jackson, Andrew: Library of Congress; Stanley F. Horn Collection, Joint University Libraries, Nashville, Tenn.; and Emil Edward Hurja Collection, Tennessee State Library and Archives.

Jefferson, Thomas: Library of Congress.

Johnson, Richard M.: Library of Congress.

Johnston, Josiah Stoddard: Historical Society of Pennsylvania.

King, Rufus: Cincinnati Historical Society and New-York Historical Society.

King, William: Maine Historical Society.

McDuffie, George: Duke University Library.

McLean, John: Library of Congress.

McLane, Louis: University of Delaware Library.

Macon, Nathaniel: North Carolina Department of Archives and History.

Madison, James: Library of Congress.

Mangum, Willie P.: Duke University Library.

Mason, Jeremiah: New Hampshire Historical Society.

Maxcy, Virgil: Galloway-Maxcy-Markoe Family Papers, Library of Congress.

Monroe, James: Lehigh University Library, Library of Congress, New-York Historical Society, New York Public Library, and University of Pennsylvania Library. In addition, there is a microfilm edition of James Monroe Letters in Virginia Repositories.

Nicolson, Joseph: Library of Congress.

Noah, Mordecai M.: American Jewish Historical Society, Waltham, Mass.

Norcross, Otis: Massachusetts Historical Society.

O'Connor, John Michael: William L. Clements Library, University of Michigan, and New-York Historical Society.

Overton, John: Tennessee State Library.

Plumer, William, Jr.: Library of Congress and New Hampshire Historical Society.

Poinsett, Joel R.: Library of Congress, Historical Society of Pennsylvania, South Carolina Historical Society, and University of Texas Library.

Porter, Peter B.: Buffalo and Erie County Historical Society.

Rice, Charles E.: Ohio Historical Society.

Rives, William C.: Library of Congress.

Rodney, Caesar A.: Library of Congress.

Rush, Richard: Princeton University Library.

Russell, Jonathan: Brown University Library.

Southard, Samuel L.: Princeton University Library.

Swift, Joseph G.: United States Military Academy Library.

Tait, Charles: Alabama Department of Archives and History.

Tallmadge, James: Massachusetts Historical Society.

Taylor, John W.: New-York Historical Society.

Thomas, Jesse B.: Illinois State Historical Library.

Trist, Nicholas P.: Virginia Historical Society.

Tyler, John: Library of Congress.

United States: Archives of the Department of State.

Van Buren, Martin: Library of Congress.

Van Deventer, Christopher: William L. Clements Library, University of Michigan.

Waddell, Moses: Library of Congress.

Warden, David Bailie: Maryland Historical Society.

Webster, Daniel: Library of Congress and New Hampshire Historical Society.

Wheaton, Henry: J. Pierpont Morgan Library, New York City.

Wirt, William: Maryland Historical Society.

Woodbury, Levi: Library of Congress.

Yancey, Bartlett: University of North Carolina Library.

PERIODICALS

Baltimore *American*.
Baltimore *Patriot and Mercantile Advertiser*.
Baltimore *Weekly Register*.
Louisville *Public Advertiser*.
New York *American*.
New York *Commercial Advertiser*.
New York *Patriot*.
North American Review.
Philadelphia *Franklin Gazette*.
Philadelphia *National Gazette*.
Portland *Evening Argus*.

Richmond *Enquirer*.
Washington *National Intelligencer*.
Washington *National Journal*.
Washington *Republican*.

AUTOBIOGRAPHIES, BIOGRAPHIES, AND COLLECTIONS OF DOCUMENTS

Aberdeen: Lady Frances Balfour, *The Life of George, Fourth Earl of Aberdeen*, 2 vols. (London: Hodder and Stoughton, 1922).

Sir Arthur Hamilton Gordon, Baron Stanmore, *The Earl of Aberdeen* (London: S. Low, Marston, and Co., 1893).

Adams, C. F.: David Donald and Aida Di Pace Donald, eds., *Diary of Charles Francis Adams*, vol. I: *January 1820-June 1825* (Cambridge, Mass.: Harvard University Press, 1964).

Adams, J. Q.: Charles Francis Adams, *Memoirs of John Quincy Adams*, 12 vols. (Philadelphia: J. B. Lippincott and Co., 1874-1877).

Samuel Flagg Bemis, *John Quincy Adams and the Foundations of American Foreign Policy* (New York: Alfred A. Knopf, 1950).

—— *John Quincy Adams and the Union* (New York: Alfred A. Knopf, 1956).

Worthington C. Ford, "John Quincy Adams and the Monroe Doctrine," *American Historical Review*, 7-8 (July, Oct. 1902).

——, ed., *The Writings of John Quincy Adams*, 7 vols. (New York: Macmillan, 1913-1917).

Samuel D. Ingham, *Exposition of the Political Character of John Quincy Adams* (Washington, D.C.: no publisher, 1827).

George A. Lipsky, *John Quincy Adams, his Theory and Ideas* (New York: Thomas Y. Crowell, 1950).

Josiah Quincy, *Memoir of the Life of John Quincy Adams* (Boston: Philips, Sampson, and Co., 1859).

Alaskan Boundary Tribunal (see United States).

Alexander I: Paul Bailleu, ed., *Correspondance inédite du roi Frédéric Guillaume III et de la reine Louise avec l'Empereur Alexandre Ier* (Leipzig: S. Hirzel, 1900).

Modest Ivanovich Bogdanovich, *Istoriya Tsarstvovovaniya Aleksandra I*, 6 vols. (St. Petersburg: Syshchinskago, 1869-1871).

Allen McConnell, *Tsar Alexander I: Paternalistic Reformer* (New York: Thomas Y. Crowell, 1970).

Grand Duke Nicholas, ed., *Scenes of Russian Court Life, being the Correspondence of Alexander I with his Sister Catherine*, English translation (London: Jarrold's, n.d.).

Grand Duke Nikolai Mikhailovich, *L'empereur Alexandre Ier: Essai d'étude historique*, 2 vols. (St. Petersburg: Papiers de l'État, 1912).

Nikolai Karlovich Shilder, *Imperator Aleksandr I, ego Zhizn i Tsarstvovanie*,

4 vols. (St. Petersburg: A. S. Suborin, 1905).

Sergei Mikhailovich Solov'ev, *Imperator Aleksandr I: Politika, Diplomatiya* (St. Petersburg: M. Stasyulevicha, 1877).

Kazimierz Waliszewski, *Le règne d'Alexandre Ier*, 3 vols. (Paris: Plon, 1923-1925).

Anderson: Alfred Tischendorf and E. Taylor Parks, eds., *The Diary and Journal of Richard Clough Anderson, Jr., 1814-1826* (Durham, N.C.: Duke University Press, 1964).

Arakcheev: Michael Jenkins, *Arakcheev, Grand Vizier of the Russian Empire* (New York: Dial Press, 1969).

Arbuthnot: Arthur Aspinall, ed., *Correspondence of Charles Arbuthnot*, Camden Society Publications, Third Series, 65 (London: Royal Historical Society, 1941).

F. Bamford and the Duke of Wellington, eds., *Mrs. Arbuthnot's Journal, 1820-1832*, 2 vols. (London: Macmillan, 1950).

Astor: Kenneth Wiggins Porter, *John Jacob Astor, Business Man* (Cambridge, Mass.: Harvard University Press, 1931).

Arthur D. H. Smith, *John Jacob Astor* (Philadelphia: J. B. Lippincott, 1929).

Barrow, John, *An Autobiographical Memoir* (London: John Murray, 1847).

Bathurst: Historical Manuscripts Commission, *Report on the Manuscripts of the Earl Bathurst* (London: H.M.S.O., 1923).

Benton, Thomas Hart, *Thirty Years View, or a History of the Working of the American Government for Thirty Years from 1820 to 1850*, 2 vols. (New York: Appleton, 1854-1856).

William N. Chambers, *Old Bullion Benton, Senator from the New West* (Boston: Little, Brown, 1956).

William M. Meigs, *Life of Thomas Hart Benton* (Philadelphia: J. B. Lippincott, 1904).

Robert E. Shalhope, "Thomas Hart Benton and Missouri Politics: A Reexamination," American Association for State and Local History *Bulletin*, 25 (April 1969).

Elbert B. Smith, *Magnificent Missourian: The Life of Thomas Hart Benton* (Philadelphia: J. B. Lippincott, 1958).

Bessborough: Arthur Aspinall and the Earl of Bessborough, eds., *Lady Bessborough and her Family Circle* (London: John Murray, 1940).

Biddle: Thomas P. Govan, *Nicholas Biddle, Nationalist and Public Banker, 1776-1844* (Chicago: University of Chicago Press, 1959).

Reginald C. McGrane, ed., *Correspondence of Nicholas Biddle, 1807-1844* (Boston: Houghton-Mifflin, 1919).

Binney: Charles C. Binney, *Life of Horace Binney* (Philadelphia: J. B. Lippincott, 1903).

Binns, John, *Recollections of his Life, written by Himself* (Philadelphia: Perry and Macmillan, 1854).

Boigne, Comtesse de, *Mémoires*, 2d ed., 4 vols. (Paris: Plon, 1907).

Boissy, Marquis de, *Mémoires, 1798-1866*, 2 vols. (Paris: E. Dentu, 1870).

Boudard, André, *Mémoires pour servir à l'histoire de Louis XVIII* (Paris: Gaillot, 1824).

Breck: Henry E. Scudder, ed., *Recollections of Samuel Breck, with Passages from his Note-Books* (Philadelphia: Porter and Coates, 1877).

Brougham: Arthur Aspinall, *Lord Brougham and the Whig Party* (Manchester: The University Press, 1927).

　　Lord Brougham, *Life and Times of Henry, Lord Brougham, written by Himself*, 3 vols. (Edinburgh and London: W. Blackwood and Sons, 1871).

　　Frances Hawes, *Lord Brougham* (London: Cape, 1957).

　　Chester W. New, *Life of Henry Brougham to 1830* (Oxford: Clarendon Press, 1961).

Buchanan: George Ticknor Curtis, *Life of James Buchanan*, 2 vols. (New York: Harper and Brothers, 1883).

　　Philip S. Klein, *President James Buchanan* (University Park, Pa.: Pennsylvania State University Press, 1962).

　　John Bassett Moore, ed., *The Works of James Buchanan, comprising his Speeches, State Papers, and Private Correspondence*, 12 vols. (Philadelphia: J. B. Lippincott, 1908-1911).

Buckingham, Duke of, *Memoirs of the Court of George IV, 1820-1830*, 2 vols. (London: Hurst and Blackett, 1859).

　　—— *Private Diary*, 2 vols. (London: Hurst and Blackett, 1862).

Butler: William MacKenzie, *The Lives and Opinions of Benjamin Franklin Butler and Jesse Hoyt* (Boston: Cook and Co., 1845).

Calhoun: Anon., ed., "Calhoun-Gouverneur Correspondence, 1823-1826," New York Public Library *Bulletin*, 3 (Aug. 1899).

　　[John C. Calhoun?], *Life of John C. Calhoun, presenting a Condensed History of Political Events from 1811 to 1834* (New York: Harper and Brothers, 1843).

　　Gerald M. Capers, *John C. Calhoun—Opportunist: A Reappraisal* (Gainsville, Fla.: University of Florida Press, 1960).

　　Margaret L. Coit, *John C. Calhoun, American Portrait* (Boston: Houghton-Mifflin, 1950).

　　Thomas Robson Hay, ed., "John C. Calhoun and the Presidential Campaign of 1824: Some Unpublished Calhoun Letters," *American Historical Review*, 40 (Oct. 1934).

　　—— "John C. Calhoun and the Presidential Campaign of 1824," *North Carolina Historical Review*, 12 (Jan. 1935).

　　W. Edwin Hemphill, ed., *The Papers of John C. Calhoun*, 8 vols. in progress (Columbia, S.C.: University of South Carolina Press, 1959—).

　　John Franklin Jameson, ed., "Correspondence of John C. Calhoun," American Historical Association *Annual Report* (1899), vol. II.

　　William M. Meigs, *Life of John Caldwell Calhoun*, 2 vols. (New York: Noble, 1917).

Albert R. Newsome, ed., "Correspondence of John C. Calhoun, George McDuffie and Charles Fisher, relating to the Presidential Campaign of 1824," *North Carolina Historical Review*, 7 (Oct. 1930).

Charles M. Wiltse, *John C. Calhoun, Nationalist, 1782-1828* (Indianapolis: Bobbs-Merrill, 1944).

Canning G.: Josceline Bagot, *George Canning and his Friends*, 2 vols. (London: John Murray, 1909).

Charles Alexander Petrie, *George Canning* (London: Eyre and Spottiswoode, 1930).

P. J. V. Rolo, *George Canning* (London: Macmillan, 1965).

Edward J. Stapleton, ed., *Some Official Correspondence of George Canning, 1821-1827* (London: Longmans, Green, 1887).

Harold W. V. Temperley, "Canning and the Conferences of the Four Allied Governments at Paris, 1823-1825," *American Historical Review*, 30 (Oct. 1924).

―――― *The Foreign Policy of Canning, 1822-1827* (London: G. Bell and Sons, 1925).

Canning, S.: Leo Byrne, *The Great Ambassador* (Columbus, Ohio: Ohio State University Press, 1964).

Elizabeth Frances Malcolm-Smith, *The Life of Stratford Canning* (London: E. Benn, 1933).

Capodistria: Lysimaque Oeconomos, *Essai sur la vie du Comte Capodistrias depuis son départ de Russie en août 1822 jusqu'à son arrivée en Grèce en janvier 1828* (Paris: Editions "Occitania," 1926).

C. M. Woodhouse, *Capodistrias* (London: Oxford University Press, 1973).

Carné, Louis, Comte de, *Souvenirs de ma jeunesse au temps de la Restauration*, 2nd ed. (Paris: Didier et Cie., 1873).

Castellane, Maréchal de, *Journal, 1804-1862*, 6 vols. (Paris: Plon, 1895).

Ruth Charlotte Sophie de Beaulaincourt-Marles, *Boniface-Louis-André de Castellane* (Paris: Plon, 1901).

Castlereagh: C. K. Webster, *The Foreign Policy of Castlereagh, 1812-1822*, 2 vols. (London: G. Bell and Sons, 1934).

Chandler: George Foster Talbot, "General John Chandler, of Monmouth, Me., with Extracts from his Autobiography," *Maine Historical Society Collections*, 9 (1887).

Charles X: Jean-Paul Garnier, *Charles X* (Paris: Fayard, 1967).

Charless: David Kaser, *Joseph Charless, Printer in the Western Country* (Philadelphia: University of Pennsylvania Press, 1963).

Chateaubriand, François René, Vicomte de, *Congrès de Vérone. Guerre d'Espagne. Negociations: colonies espagnoles*, 2 vols. (Paris: Béthune et Plon, 1838).

―――― "Supplement au Congrès de Vérone," *Revue politique et littéraire* (Nov. 2, 1912).

Henry Contamine, "Les conditions du travail ministeriel de Chateaubriand," *Revue d'histoire diplomatique*, 69 (July-Sept., 1955).

E. Beau de Loménie, *La carrière politique de Chateaubriand de 1814 à 1830*, 2 vols. (Paris: Plon, 1929).

Marie Louis, Comte de Marcellus, *Chateaubriand et son temps* (Paris: M.′ Lévy Frères, 1859).

Pierre Moreau, *Chateaubriand* (Paris: Hatier Boivin, 1956).

J. Peuch, *Chateaubriand au Congrès de Vérone* (Paris: E. Bacard, 1939).

Louis Thomas, ed., *Correspondance générale de Chateaubriand*, 5 vols. (Paris: Édouard Champion, 1912-1924).

Cahiers de Madame de Chateaubriand (Paris: no publisher, 1909).

Lettres inédites de Madame de Chateaubriand (Bordeaux: Ferot et Fils, 1888).

Choiseul-Gouffier, Sophie, Comtesse de, *Historical Memoirs of the Emperor Alexander I and the Court of Russia*, English translation (Chicago: A. C. McClurg, 1900).

Clay: James F. Hopkins, ed., *The Papers of Henry Clay*, 4 vols. in progress (Lexington, Ky.: University of Kentucky Press, 1959—).

Clement Eaton, *Henry Clay and the Art of American Politics* (Boston: Little, Brown, 1957).

Bernard Mayo, *Henry Clay, Spokesman of the New West* (Boston: Houghton-Mifflin, 1937).

Glyndon G. Van Deusen, *Henry Clay* (Boston: Little, Brown, 1937).

Clermont-Tonnerre: Camille Rousset, *Un ministre de la Restauration: le Marquis de Clermont-Tonnerre* (Paris: Plon, 1885).

Clinton: John Bigelow, "Dewitt Clinton as a Politician," *Harper's*, 50 (Feb. 1875).

Dorothie Bobbé, *De Witt Clinton* (New York: Minton, Balch, and Co., 1933).

Colton: Alfred A. Cave, *An American Conservative in the Age in Jackson: The Political and Social Thought of Calvin Colton* (Fort Worth, Tex.: Texas Christian University Press, 1969).

Crawford: Philip J. Green, *The Public Life of William H. Crawford* (Chicago: no publisher, 1938).

Chase C. Mooney, *William H. Crawford, 1772-1834* (Lexington, Ky.: University of Kentucky Press, 1974).

J. E. D. Shipp, *Giant Days, or the Life and Times of William H. Crawford* (Americus, Ga.: Southern Printers, 1909).

Creevey: J. Gore, *Creevey's Life and Times: A Further Selection from the Correspondence of Thomas Creevey* (London: John Murray, 1934).

Sir Herbert Maxwell, ed., *The Creevey Papers*, 2 vols. (London: John Murray, 1904).

Croker: Louis J. Jennings, ed., *The Croker Papers: The Correspondence and Diaries of . . . John Wilson Croker*, 2 vols. (New York: Charles Scribner's Sons, 1884).

Cussy, Chevalier de, *Souvenirs . . . 1795-1866*, vol. I (Paris: Plon, 1909).

Cutler: Julia Perkins Cutler, *Life and Times of Ephraim Cutler* (Cincinnati, Ohio: R. Clarke and Co., 1890).

Damas, Baron, *Mémoires*, 2 vols. (Paris: Plon, 1923).

Daniel: John P. Frank, *Justice Daniel Dissenting: A Biography of Peter V. Daniel, 1784-1860* (Cambridge, Mass.: Harvard University Press, 1964).

Doudeauville, Duc de, *Une politique française au dix-neuvieme siècle* (Paris: Honoré Champion, 1927).

Duane, William, *A Visit to Colombia in the Years 1822 and 1823* (Philadelphia: T. H. Palmer, 1826).

DuPont: B. G. DuPont, ed., *Life of Eleuthère Irenée duPont from Contemporary Correspondence*, 12 vols. (Newark, Del.: University of Delaware Press, 1923-1926).

Duras: Gabriel Pailhes, *La duchesse de Duras et Chateaubriand* (Paris: Perrin et Cie., 1910).

Edwards, Ninian W., *History of Illinois, 1778-1833 and Life and Times of Ninian Edwards* (Springfield, Ill.: Illinois State Journal Co., 1870).

    C. B. Washburne, ed., "Ninian Edwards Papers," Chicago Historical Society *Collections*, 3 (1884).

Eldon: Horace Twiss, *The Public and Private Life of Lord Chancellor Eldon*, 2 vols. (London: John Murray, 1844).

Ellicott: William Chazanof, *Joseph Ellicott and the Holland Land Company: The Opening of Western New York* (Syracuse, N.Y.: Syracuse University Press, 1970).

Everett: Worthington C. Ford, ed., "Letters between Edward Everett and John McLean, 1828," Massachusetts Historical Society *Proceedings*, Third Series, 1 (1907-1908).

    Paul R. Frothingham, *Edward Everett, Orator and Statesman* (Boston: Little, Brown, 1925).

Favre (see Pasquier).

Floyd: Charles H. Ambler, *The Life and Diary of John Floyd* (Richmond, Va.: Richmond Press, 1918).

Ford, Worthington C. (see Adams, J. Q., and United States).

Forsyth: Alvin L. Duckett, *John Forsyth, Political Tactician* (Athens, Ga.: University of Georgia Press, 1962).

Frénilly, Auguste, Marquis de, *Souvenirs, 1768-1828* (Paris: Plon, 1908).

Frere: Gabrielle Festing, *John Hookham Frere and his Friends* (London: J. Nisbet and Co., 1899).

Gallatin: Henry Adams, ed., *Writings of Albert Gallatin*, 3 vols. (Philadelphia: J. B. Lippincott, 1879).

    Frederick Merk, *Albert Gallatin and the Oregon Problem* (Cambridge, Mass.: Harvard University Press, 1950).

    Raymond Walters, Jr., *Albert Gallatin* (New York: Macmillan, 1957).

George IV: Arthur Aspinall, ed., *The Letters of King George IV*, 3 vols. (Cambridge, Eng.: Cambridge University Press, 1938).

Gibson: T. P. Roberts, ed., *Memoirs of John Bannister Gibson* (Pittsburgh: J. Eichbaum and Co., 1890).

Giles: Dice R. Anderson, *William Branch Giles: A Study in the Politics of Virginia and the Nation from 1790 to 1830* (Menasha, Wis.: George Banta, 1915).

Goodrich, S. G., *Recollections of a Lifetime*, 2 vols. (New York: Miller, Orton, and Mulligan, 1856).

Gore: Helen R. Pinkney, *Christopher Gore, Federalist of Massachusetts, 1758-1827* (Waltham, Mass.: Gore Place Society, 1969).

Graham, Gerald S. (see Great Britain).

[Grant, James], *Travels in Town*, 2 vols. (London: Saunders and Ottley, 1839).

Great Britain: Gerald S. Graham and R. A. Humphries, ed., *The Navy and South America, 1807-1823: Correspondence of the Commanders-in-Chief on the South American Station* (London: Navy Records Society, 1962).

   Bradford Perkins, "The Suppressed Dispatch of H. U. ·Addington, Washington, November 3, 1823," *Hispanic American Historical Review*, 37 (Nov. 1957).

   C. K. Webster, ed., *Britain and the Independence of Latin America: Select Documents from the Foreign Office Archives*, 2 vols. (London: Oxford University Press, 1938).

Green, Duff. *Facts and Suggestions, Biographical Historical, Financial and Political, addressed to the People of the United States* (New York: Richardson and Co., 1866).

Greville: Lytton Strachey and Roger Fulford, eds., *The Greville Memoirs, 1814-1860*, 8 vols. (London: Macmillan, 1938).

Guernon-Ranville, Comte de, *Journal d'un ministre* (Caen: Blanc-Hardel, 1873).

Hall, Basil, *Travels in North America in the Years 1827 and 1828*, 2 vols. (Philadelphia: Carey, Lea and Carey, 1829).

Hall, J.: Randolph C. Randall, *James Hall, Spokesman of the New West* (Columbus, Ohio: Ohio State University Press, 1964).

Hamilton, James A., *Reminiscences . . . or Men and Events at Home and Abroad* (New York: Charles Scribner and Co., 1869).

Hammond: William Henry Smith, *Charles Hammond and his Relations to Henry Clay and John Quincy Adams* (Chicago: Chicago Historical Society, 1885).

Haussez, Charles, Baron d', *Mémoires*, 2 vols. (Paris: Calmann-Lévy, 1896-1897).

Haussonville, Joseph, Comte de, *Ma jeunesse, 1814-1830* (Paris: Calmann-Lévy, 1885).

Hauterive: A. F. Artaud de Montour, *Histoire de la vie et des travaux politiques du Comte d'Hauterive* (Paris: Adrien LeClerc et Cie., 1839).

Hay, Robert P., "'The Presidential Question': Letters to Southern Editors, 1823-1824," *Tennessee Historical Quarterly*, 30 (Summer 1972).

Hayne: Theodore D. Jervey, *Robert Y. Hayne and his Times* (New York: Macmillan, 1909).

Hertslet, Sir Edward, *Recollections of the Old Foreign Office* (London: John Murray, 1901).

Hill: Cyrus P. Bradley, *Biography of Isaac Hill* (Concord, N.H.: J. F. Brown, 1835).

Hobhouse: Arthur Aspinall, ed., *The Diary of Henry Hobhouse, 1820-1827* (London: Hume and van Thal, 1947).

John Cam Hobhouse, Lord Broughton, *Recollections of a Long Life*, 6 vols. (London: John Murray, 1909-1911).

Holland, Lord, *Further Memoirs of the Whig Party, 1807-1821* (New York: no publisher, 1905).

Hoyt, J. (see Butler).

Huskisson: Alexander Brady, *William Huskisson and Liberal Reform* (London: Oxford University Press, 1928).

Hyde de Neuville, Jean Guillaume, Baron, *Mémoires et souvenirs*, 3 vols. (Paris: Plon, 1888-1892).

Ingersoll: William M. Meigs, *Life of Charles Jared Ingersoll* (Philadelphia: J. B. Lippincott, 1897).

Ingham: W. A. Ingham, *Samuel Delucemma Ingham* (n.p.: no publisher, 1910).

Jackson: John S. Bassett and J. Franklin Jameson, eds., *The Correspondence of Andrew Jackson*, 7 vols. (Washington, D.C.: Carnegie Institution, 1926-1935).

Henry F. DuPuy, "Some Letters of Andrew Jackson," American Antiquarian Society *Proceedings*, New Series, 31 (1921).

Marquis James, *Andrew Jackson*, 2 vols. (Indianapolis: Bobbs-Merrill, 1933-1937).

Robert V. Remini, *Andrew Jackson* (New York: Twayne, 1966).

John William Ward, *Andrew Jackson, Sumbol for an Age* (New York: Oxford University Press, 1955).

Kent: William Kent, ed., *Memoirs and Letters of James Kent* (Boston: Little, Brown, 1898).

King: Robert Ernst, *Rufus King: American Federalist* (Chapel Hill: University of North Carolina Press, 1968).

Charles R. King, ed., *The Life and Correspondence of Rufus King*, 6 vols. (New York: G. P. Putnam's Sons, 1894-1900).

Lamartine, Alphonse de, *Mémoires politiques*, 4 vols. (Paris: no publisher, 1863).

LaRochefoucauld, Sosthène, Vicomte de (Duc de Doudeauville), *Mémoires*, 5 vols. (Paris: Allardin, 1837).

Lebzeltern: Grand Duke Nikolai Mikhailovich, ed., *Les rapports diplomatiques de Lebzeltern, Ministre d'Autriche à la Cour de Russie (1816-1826)* (St. Petersburg: Gosudarstvennie Bumag', 1913).

Emmanuel de Lévis-Mirepoix, Prince de Robach, *Un collaborateur de Metternich: Mémoires et papiers de Lebzeltern* (Paris: Payot, 1949).

Lieven: Peter Quennell, ed., *Private Letters of Princess Lieven to Prince Metternich, 1820-1826* (London: John Murray, 1937).

Lionel G. Robinson, ed., *Letters of Dorothea, Princess Lieven . . . 1812-1834* (London: Longmans, Green, 1902).

Harold W. V. Temperley, ed., *The Unpublished Diary and Political Sketches, of Dorothea, Princess Lieven* (London: J. Cape, 1925).

Liverpool: W. R. Brock, *Lord Liverpool and Liberal Toryism* (Cambridge, Eng.: Cambridge University Press, 1941).

Charles Alexander Petrie, *Lord Liverpool and his Times* (London: Barrie, 1954).

Charles D. Yonge, *Life and Administration of Robert Banks Jenkinson, Second Earl of Liverpool*, 3 vols. (London: Macmillan, 1868).

Louis XVIII: Alphonse de Beauchamp, *Vie de Louis XVIII*, 2 vols. (Paris: J.-J. Naudin, 1825).

Jean Lucas-Dubreton, *Louis XVIII* (Paris: A. Michel, 1925).

Etienne León, Baron de Lamothe-Langon, *Mémoires d'une femme de qualité sur Louis XVIII, sa cour, et son règne* (Paris: Manse et Delaunay-Vallée, 1830).

Lowndes: Harriet H. Ravenel, *Life and Times of William Lowndes, 1782-1822* (Boston: Houghton-Mifflin, 1901).

McKenney, Thomas L., *Memoirs* (New York: Paine and Burgess, 1846).

Macon: Kemp B. Battle, ed., *Letters of Nathaniel Macon, John Steele, and William Barry Grove, with Sketches and Notes* (Chapel Hill: University of North Carolina Press, 1902).

W. K. Boyd, ed., "Letters of Nathaniel Macon to Judge Charles Tait," Historical Society of Trinity College (Durham, N.C.), *Annual Publication of Historical Papers*, Series 8 (n.d.).

William E. Dodd, *Life of Nathaniel Macon* (Raleigh, N.C.: Edwards and Broughton, 1903).

Edwin Mood Wilson, *The Congressional Career of Nathaniel Macon* (Chapel Hill: University of North Carolina Press, 1900).

Malmesbury, James Harris, First Earl of, *Diaries and Correspondence*, 4 vols. (London: R. Bentley, 1845).

Manning, William R. (see United States).

Mansfield, E. D., *Personal Memories, Social and Political, with Sketches of Many Noted People, 1803-1843* (Cincinnati: R. Clarke and Co., 1879).

Marcy: Ivor Debenham Spencer, *The Victor and the Spoils: A Life of William L. Marcy* (Providence, R.I.: Brown University Press, 1959).

Marmont, Maréchal (Duc de Raguse), *Mémoires . . . 1792 à 1832*, 9 vols. (Paris: Perrotin, 1857).

Martens, F. F. (see Russia).

Martin: Paul S. Clarkson and R. Samuel Jett, *Luther Martin of Maryland* (Baltimore: The Johns Hopkins University Press, 1970).

Mason: George S. Hilliard, ed., *Memoir and Correspondence of Jeremiah Mason* (Cambridge, Mass.: Riverside Press, 1873).

Maxcy: J. Franklin Jameson, ed., "Virgil Maxcy on Calhoun's Political Opinions and Prospects, 1823," *American Historical Review*, 12 (April 1907).

Melbourne: Lloyd C. Sanders, ed., *Lord Melbourne's Papers* (London: Longmans, Green, 1889).

Metternich: G. de Bertier de Sauvigny, *Metternich and his Times*, English translation (London: Darton, Longman, and Todd, 1962).

_____ *Metternich et la France après le Congrés de Vienne*, 3 vols. (Paris: Hachette, 1968-1971).

Mills: Henry Cabot Lodge, ed., "Extracts from the Familiar Correspondence of the Hon. Elijah H. Mills," Massachusetts Historical Society *Proceedings*, 19 (1881-1882).

Molé: Hélie Noailles, *Le Comte Molé, sa vie—ses mémoires*, 6 vols. (Paris: Édouard Champion, 1922-1930).

Monroe: Harry Ammon, *James Monroe and the Quest for National Identity* (New York: McGraw-Hill, 1971).

William P. Cresson, *James Monroe* (Chapel Hill: University of North Carolina Press, 1946).

Stanislaus Murray Hamilton, ed., *The Writings of James Monroe*, 7 vols. (New York: G. P. Putnam's Sons, 1898-1903).

Barnes F. Lathrop, "Monroe on the Adams-Clay Bargain," *American Historical Review*, 42 (Jan. 1937).

Arthur Styron, *The Last of the Cocked Hats: James Monroe and the Virginia Dynasty* (Norman, Okla.: University of Oklahoma Press, 1945).

Montesquiou-Fezensac, Anatole, Comte de, *Souvenirs* (Paris: Plon, 1961).

Montmorency: E. Beau de Loménie, "Une amie dévote de Mme. Recamier," *Revue universelle*, 1 (Jan. 15, 1923).

Mordvinov: V. A. Bil'basov, ed., *Arkhiv Grafov' Mordvinovykh*, 6 vols. (St. Petersburg: I. N. Skorokhodova, 1902).

Murphey: William Henry Hoyt, ed., *The Papers of Archibald D. Murphey*, 2 vols. (Raleigh, N.C.: E. M. Uzzell and Co., 1914).

Nesselrode: A. De Nesselrode, ed., *Lettres et papiers du chancelier comte de Nesselrode, 1760-1850*, 12 vols. (Paris: A. Lahure, 1908-1912).

Otis: Samuel Eliot Morison, *The Life and Letters of Harrison Gray Otis, 1765-1848*, 2 vols. (Boston: Houghton-Mifflin, 1913).

Palfrey: Frank Otto Gatell, *John Gorham Palfrey and the New England Conscience* (Cambridge, Mass.: Harvard University Press, 1963).

Palmerston: Evelyn Ashley, *Life of Henry John Temple, Viscount Palmerston, with Selections from his Diaries and Correspondence*, 3 vols. (London: R. Bentley, 1870-1874).

Pasquier: L. Favre, *Pasquier . . . , souvenirs de son dernier sécretaire* (Paris: Didier et Cie., 1870).

Chancellier Pasquier, *Mémoires*, 6 vols. (Paris: Plon, 1894).

Paulding: Ralph M. Aderman, *The Letters of James Kirke Paulding* (Madison, Wis.: University of Wisconsin Press, 1962).

Peel: Norman Gash, *Mr. Secretary Peel, The Life of Sir Robert Peel to 1830* (Cambridge, Mass.: Harvard University Press, 1961).

Charles Stuart Parker, *Sir Robert Peel from his Private Papers*, 3 vols. (London: John Murray, 1891-1899).

Sir Robert Peel, *Memoirs*, 2 vols. (London: John Murray, 1857).

Perkins, Bradford (see Great Britain).

Perkins, Samuel, *Historical Sketches of the United States, 1815-1830* (New York: S. Converse, 1830).

Pintard: Dorothy C. Barck, ed., *Letters from John Pintard to his Daughter, Eliza Noel Pintard Davidson*, 4 vols. (New York: New-York Historical Society, 1940-1941).

Plumer: Everett S. Brown, ed., *The Missouri Compromise and Presidential Politics, 1820-1825, from the Letters of William Plumer, Junior* (St. Louis: Missouri Historical Society, 1926).

    William Plumer, Jr., *Life of William Plumer* (Boston: Phillips, Sampson, and Co., 1857).

    Lynn W. Turner, *William Plumer of New Hampshire, 1759-1850* (Chapel Hill: University of North Carolina Press, 1962).

Poinsett: J. Fred Rippy, *Joel Roberts Poinsett, Versatile American* (Durham, N.C.: Duke University Press, 1935).

Poletica: Mykhaylo Huculak, *When Russia was America: The Alaskan Boundary Treaty Negotiations, 1824-1825, and the Role of Pierre de Poletica* (Vancouver: Mitchell Press, 1971).

    Petr Ivanovich Poletika, *A Sketch of the Internal Condition of the United States of America*, English translation (Baltimore: E. J. Coale, 1826).

    ——— "Vospominaniya," *Russky Arkhiv*, 3 (1885).

Polk: Charles G. Sellers, *James K. Polk, Jacksonian, 1795-1843* (Princeton: Princeton University Press, 1957).

    Herbert Weaver, ed., *Correspondence of James K. Polk, vol. I: 1817-1832* Nashville, Tenn.: Vanderbilt University Press, 1969).

Polovtsov, A. (see Richelieu, Russia).

Pozzo di Borgo: Adrien, Vicomte Maggiolo, *Corse, France et Russie: Pozzo di Borgo, 1764-1842* (Paris: Calmann Lévy, 1890).

    Pierre Ordioni, *Pozzo di Borgo, Diplomate de l'Europe française* (Paris: Plon, 1935).

Prince: *The Journals of Hezekiah Prince, 1822-1828*, with an introduction by W. M. Whitehill and a foreword by R. G. Albion (New York: Crown, 1965).

"Protocols of Conferences of the Representatives of the Powers respecting Spanish America, 1824-1825," *American Historical Review*, 22 (April 1917).

Quincy: Edmund Quincy, *Life of Josiah Quincy* (Boston: Ticknor and Fields, 1865).

Reeve: John Knox Laughton, *Memoirs of the Life and Correspondence of Henry Reeve*, 2 vols. (London: Longmans, Green, 1898).

Rémusat, Charles, Comte de, *Mémoires de ma vie*, 5 vols. (Paris: Plon, 1958-1967).

Richelieu: A. A. Polovtsov, ed., *Armand Emmanuel Richelieu, Correspondance et Documents, 1766-1822* (St. Petersburg: Papiers de l'État, 1887).

Ritchie: Charles H. Ambler, *Thomas Ritchie: A Study in Virginia Politics* (Richmond: Bell Book and Stationery Co., 1913).

Robbins: Increase N. Tarbox, ed., *Diary of Thomas Robbins, D.D., 1796-1854*, 2 vols. (Boston: T. Todd, 1886-1887).

Roberts: Philip S. Klein, ed., "Memoirs of a Senator from Pennsylvania:

Jonathan Roberts, 1771-1854," *Pennsylvania Magazine of History and Biography,* 62 (Oct. 1937-Jan. 1939).

Royall, Anne, *Sketches of History, Life and Manners in the United States* (New Haven: no publisher, 1826).

Ruffin: J. G. de Roulhac Hamilton, ed., *The Papers of Thomas Ruffin,* 4 vols. (Raleigh, N.C.: Edwards and Broughton, 1918-1920).

Rush: Anthony M. Brescia, "The American Navy, 1817-1822: Comments of Richard Rush," *American Neptune,* 30 (July 1971).

J. H. Powell, *Richard Rush, Republican Diplomat* (Philadelphia: University of Pennsylvania Press, 1942).

Richard Rush, *Memoranda of a Residence at the Court of London* (Philadelphia: Key and Biddle, 1833).

_____ *Memoranda of a Residence at the Court of London, comprising Incidents Official and Personal from 1819 to 1825* (Philadelphia: Key and Biddle, 1845).

Russell, Lord John, *Recollections and Suggestions, 1813-1873* (London: Longmans, Gree, 1875).

Rollo Russell, ed., *The Early Correspondence of Lord John Russell, 1805-1840,* 2 vols. (London: T. F. Unwin, 1913).

Sir Spencer Walpole, *Life of Lord John Russell,* 2 vols. (London: John Murray, 1889).

Russia: "Correspondence of Russian Ministers in Washington, 1818-1825," *American Historical Review,* 18 (Jan. 1913).

Fedor Fedorovich Martens, ed., *Recueil des traités et conventions conclus par la Russie avec les puissances étrangères,* 15 vols. (St. Petersburg: Ministère des voies et communications, 1874-1909).

A. A. Polovtsov, ed., *Correspondance diplomatique des ambassadeurs et ministres de la Russie en France et de la France en Russie avec leur gouvernements de 1814 à 1830,* 3 vols. (St. Petersburg: no publisher, 1902-1907); actually goes only to 1820.

Ryleev, Kondratii Fedorovich, *Polnoe sobranie sochinenii* (Moscow: "Academia," 1934).

Sargent, Nathan, *Public Men and Events,* 2 vols. (Philadelphia: J. B. Lippincott, 1875).

Saunders: A. R. Newsome, ed., "Letters of Romulus M. Saunders to Bartlett Yancey, 1821-1828," *North Carolina Historical Review,* 8 (Oct. 1931).

Seaton: Josephine Seaton, *William Winston Seaton of the "National Intelligencer": A Biographical Sketch* (Boston: James P. Osgood and Co., 1871).

Sidmouth: G. Pellew, ed., *Life and Correspondence of Henry Addington, Lord Sidmouth,* 3 vols. (London: John Murray, 1847).

Smith, J.: William W. Andrews, ed., *The Correspondence and Miscellanies of the Hon. John Cotton Smith, formerly Governor of Connecticut* (New York: Harper and Brothers, 1847).

Smith, M.: Gaillard Hunt, ed., *The First Forty Years of Washington Society in the Family Letters of Margaret Bayard Smith* (New York: Frederick Ungar, 1906).

Smith, S.: Frank A. Cassell, *Merchant Congressman in the New Republic: Samuel Smith of Maryland, 1752-1839* (Madison: University of Wisconsin Press, 1971). John Pancake, *Samuel Smith and the Politics of Business, 1752-1839* (University, Ala.: University of Alabama Press, 1973).

Speransky: Marc Raeff, *Michael Speransky: Statesman of Imperial Russia, 1772-1839* (The Hague: Martinus Nijhoff, 1957).

Story: William W. Story, ed., *Life and Letters of Joseph Story*, 2 vols. (Boston: Charles C. Little and James Brown, 1851).

Swift: Harrison Ellery, ed., *The Memoirs of Gen. Joseph Gardner Swift* (Worcester, Mass.: F. S. Blanchard and Co., 1890).

Talaru: François Rousseau, "L'ambassade du marquis de Talaru en Espagne, juillet 1823-août 1824," *Revue des questions historiques*, 90 (July 1911).

Talleyrand: G. Lacour-Gayet, *Talleyrand, 1754-1838*, 3 vols. (Paris: Payot, 1947).

Taney: Carl Brent Swisher, *Roger B. Taney* (New York: Macmillan, 1935).

Temperley, H. W. V., "Documents illustrating the Reception and Interpretation of the Monroe Doctrine in Europe, 1823-1824," *English Historical Review*, 39 (Oct. 1924) (see also under Canning).

Tompkins: Ray W. Irwin, *Daniel D. Tompkins, Governor of New York and Vice President of the United States* (New York: New-York Historical Society, 1968).

Trimble: "Papers of Governor Allen Trimble," *Old Northwest Genealogical Quarterly*, 10 and 11 (July-Oct. 1889).

Turgenev, Nikolai I., *La Russie et les Russes*, 3 vols. (Paris: Imprimeurs-Unis, 1847).

United States: 59th Congress, 2d session, Senate Document No. 162, "Proceedings of the Alaskan Boundary Tribunal" (Washington, D.C.: G.P.O., 1904).

    American State Papers, 5 vols. (Washington, D.C.: Gales and Seaton, 1834).

    Annals of Congress.

    Nikolai N. Bolkhovitinov and Basil Dmytryshyiz, "Russia and the Declaration of the Monroe Doctrine: New Archival Evidence," *Oregon Historical Quarterly*, 72 (June 1971).

    Worthington C. Ford, ed., "Some Original Documents on the Genesis of the Monroe Doctrine," *Massachusetts Historical Society Proceedings*, Second Series, 15 (1901-1902).

    William R. Manning, ed., *Diplomatic Correspondence of the United States: Canadian Relations, 1784-1860*, 3 vols. in progress (Washington, D.C.: Carnegie Endowment, 1940—).

    —— ed., *Diplomatic Correspondence of the United States concerning the Independence of the Latin American Nations*, 3 vols. (New York: Oxford University Press, 1925).

    James D. Richardson, ed., *A Compilation of the Messages and Papers of the Presidents*, 9 vols. (n.p.: Bureau of National Literature and Art, 1903).

Upshur: Claude H. Hall, *Abel Parker Upshur, Conservative Virginian, 1790-1844* (Madison: University of Wisconsin Press, 1963).

Van Buren: James C. Fitzpatrick, ed., "The Autobiography of Martin Van

Buren," American Historical Association *Annual Report* (1918), vol. II.

    Robert V. Remini, *Martin Van Buren and the Making of the Democratic Party* (New York: Columbia University Press, 1959).

Van Ness: T. D. Seymour Bassett, "The Rise of Cornelius Peter Van Ness, 1782-1826," Vermont Historical Society *Proceedings*, New Series, 10 (March 1942).

Villèle: Jean Fourcassié, *Villèle* (Paris: Arthéme Fayard, 1954).

    Joseph, Comte de Villèle, *Mémoires et correspondance*, 6 vols. (Paris: Perrier et Cie., 1889).

Walker: James P. Shenton, *Robert John Walker, A Politician from Jackson to Lincoln* (New York: Columbia University Press, 1961).

Watterston, George, *Letters from Washington . . . 1817-1818* (Washington, D.C.: no publisher, 1818).

Webster, C. K. (see Great Britain).

Webster, D.: Claude M. Fuess, *Daniel Webster*, 2 vols. (Boston: Little, Brown, 1930).

    J. W. McIntyre, ed., *The Writings and Speeches of Daniel Webster*, 18 vols. (Boston: Little, Brown, 1903).

Weed: Harriet A. Weed, ed., *Autobiography of Thurlow Weed* (Boston: Houghton-Mifflin, 1883).

    Glyndon G. Van Deusen, *Thurlow Weed, Wizard of the Lobby* (Boston: Little, Brown, 1947).

Wellington: Elizabeth Pakenham, Lady Longford, *Wellington*, 2 vols. (London: Weidenfeld and Nicolson, 1969-1972).

    Despatches, Correspondence and Memoranda of the Duke of Wellington, Third Series, 8 vols. (London: John Murray, 1867-1880).

Wheaton: Elizabeth Feaster Baker, *Henry Wheaton, 1785-1848* (Philadelphia: University of Pennsylvania Press, 1939).

Wirt, J. P. Kennedy, *Memoirs of the Life of William Wirt, Attorney General of the United States*, 2 vols. (Philadelphia: Lea and Blanchard, 1849).

Wright: John Garraty, *Silas Wright* (New York: Columbia University Press, 1949).

MONOGRAPHS AND HISTORIES

Abernethy, Thomas Perkins, *The Formative Period in Alabama, 1815-1828* (University, Ala.: University of Alabama Press, 1965).

    ——— *From Frontier to Plantation in Tennessee* (Chapel Hill: University of North Carolina Press, 1932).

Accioly, Hildebrando P. P., *O reconhecimento do Brasil pelos Estados Unidos da América* (Sâo Paulo: Companhia Editora Nacional, 1936).

Adams, Henry, *History of the United States during the Administrations of Thomas Jefferdon and James Madison*, 9 vols. (New York: Charles Scribner's Sons, 1891-1896).

Alexander, David Stanwood, *Political History of New York, 1774-1882*, 3 vols. (New York: Henry Holt and Co., 1906-1909).

Ambler, Charles H., *Sectionalism in Virginia from 1776 to 1851* (Chicago: University of Chicago Press, 1910).

Amburger, Erik, *Geschichte der Behördenorganisation Russlands von Peter dem Grossen bis 1917* (Leiden: Brill, 1966).

Ammon, Harry, "The Richmond Junto, 1880-1824," *Virginia Magazine of History and Biography*, 61 (Oct. 1953).

Arsen'ev, Konstantin Ivanovich, *The Statistical Sketches of Russia* (Edinburgh: W. F. Cuthbertson, 1856).

Aspinall, A., *The Cabinet Council, 1783-1835* (London: Cumberlege, 1952).

—— *Lord Brougham and the Whig Party* (Manchester: University Press, 1927).

—— *Politics and the Press, 1780-1850* (London: Home and Van Thal, 1949).

Bailey, Hugh C., "John W. Walker and the Georgia Machine' in Early Alabama Politics," *Alabama Review*, 8 (Dec. 1955).

Banner, James M., Jr., *To the Hartford Convention: The Federalists and the Origins of Party Politics in Massachusetts, 1789-1815* (New York: Alfred A. Knopf, 1970).

Bartlett, C. J., *Great Britain and Sea Power, 1815-1853* (Oxford: Clarendon Press, 1963).

Baumgarten, Hermann, *Geschichte Spaniens vom Ausbruch der französischen Revolution bis auf unsere Tage*, 3 vols. (Leipzig: no publisher, 1865-1871).

Belgrano, Mario, *La Francia y la monarquiá en el Plata (1818-1820)* (Buenos Aires: A. García Santos, 1933).

Benson, Lee, *The Concept of Jacksonian Democracy: New York as a Test Case* (Princeton: Princeton University Press, 1961).

Bertier de Sauvigny, G. de, *The Bourbon Restoration*, English translation (Philadelphia: University of Pennsylvania Press, 1967).

Billingsley, Edward Baxter, *In Defense of Neutral Rights: The United States Navy and the Wars of Independence in Chile and Peru* (Chapel Hill: University of North Carolina Press, 1967).

Blue, Verne, "The Oregon Question, 1818-1828: A Study of Dr. John Floyd's Efforts in Congress to Secure the Oregon Country," *Oregon Historical Quarterly*, 23 (Sept. 1922).

Bolkhovitinov, Nikolai N., *Doktrina Monro (Proiskhozhdenie i Kharakter)* (Moscow: Instituta Mezhundarodnykh Otnoshenii, 1959).

Bonney, Catharine V. R., *A Legacy of Historical Gleanings*, 2 vols. (Albany, N.Y.: J. Munsell, 1875).

Bornholdt, L., "The Abbé de Pradt and the Monroe Doctrine," *Hispanic American Historical Review*, 24 (May 1944).

Bourquin, Maurice, *Histoire de la sainte alliance* (Geneva: Georg, 1954).

Briggs, Sir John Henry, *Naval Administration, 1827-1892* (London: S. Low, Marston and Co., 1897).

Brooks, Philip Coolidge, *Diplomacy and the Borderlands: The Adams-Onís Treaty of 1819* (Berkeley: University of California Press, 1939).

Brown, Everett S., "The Presidential Election of 1824-25," *Political Science Quarterly*, 40 (March 1927).

Buley, R. Carlyle, *The Old Northwest: Pioneer Period, 1815-1840*, 2 vols. (Indianapolis: Indiana Historical Society, 1950).

Butkovskii, Yakov N., *Sto let politiki v vostochnom voproce* (St. Petersburg: no publisher, 1888).

Capefigue, Jean Baptiste Honoré Raymond, *Histoire de la Restauration*, 8 vols. (Brussels: Wouten, Raspoet et Cie., 1843).

Capowski, Vincent J., "The Era of Good Feelings in New Hampshire: The Gubernatorial Campaigns of Levi Woodbury, 1823-1824," *Historical New Hampshire*, 21 (Winter 1966).

Carroll, Charles, *Rhode Island: Three Centuries of Democracy*, 4 vols. (New York: no publisher, 1932).

Cave, Alfred A., *Jacksonian Democracy and the Historians* (Gainesville: University of Florida Press, 1964).

Chambers, William Nisbet and Walter Dean Burnham, *The American Party System: Stages of Political Development* (New York: Oxford University Press, 1967).

Chapelle, Howard I., *The History of the American Sailing Navy* (New York: Norton, 1949).

Chase, James S., "Jacksonian Democracy and the Rise of the Nominating Convention," *Mid-America*, 45 (Oct. 1963).

Clark, Thomas D., *A History of Kentucky* (New York: Prentice-Hall, 1937).

Cleland, Robert Glass, "Asiatic Trade and the American Occupation of the Pacific Coast," American Historical Association *Annual Report* (1914), vol. I.

Cline, Myrtle Agnes, *American Attitude toward the Greek War of Independence* (Atlanta: Higgins-McArthur Co., 1930).

Cohen, Emmeline W., *The Growth of the British Civil Service, 1780-1939* (London: G. Allen and Unwin, 1941).

Cole, Donald B., *Jacksonian Democracy in New Hampshire, 1800-1851* (Cambridge, Mass.: Harvard University Press, 1970).

Connelly, W. E., and E. M. Coulter, *History of Kentucky*, 5 vols. (Chicago: American Historical Society, 1922).

Contamine, Henry, *Diplomatie et diplomates sous la Restauration, 1814-1830* (Paris: Hachette, 1970).

Coughlin, Magdalen, "Commercial Foundations of Political Interest in the Opening Pacific, 1789-1829," *California Historical Quarterly*, 50 (March 1971).

Cox, Montagu H. and Philip Norman, eds., *London County Council Survey of London*, vol. XIV: *The Parish of St. Margaret, Westminster*: Part III, vol. II: *Neighborhood of Whitehall* (London: B. T. Botsford, 1931).

Crockett, Walter Hill, *Vermont: The Green Mountain State*, 3 vols. (New York: Century History Co., n.d.).

Crosby, Alfred W., *America, Russia, Hemp, and Napoleon: American Trade with*

Russia and the Baltic, 1783-1812 (Columbus, Ohio: Ohio State University Press, 1965).

Dakin, Douglas, *The Greek Struggle for Independence, 1821-1833* (Berkeley and Los Angeles: University of California Press, 1973).

Dangerfield, George, *The Awakening of American Nationalism, 1815-1828* (New York: Harper, 1965).

———— *The Era of Good Feelings* (New York: Harcourt Brace, 1952).

Darling, Arthur B., *Political Changes in Massachusetts, 1824-1848* (New Haven: Yale University Press, 1925).

Driault, E., *Histoire diplomatique de la Grèce de 1821 à nos jours,* vol. I (Paris: Presses Universitaires, 1925).

Earle, Edward M., "American Interest in the Greek Cause, 1821-1827," *American Historical Review,* 33 (July 1927).

Edgington, Thomas Benton, *The Monroe Doctrine* (Boston: Little, Brown, 1904).

Eroshkin, Nikolai Petrovich, *Istoriya gosudarstvennykh uchrezhdenii dorevoliutsionnii Rossii,* 2d ed. (Moscow: no publisher, 1968).

Esarey, Logan, *History of Indiana,* 3 vols. (Indianapolis: W. K. Stewart Co., 1915-1923).

Fadeev, A. V., *Rossiya i vostochnyi krizis 20kh godov XIX v.* (Moscow: Akademii Nauk, 1958).

Fee, Walter, *The Transition from Aristocracy to Democracy in New Jersey, 1789-1829* (Somerville, Mass.: Somerville Press, 1933).

Field, James A., Jr., *America and the Mediterranean World, 1776-1883* (Princeton: Princeton University Press, 1969).

Fox, Dixon Ryan, *The Decline of Aristocracy in the Politics of New York* (New York: Columbia University Press, 1919).

Freehling, William W., *Prelude to Civil War: The Nullification Controversy in South Carolina, 1816-1836* (New York: Harper, 1966).

García Samudia, Nicolás, *Capítulos de historia diplomatica* (Bogotá: Imprenta Nacional, 1925).

———— *La mision de Don Manuel Torres en Washington y los orígenes suramericanos de la Doctrina Monroe* (Bogotá: Imprenta Nacional, 1941).

Garrison, Curtis Wiswell, "The National Election of 1824," Ph. D. dissertation, The Johns Hopkins University, 1928.

Gervinus, Georg Gottfried, *Geschichte des neunzehnten Jahrhunderts seit den Wiener Verträgen,* 8 vols. (Leipzig: W. Engelmann, 1855-1866).

Geotzmann, William H., *When the Eagle Screamed: The Romantic Horizon in American Diplomacy* (New York: John Wiley, 1966).

Goldberg de Flichman, Marti B., "Los intereses económicos que influyeron en la orientación diplomatica norteamericana en el Río de la Plata (1810-1823)," *Boletín del Instituto de Historia de la Argentina "Dr. Emilio Ravignani,"* Second Series, 12 (1969).

Goodman, Paul, *The Democratic-Republicans of Massachusetts: Politics in a Young Republic* (Cambridge, Mass.: Harvard University Press, 1964).

Grabill, Joseph L., *Protestant Diplomacy and the Near East: Missionary Influence on American Policy, 1810-1927* (Minneapolis: University of Minnesota Press, 1971).

Green, Constance M., *Washington, Village and Capital, 1800-1878* (Princeton: University Press, 1962).

Green, Fletcher M., *Constitutional Development in the South Atlantic States, 1776-1860* (Chapel Hill: University of North Carolina Press, 1930).

Griffin, Charles Carroll, *The United States and the Disruption of the Spanish Empire, 1810-1822* (New York: Columbia University Press, 1937).

Grimsted, Patricia Kennedy, *The Foreign Ministers of Alexander I: Political Attitudes and the Conduct of Russian Diplomacy, 1801-1825* (Berkeley and Los Angeles: University of California Press, 1969).

Gujer, Bruno, *Free Trade and Slavery: Calhoun's Defense of Southern Interests against British Interference, 1811-1848* (Zürich: aku Fotodrück, 1971).

Gutkina, I. G., "Grecheskii vopros i diplomaticheskie otnosheniya derzhav," *Istoricheskikh Nauk, Uchenye zapiski Leningradskogo Universitet,* 130 (1951).

Hailperin, Herman, "Pro-Jackson Sentiment in Pennsylvania, 1820-1828," *Pennsylvania Magazine of History and Biography,* 50 (July 1926).

Haller, Mark H., "The Rise of the Jackson Party in Maryland, 1820-1829," *Journal of Southern History,* 28 (Aug. 1962).

Hammond, Jabez D., *The History of Political Parties in the State of New York,* 2 vols. (Cooperstown, N.Y.: H. and E. Phinney, 1846).

Hartz, Louis, *Economic Policy and Democratic Thought: Pennsylvania, 1776-1860* (Cambridge, Mass.: Harvard University Press, 1948).

Hatch, Louis C., and others, eds., *Maine: A History,* 5 vols. (New York: American Historical Society, 1919).

Hay, Thomas R. (see previous section, under Calhoun).

Heinz, Georg, *Die Beziehungen zwischen Russland, England, und Nordamerika im Jahre 1823* (Berlin: E. Ebering, 1911).

Higginbotham, Sanford W., *The Keystone in the Democratic Arch: Pennsylvania Politics, 1800-1816* (Harrisburg, Pa.: Pennsylvania Historical and Museum Commission, 1952).

Hoffmann, William S., *Andrew Jackson and North Carolina Politics* (Chapel Hill: University of North Carolina Press, 1958).

Hofstadter, Richard, *The Idea of a Party System: The Rise of Legitimate Opposition in the United States, 1780-1840* (Berkeley and Los Angeles: University of California Press, 1969).

Huculak, Mykhaylo (see previous section, under Poletica).

Huerta Garrastachu, Fernando, *Estudio analítico genético del mensaje Monroe* (Mexico, D.F.: Universidad Nacional, 1940).

Isambert, Gaston, *L'independance grecque et l'Éurope* (Paris: Plon, 1900).

Jack, Theodore H., *Sectionalism and Party Politics in Alabama, 1819-1842* (Menasha, Wis.: George Banta Co., 1919).

Jelavich, Barbara, *A Century of Russian Foreign Policy, 1814-1914* (Philadelphia: J. B. Lippincott, 1964).

Kass, Alvin, *Politics in New York State, 1800-1830* (Syracuse, N.Y.: Syracuse University Press, 1965).

Kehl, James A., *Ill Feeling in the Era of Good Feeling: Western Pennsylvania Political Battles, 1815-1825* (Pittsburgh: University of Pittsburgh Press, 1956).

Klein, Philip S., *Pennsylvania Politics, 1817-1822, A Game without Rules* (Philadelphia: Historical Society of Pennsylvania, 1940).

Leonard, Adam A., "Personal Politics in Indiana, 1816 to 1840," *Indiana Magazine of History*, 19 (March, June, and Sept. 1923).

Lévis-Mirepoix, Emmanuel de, *Le ministère des affaires étrangères, organisation de l'administration centrale et des services extérieures (1793-1933)* (Angers: Éditions de l'ouest, 1934).

Livermore, Shaw, Jr., *The Twilight of Federalism: The Disintegration of the Federalist Party, 1815-1830* (Princeton: Princeton University Press, 1962).

Ludlum, David M., *Social Ferment in Vermont, 1791-1850* (New York: Columbia University Press, 1939).

Luetscher, George D., *Early Political Machinery in the United States* (Philadelphia: no publisher, 1903).

Lynch, William O., *Fifty Years of Party Warfare, 1789-1837* (Indianapolis: Bobbs-Merrill, 1931).

Lyon, William H., *The Pioneer Editor in Missouri, 1808-1860* (Columbia, Mo.: University of Missouri Press, 1965).

McCandless, Perry, *A History of Missouri*, vol. II: *1820 to 1860* (Columbia, Mo.: University of Missouri Press, 1972).

McCormick, Richard P., *The Second American Party System: Party Formation in the Jacksonian Era* (Chapel Hill: University of North Carolina Press, 1966).

McDowell, Robert B., *Public Opinion and Government Policy in Ireland, 1801-1846* (London: Faber and Faber, 1952).

McGee, Gale W., "The Monroe Doctrine—A Stopgap Measure," *Mississippi Valley Historical Review*, 38 (Sept. 1951).

McMahon, John V. L., *An Historical View of the Government of Maryland* (Baltimore: F. Lucas, Jr., 1831).

Merk, Frederick, *The Oregon Question: Essays in Anglo-American Diplomacy and Politics* (Cambridge, Mass.: Harvard University Press, 1967) (see also previous section, under Gallatin).

Miles, Edwin Arthur, *Jacksonian Democracy in Mississippi* (Chapel Hill: University of North Carolina Press, 1960).

Mitchell, Austin, *The Whigs in Opposition, 1815-1830* (Oxford: Oxford University Press, 1967).

Moore, Glover, *The Missouri Compromise, 1819-1821* (Lexington, Ky.: University of Kentucky Press, 1953).

Morse, Jarvis M., *A Neglected Period of Connecticut's History, 1818-1850* (New Haven: Yale University Press, 1933).

Nettement, Alfred, *Histoire de la Restauration*, 8 vols. (Paris: Lecoffre fils, 1860-1872).

Newsome, A. R., *The Presidential Election of 1824 in North Carolina* (Chapel Hill: University of North Carolina Press, 1939).

Nichols, Irby C., Jr., *The European Pentarchy and the Congress of Verona, 1822* (The Hague: Martinus Nijhoff, 1971).

────── "The Russian Ukase and the Monroe Doctrine: A Reevaluation," *Pacific Historical Review*, 36 (Feb. 1967).

Nichols, Roy F., *The Invention of the American Political Parties* (New York: Macmillan, 1967).

Ocherk istorii ministerstva inostrannykh del 1802-1902 (St. Petersburg: R. Golike and A. Vil'borg, 1902).

Okun, S. B., *The Russian-American Company*, English translation (Cambridge, Mass.: Harvard University Press, 1951).

Pease, Theodore C., *The Frontier State, 1818-1840* (Chicago: A. C. McClurg Co., 1922); vol. II in *The Centennial History of Illinois*.

Perkins, Bradford, *Castlereagh and Adams: England and the United States, 1812-1823* (Berkeley and Los Angeles: University of California Press, 1964).

Perkins, Dexter, *The Monroe Doctrine, 1823-1826* (Cambridge, Mass.: Harvard University Press, 1932).

Pessen, Edward, *Jacksonian America: Society, Personality, and Politics* (Homewood, Ill.: Dorsey Press, 1969).

Porritt, Edward and Annie G., *The Unreformed House of Commons, Parliamentary Representation before 1823*, 2 vols. (Cambridge, Eng.: Cambridge University Press, 1903).

Prince, Carl E., *New Jersey's Jeffersonian Republicans: The Genesis of an Early Party Machine* (Chapel Hill: University of North Carolina Press, 1967).

Prokesch von Osten, Anton, *Geschichte des Abfalls der Griechen*, 6 vols. (Vienna: C. Gerolds Sohn, 1867).

Pypin, Aleksandr N., *Obshchestvennoe dvizhenie v Rossii pri Alexandre I* (St. Petersburg: M. M. Stasiulevicha, 1908).

Rammelkamp, C. H., "The Campaign of 1824 in New York," American Historical Association *Annual Report* (1904).

Rashin, Adol'f G., *Naselenie Rossii za 100 let (1811-1913 gg): Statisticheskie ocherki* (Moscow: Gosstatizdat, 1956).

Remini, Robert V., *The Election of Andrew Jackson* (Philadelphia: J. B. Lippincott, 1963) (see also previous section, under Jackson and Van Buren).

Rémond, René, *Les États-Unis devant l'opinion française, 1815-1852*, 2 vols. (Paris: Fondation Nationale des Sciences Politiques, 1962).

Risjord, Norman K., *The Old Republicans: Southern Conservatism in the Age of Jefferson* (New York: Columbia University Press, 1965).

Robertson, William Spence, *France and Latin American Independence* (Baltimore: Johns Hopkins University Press, 1939).

────── "Russia and the Emancipation of Spanish America," *Hispanic American Historical Review*, 21 (May 1941).

Robinson, William A., *Jeffersonian Democracy in New England* (New Haven: Yale University Press, 1916).

Rosebloom, Eugene H., "Ohio in the Presidential Election of 1824," *Ohio Archeological and Historical Quarterly*, 26 (April 1917).

Rothbard, Murray N., *The Panic of 1819, Reactions and Policies* (New York: Columbia University Press, 1962).

Rousseau, François (see previous section, under Talaru).

Ruiz Ruiz, Ramón, *Doctrina de Monroe, su génesis antes y después del Congreso de Verona de 1822 y sus interpretaciones* (León, Nic.: no publisher, 1949).

Scharf, J. Thomas, *History of Maryland from the Earliest Period to the Present Day*, 3 vols. (Baltimore: State Printing Office, 1876).

Schefer, Christian, *La France moderne et le problème colonial* (Paris: F. Alcan, 1907).

Schellenberg, T. R. "The Secret Treaty of Verona: A Newspaper Forgery," *Journal of Modern History*. 8 (Sept. 1935).

Schuyler, Robert L., *The Fall of the Old Colonial System: A Study in British Free Trade, 1770-1870* (New York: Oxford University Press, 1945).

Scott, Ivan, "Counter-Revolutionary Diplomacy and the Demise of Anglo-Austrian Cooperation, 1820-1823," *Historian*, 34 (May 1972).

Semmel, Bernard, *The Rise of Free Trade Imperialism: Classical Political Economy, the Empire of Free Trade and Imperialism, 1750-1850* (New York: Cambridge University Press, 1970).

Shalhope, Robert E. (see previous section, under Benton).

Shpara, O., "Rol" Rossii v bor'be Gretsii za nezavisimost'," *Voprosy Istorii* (1949), no. 8.

———— "Vneshnyaya politika Kanninga i grechskii vopros," *Voprosy Istorii* (1947), no. 12.

Simms, H. H., *The Rise of the Whigs in Virginia, 1824-1840* (Richmond: William Byrd Press, 1929).

Sonne, Niels Henry, *Liberal Kentucky, 1780-1828* (New York: Columbia University Press, 1939).

Stevens, Harry R., *The Early Jackson Party in Ohio* (Durham, N.C.: Duke University Press, 1957).

Sydnor, Charles S., *The Development of Southern Sectionalism, 1819-1848* (n.p.: Louisiana State University Press, 1948).

Tankard, James W., Jr., "Public Opinion Polling by Newspapers in the Presidential Election Campaign of 1824," *Journalism Quarterly*, 49 (Summer 1972).

Tatum, Edward H., *The United States and Europe, 1815-1823* (Berkeley: University of California Press, 1936).

Temperley, Harold W. V., "French Designs on Spanish America in 1820-5," *English Historical Review*, 40 (Jan. 1925) (see also previous section, under Canning and Temperley).

Thompson, C. S., *An Essay on the Rise and Fall of the Congressional Caucus* (New Haven: Yale University Press, 1902).

Tikhemenev, I. P., *Istoricheskoe obozrenie obrazovaniya Rossiiski-Amerikanskoi Kompanii* (St. Petersburg: no publisher, 1861-1862).

Torke, Hans Joachim, "Das russische Beamtentum in der ersten Hälfte des 19. Jahrhunderts," *Forschungen zur osteuropäischen Geschichte*, 13 (1967).

Turberville, A. S., *The House of Lords in the Age of Reform, 1784-1837* (London: Faber and Faber, 1958).

Turner, Frederick Jackson, *The Rise of the New West, 1818-1829* (New York: Harper and Brothers, 1906).

Viel-Castel, Louis, Baron de, *Histoire de la Restauration*, 20 vols. (Paris: Michel Lévy frères, 1860-1878).

Villanueva, Carlos A., *Fernando VII y los Nuevos Estados* (Paris: P. Ollendorff, 1912).

———— "La diplomatie française et la reconnaissance de l'indépendance de Buenos Aires, de la Colombie et du Mexique par l'Angleterre (1825)," *Bulletin de la bibliothèque américaine*, 13 (Oct. 1912).

Wallace, Michael, "Changing Concepts of Party in the United States: New York, 1815-1828," *American Historical Review*, 74 (Dec. 1968).

Webster, C. K. (see previous section, under Castlereagh and Great Britain).

Webster, Homer J., "History of Democratic Party Organization in the Northwest, 1820-1840." *Ohio Archeological and Historical Quarterly*, 24 (July 1915).

Weiner, Alan S., "John Scott, Thomas Hart Benton, David Barton and the Presidential Election of 1824," *Missouri Historical Review*, 60 (July 1966).

Whitaker, Arthur Preston, *The United States and the Independence of Latin America, 1800-1830* (Baltimore: The Johns Hopkins University Press, 1941).

White, Lonnie J., *Politics on the Southwestern Frontier, 1819-1830* (Memphis: Memphis State University Press, 1964).

Williamson, Chilton, *American Suffrage from Property to Democracy, 1760-1860* (Princeton: Princeton University Press, 1960).

———— *Vermont in Quandary, 1763-1825* (Montpelier: Vermont Historical Society, 1949).

Young, James Sterling, *The Washington Community, 1800-1828* (New York: Columbia University Press, 1966).

Zhigarev, Sergei, *Russkaya politika v' vostochnom vopros'*, 2 vols. (Moscow: no publisher, 1896).

Zorin, Valerian A., and others, *Istoriya diplomatii*, vol. I (Moscow: Gospolitizdat, 1959).

Index